CÉLESTINE

Voices from a French Village

Gillian Tindall is the author of two
enduring books on the history of places
and a study of the meaning of place to
writers. Two of her novels deal with
rural France under the Occupation. An
early novel, which won the Somerset
Maugham Award, is set in Paris.

Also by Gillian Tindall

GILLIAN TINDALL

CÉLESTINE

Voices from a French Village

Minerva

A Minerva Paperback
CÉLESTINE

First published in Great Britain 1995
by Sinclair-Stevenson
This Minerva edition published 1996
by Mandarin Paperbacks
an imprint of Reed International Books Limited
Michelin House, 81 Fulham Road, London SW3 6RB
and Auckland, Melbourne, Singapore and Toronto
www.minervabooks.com

Reprinted 1996 (four times)

A CIP catalogue record for this title
is available from the British Library
ISBN 0 7493 2025 7

Printed and bound in Great Britain
by Cox & Wyman Ltd, Reading, Berkshire

Once, on this earth, once, on this familiar spot of ground, walked other men and women, as actual as we are today, thinking their own thoughts, swayed by their own passions, but now all gone, one generation vanishing after another, gone as utterly as we ourselves shall shortly be gone like ghosts at cockcrow.

G. M. Trevelyan, *An Autobiography and Other Essays*

The written history of these regions is odd. It opens extremely late: there is very little, it seems, till the nineteenth century. The country people who lived there, far from towns and main roads, remained for a long time without a voice of their own or anyone else to speak for them. They were nevertheless there; they did things, cared about things, and thus had their effect, without anyone realizing it, on the heart and soul of the nation.

Daniel Halévy, *Visites aux Paysans du Centre (1907–1934)*

Contents

Author's Note

This book is all true. I have not been able to discover everything that I would have liked, but nothing has been invented
or imagined. A number of people both in England and France,
and from varying walks of life, have contributed greatly to its
writing, either through their own writings and specialized
knowledge, through family papers they have lent to me or
through conversations I have been privileged to have with
them. In particular, several Chassignolles citizens, all of whom
are, with their consent, mentioned under their real names,
have shown me a generosity and interest without which my
re-creation of a past world would have been impossible. I
hope they will accept this work as a tribute, however foreign,
to themselves, their ancestors, and to the tenacious traditions
of rural French society.

To all the living, and to the known and much-remembered
dead, my humble thanks. To all those dead I never knew in
person, whose shadowy lives I have tried to call up from the
gulf of time – my grateful salutations.

Gillian Tindall

I

The Making
of a World

Chapter 1

One autumn day in the 1970s an old man left his small house in a village near the geographical heart of France and caught the weekly bus into the nearby market town.

He was not a Frenchman, though he had spent every summer in the village for many years, since long before foreigners were generally seen in the French countryside. He was by birth an Australian and by vocation a painter: he had harvested the landscapes, the skies, the light and the stone of the Berry in his pictures, and these were, in token of friendship, disseminated in many houses in the village and neighbouring farms. He had come to France as a soldier in 1916; the Second World War found him in Paris again at the Liberation in a liaison job. There, no longer a young man, he encountered a secretary of charm and intelligence who was not young either. In due course she took him back to the house she had inherited from her parents and introduced him to the covertly amused but respectful neighbours she had known since childhood.

These neighbours were not entirely surprised. They had always known that Zénaïde – rather a fancy name for a local girl, what do you expect? – was a bit of a dreamer, with tastes and expectations outside their ken, and anyway look at the family she came from ... Her mother going odd in that way. And her father: an amiable man but no head at all for business. And her grandmother

3

– such a refined yet open-hearted person. People a bit out of the ordinary run and long remembered.

Although the painter was known to have another life, and another wife, in England, that was a long way off and the fact was politely unmentioned. The summers together continued for ten years till Zénaïde herself died before she reached old age. She left the small house and its contents to her painter for his lifetime. A handyman, he had embellished the classic French exterior with a veranda and a blue-painted trellis, so that it now resembled an English *cottage orné* of the Edwardian era. He also converted the grain loft into bedrooms reached by an inside boxed ladder, and built on a kitchen and bathroom in a lean-to with a soakaway to a covered pit beyond the apple trees – at a time when hardly another house in the village had plumbing. The two main rooms, however, were left as they were and had always been. He continued to return and open the place up every summer, spending months at a time in the décor of past lives he had never actually known. In the 1960s and '70s the polished press in the bigger room was full of the linen sheets, square, lace-edged pillowcases and towel-sized table-napkins with initials in the damask that had been a bride's dowry in the 1890s. The padded *prie-dieu* stood where it always had, and so did the wood-burning stove. So did the footstool with the *gros point* cat upon it, worn now but still as lifelike as when it was worked long ago by Zénaïde's grandmother, when she was still a pretty girl, before her own life became harder and sadder.

Leaving the house, the painter carefully secured the shutters as usual and turned the heavy iron key, locking up all those things again in timeless suspension along with his own paintings, his cream flannel suits and his old straw hat with the brush marks on it. The bed in his attic room was left made up, there were packets and tins in the kitchen cupboards; a carton with a little milk left in it stood overlooked by the stove. He meant to return within two or three weeks. He never did. The vivid autumn of central France declined into the bleached landscape of winter. In the house, only the mice and rats moved. The stool cat sat on with her happy face. The unmoving air, ventilated only by the chimney, took on the taint of soot. The forgotten milk became a brownish, transparent liquid, infinitely antique. Dead leaves silted up in the back porch by the makeshift bathroom. The weeks grew into months. People

4

in the village began to worry, to recall how vague the old man had seemed that summer, and to ask one another what should be done. Eventually, fumblingly, enquiries were made, someone was contacted, someone else was found to translate a lawyer's letter, the wheels of necessary destruction began cumbersomely to turn, finally rendering Zénaïde's forebears and their home extinct long after their own deaths.

The following summer the house was at last cleared. It would be sold by its inheritors, Zénaïde's distant cousins. They took most of the contents, except for a few things that were given away. They left behind, on a corner of the mantelshelf in the darkened, empty room behind the shutters, a small cardboard case meant to contain those cards that are distributed in pious families to commemorate baptisms, first communions and Masses said for the dead. Perhaps they assumed that cards were what was still in it and therefore, with some half-formed sense of respect or superstition, refrained from putting it on the great garden bonfire which had already consumed so many long-paid bills, so many mildewed cushions, wormy chairs, quilts sticky with moths' eggs, and mouse-wrecked packets of sugar.

Had Zénaïde's cousins looked, as I did when I came to the house, they would have found that the case was packed tight with seven letters, two of them in their small envelopes, the others showing traces of having been simply folded and sealed. In the late afternoon light coming through the door that I had left open behind me, I peered at them and found a date – 1862 – and then another. The copybook handwritings varied: I saw that the letters could not all be from one person, but the ink was faded and even a cursory glance through the soft wads of paper delicate as old skin showed that some of the French was very odd.

I had come to collect the cat footstool, which had been promised me. Now I creaked open the shutter over the stone sink in the smaller room, dusted the long-dried surface with my handkerchief and carefully spread the letters out.

The Célestine to whom they were all addressed I knew to have been Zénaïde's grandmother. I knew almost nothing else about her at that time, but she had been a young girl in this village; she must have kept the letters all her life and her granddaughter had continued to do so after her death. They were all from suitors, except for one from a young soldier brother, and all, except that last letter, dated from the early 1860s. One was from a local schoolmaster, another from a salesman travelling for a wine merchant. Others came from a bakery, from a village where rural iron foundries then were, and from another known for its annual cattle fair: these writers expressed themselves with more difficulty in the unfamiliarity of the written word. From the way they were addressed – variations on 'Mademoiselle Célestine Chaumette, in her father's house, the Auberge at Chassignolles' – I saw that she had been the daughter of the local innkeeper; as such, she must have had the opportunity to meet and attract a wider range of admirers than most country girls at that date.

Some sentences sprang fresh as flowers from the pages; others seemed for the moment impenetrable. I found that each letter was in a different hand except for two that were from the same young man, writing first in hope and then in bitter disappointment. Even so, he was not bitter at Célestine: she seems to have had the gift of inspiring respect and affection in youth as in old age: '... I havent put myself about to talk to your parents because it wouldnt be any use, I wanted to know what you thought first of all tho' I do think they wouldnt a been averse ... All I can say is, I wish you from the bottom of my heart a husband who will always be faithful to you, for you dont deserve to be Cheated on [... *je te souhaite du plus profond de moncoeur un marie qui te soie toujours fidelle car tu merite pas detre Trompé*].'

In the dusk, which in that part of France, south of the Loire but just north of the mountains, descends with a pinkish, theatrical light, I returned to my own cottage on the other side of the village. I took with me the cat footstool, Célestine's cat with its worn, wool smile. I also took the letters. Once ephemeral as butterflies, they had been cherished and kept for reasons of obscure pride, comfort or regret; messages from a life already past to Célestine, they had undergone a long hibernation. They had been transformed into messages of another kind, making 'for ever' come true in a different way from the one the writers originally, bravely intended; they were to be cherished for new reasons. Now, when Célestine herself, all her correspondents, every single person they knew and most of those they were ever going to know, had vanished as if they had never been, I would bring them to life again.

6

Chapter 2

I had come to the village some dozen years earlier on just such an evening of unearthly light. I arrived there by chance, with my husband and our then small son, driving south on minor roads, hesitating before obscure signposts by fields where white Charolais cattle drifted in ghostly herds and mistletoe hung in swags from the trees. It was a relief when we saw a church spire and a water-tower ahead and at last drove into an irregular square with a café and two petrol pumps and a tree. We stayed the night in one of the café's four hotel rooms, ate a home-cooked meal, went for a brief walk round unknowable houses in the starry dark that surprised us by its sudden cold. In the hot May sun of the following morning we played ball with our child in the hotel yard, packed up the car and drove off, mentally rolling up behind us like a map this unremarkable village. However, by chance we returned, in a different season. And then returned again. The place's situation near the geographical centre of France, an area crossed by many itineraries yet generally consigned by the French themselves to that unexplored and apparently unexplorable region *la France profonde*, began to speak to us.

On our fourth or fifth visit we asked the owner of the café-hotel, Suzanne Calvet, who had inherited it from her father when it was a plain village inn, if she knew of any houses for sale? It was 1972, the autumn before the Common Market was due to include Britain in its reluctant embrace.

'I'll go and ask the men in the bar,' she said.

These, since it was morning, were a coterie of elderly citizens all wearing the striped trousers and black alpaca jackets that had indicated respectability in their youth. The consensus was that there were two possible houses for us. One was a pretty but large and dilapidated property by the cemetery. (It was later bought by a local faith-healer and teller of fortunes, but good fortune it did not bring him.) The other house was agreed by all to be extremely tiny but in good condition. Georges Bernardet, who had acquired it in 1938 for the widowed aunt who had brought him up, was known to be a conscientious owner. 'The Proprietor' was his village nickname.

'Bought it for her out of what he saved when he was doing his military service, he did.'

'How he managed to save beats me. But that's him all over.' Comfortable, slightly malicious chuckles. They were café-frequenters; Georges Bernardet was not.

'Ah, it's so small, it wouldn't have cost much then. Doesn't cost much now, come to that. Same price as a small car.' To me: 'You buy it, Madame, you won't regret it, the roof's sound . . . Well, go and look at it anyway. Last house in the village on the Séchère road, the corner by the cross. Its garden's all down to cabbages this year. Georges never leaves land idle . . . You can't miss it.'

Four months later, on a day when January hoar-frost was petrifying every leaf, blade of grass and spider's web, the house became ours. Or, more accurately, it became mine, since I was the one able to be present in the attorney's office in La Châtre for the ceremonial signing of documents that French law requires.

Bernardet had ridden in on his mobylette. I did not then know, but came later to understand, what an exceptional event it had to be to bring him into the town. Tall, heavy, battered-looking but wearing his sixty years well, he was ill at ease, constantly resettling his cap on his thick grey hair. He was mistrustful of the lawyer, the traditional enemy. Some months later, when it became apparent that an extra and wrong land registry number had been put in by mistake on the purchase document, Bernardet was not so much annoyed as grimly triumphant to have his suspicions vindicated, and gave the attorney a piece of his mind.

8

That day he was circumspect, however; disposed to be amiable to me but on his guard, sizing me up over an exceptional, cere-monial drink in the café afterwards. Was I going to like his house – understand how to live in it? Would I and my husband really be happy for the time being with the earth closet he had rashly agreed to construct for us at the bottom of the garden? He spoke carefully in his elegant, Sunday-best French, which was different from the tongue he employed at home. When the subject of the cabbage-patch garden came up, however, he became more animated, even gallant.

'I myself will do the garden for you, Madame, as I mentioned to you when you first looked at the house. That's good earth you've got there. I like to see it put to proper use.'

The next summer, and for sixteen summers after, the garden in late summer was a neat vision of potatoes, carrots, leeks, lettuces, haricot beans and tomatoes. Once in a while there was a coolness from him if we failed to be there at the right time to harvest everything he provided. We would beg him to use the stuff himself, but this was not part of his plan. He never entirely came to terms with our itinerant habits, but after many years he relented so far as to regard these as our fate and our misfortune rather than our own foolish choice. Once or twice, coming upon me with papers spread out on the table, he expressed sympathy for me – it must be hard on the brain, I ought to take care not to overdo it – and general relief that he himself had never been constrained by a Higher Authority to take up book-work.

Choice and free will were things of which life had provided him with little experience, yet he had turned his own fate to good advantage. Born into a large and poor family, bred to labour on the land of others, he set himself to acquire territory of his own. Over many years, intelligently and persistently, he worked his way into a position of modest comfort and universal respect: this was the real drama of his life.

Its one great adventure was a different matter. Called up at the beginning of the Second World War, he was taken prisoner at the fall of France along with half a million other Frenchmen. He was sent to a transit camp on the borders of Belgium, where his job was to get requisitioned horses ready for transport to Germany. It was clear to him that soon it would be men who were being deported thence, and having established an image of himself as a

9

trusty, he made his plans to escape and did so. How he managed, without papers, money or civilian clothes, to make his way over hundreds of miles of occupied France was something I never entirely understood. Once, in conversation alone with me, he mentioned that *une personne* had been of crucial assistance at one point. French uses the female form to describe any person, so the word was opaque, but I felt that if his helper had been a man he would have said *quelqu'un* or *un type* (a chap). At other times he said that whenever he sensed a German patrol might be near he would take to the fields and pretend to be tending the crops, a role in which he presumably looked so convincing that he was never questioned. Once he hastily joined a family who were digging up potatoes, muttering to them 'I'm your cousin . . .' Potatoes, cabbages and turnips – the main crops at that season in the chilly north – also provided his food. The motorized and provisioned troops of 1940 covered territory at speed; half France was in German hands almost before the distraught populace had grasped the scale of the defeat. But stragglers, deserters, escaped prisoners, and refugees were back to the pace of foot-soldiers living off the land, as in the days when France was 'sixteen days wide and twenty-two days long'.

His keenest anxiety during that journey was that he did not know whether his home country, that *pays* to which he was pertinaciously, almost instinctively making his way, was now in the Occupied Zone or in Pétain's nominally Free one. In fact the Department of the Indre was just within the Free Zone: the line of demarcation was the River Cher, which bisects the old province of the Berry into two Napoleonic Departments, each named after its river. Bernardet only discovered the position of the frontier when he reached its banks. There he wandered for hours, avoiding the bridges which were now equipped with gun posts, gazing morosely at the farther shore. From any deserted water-meadow a swimmer could have made it easily to the other side. However, the rivers that criss-cross Bernardet's landlocked native countryside are all smaller than the Cher. The Indre there is easily fordable; the larger Creuse is twenty miles away. So Bernardet had never learnt to swim.

His saviour, who appeared at last as night was falling, was that classic figure of French folk-tale, a small boy herding cows. The child showed him where he could wade across, armpit deep. Some sixteen hours later, having walked in exhilaration all through the night, he strode into his own village. He went straight to his aunt, in the house that is now ours.

He never travelled again after that. He had done it, and that was enough. Why should he wander in other people's kingdoms when his own, so intimately known to him in all its rises and descents, its variations in soil, its pastures and crop fields, vineyards, copses and vegetable gardens, was there demanding his attention?

Late in life, he did occasionally get on the train to visit his daughter, established in the suburbs of Paris, but this was on the understanding that her garden needed expert attention which her garage-mechanic husband could not be expected to provide. Each to his own skill. I believe that in his seventies, also, he did once relent so far as to accompany his wife on a day trip to the Atlantic coast, but till then it had been almost a matter of pride to him that he had never seen the sea.

After the war, when the aged, limiting structure of French rural life was at last cracking open a little, one or two friends suggested to him that a man of his acknowledged capabilities might aspire now to a different job. The local Gendarmerie, perhaps, where a good friend was established? Or the railways? His army sergeant, in civilian life a railway worker, would put in a good word for him there. Bernardet considered these propositions but turned them down: the thought of a life unencumbered by the demands of either the fields or the animals that meant so much to him did not, after all, appeal.

He grumbled furiously at times, but that is a general trait in farmers, subject as they are to forces of God and Government perpetually beyond their control. Not that he believed much in God, and he had a covert contempt for all forms of organized government from the Élysée Palace to the village municipal council. His ethic and his passion was work; it was his pride that, apart from all his farming skills, both current and remembered, he could turn his hand to a whole range of other things: he made gates, ladders and wheelbarrows, chicken coops and pigsties, he retiled roofs, laid hedges.

His great model in life, his personal version of the admired grown-up that is internalized within us, was his maternal grandfather. 'Ah, my grandfather could have told you that,' he would say, when I sought some piece of knowledge about the village's past. This man, whom I eventually discovered to have been a contemporary of Célestine Chaumette, grew up within a mile of her. They must have been acquainted: in those days the inhabitants of a rural area hardly ever encountered a face to which they were unable to put a name. But socially there would have been a gap between them. He was the son of a day-labourer, while the daughter of the innkeeper was almost a member of the bourgeoisie. The word originally indicated no more than those who lived *au bourg* – that is, within a little town or village however rural, as opposed to those who lived on a more remote farm or hamlet among the fields – but certain social differences tended to follow from these different circumstances, and still exist today. In the last century the differences would have been more marked. Clearly, Célestine could read and write herself (so, as we shall see, could her father) whereas Bernardet's grandfather was completely illiterate. He is said, however, to have been able to 'calculate anything in his head'. When still in his teens and working long days on someone else's farm, he took to fetching stone in the evenings from a local quarry with a hand-made cart and a borrowed mule. He fetched lime, too, from a river-bank, sawed wood and seasoned it. With infinite labour in snatched hours, he built a two-roomed house for himself and his future wife outside the village. It is standing to this day.

From the vantage-point of the present Bernardet himself now seems a figure from another era, one of those people who are irreplaceable because they can no longer be made: the mould is broken. It is a comfort, of a sort, to realize that the idea that the modern world has invaded and destroyed an ageless, unchanging peasant culture at some recent date (1950? 1939? 1914?) is to some extent an optical illusion. Moulds have repeatedly been broken over the previous centuries; peasant cultures, however apparently static, have often before been in a state of deep-seated change: otherwise, paradoxically, they could not have survived. Bernardet, in his turn, regarded his grandfather as a representative of the world he felt had slipped away already by his own youth: the world of the reaping hook, the wolves, the fairies and the all-night *veillées* where nuts were shelled for oil and wool was carded, and where the folk memories of unlettered men and women went back before the Revolution.

In old age, when he had retired from the heaviest farm labours, Bernardet softened his work ethic to the extent of adding a few flowers among the regimented vegetables in our garden. He had always, till then, regarded flowers as 'the wife's department'. A hedge of pink escallonia that we planted ourselves particularly took his fancy, and in the early summer of 1988 we received a letter from him that for once conveyed no practical message but simply told us: 'your primroses [*vos prime verts*] are a marvel to see.'

It was to be the last year he saw them.

Bernardet, though unique in his way, was in many respects a far more typical inhabitant of the village than were Célestine and her descendants. He and his family and his shadowy ancestors belong to the great but largely silent tradition of French peasantry, those who 'come; and till the soil, and lie beneath', but whose anonymous presence is still widely perceived in France as the country's moral foundation. He figures here not just for his own sake but as a rural norm against which the different, more ambitious and yet more fortune-tossed lives of Célestine and her kind need to be seen.

Chapter 3

You have most likely passed through the village, or its prototype. Anybody who has travelled across the large, beautiful, essentially reclusive countryside of France has been to it, in one of its thousand variants. In the language of bureaucracy, it is the *chef-lieu* of a Commune: the basic, untranslatable unit of French local government that is presided over by its own elected mayor. The Commune is home to some six hundred people, but that includes the population of a dozen outlying farm-hamlets as well.

In the village itself there is a fine church dating from the thirteenth century but much altered since, a Mairie built after 1870 which used to house the boys' school as well but does no longer, and a modern primary school for both sexes constructed out of the girls' school that was the latest thing in the 1900s. There is a diminutive post office, open four hours a day, where a new centralized computer performs manoeuvres to do with pensions and electricity that a few years ago were achieved just as efficiently with handwritten entries in small books. There is a busy garage, another down the road that attends to two-stroke motors and agricultural machinery, a Tabac run by the garage owner's wife as a service to the village, and the café-restaurant. Two other modest cafés have closed in the last twenty years, when their elderly owners wished to collect their trade-related pensions and could find no one who felt it was worth taking on such small businesses;

one of these was the place where Célestine Chaumette served customers a hundred years earlier.

Shut now, for the same reason, are the barber's and the forge. The last working horse clopped to his rest about fifteen years ago on the death of his master – similarly shod in name at least, since horseshoes and clogs are both called *sabots*. The thriving baker's shop still works seven days a week, sustaining the French tradition that daily bread should mean just that. When not at his ovens, the baker himself delivers the warm loaves for miles around. Since he and his wife are not getting any younger either, the village surrounds them with a nervous appreciation. 'During that terrible weather, five years ago now, when it got down to twelve below freezing, do you know Monsieur Meyer *never missed a round*? Some of the farm tracks were quite snowed up, and he went *on foot* to the doors to make sure people got their bread. Such devotion . . .' In France the baker plays the role taken in England by the milkman. It is the baker who finds yesterday's bread still in the bird-proof box by the farm gate, penetrates the unlocked kitchen and discovers the owner incapacitated beside the stove, or ranges the barns and orchards calling a name till a feeble voice responds from beside a fallen ladder or a toppled straw stack.

There is no grocer's in the village today. Once, counting those 'in a small way' there were five. A grocer's van from the town calls weekly, trumpeting its horn as it comes to rest in the square behind the church, opening up flaps and extensions in a minor transformation scene that leaves you wondering if the houses around might not embark on the same trick – but all that happens is that customers emerge from doors like weathermen. The last proper grocer's shop, which closed some ten years ago, is much missed. It was almost always open, Madame Démeure having been brought up in the business from childhood and having the interests of her customers truly at heart (said everyone). She was sometimes heard to wail, 'It's no use my saying I'm shut for the afternoon – people keep coming in just the same', but she must have liked it that way, since she did not lock the door. She sold a great many things: not just perishable and tinned food and cleaning stuffs, but saucepans, underclothes, babywear, old men's flannel shirts, slippers, wellingtons, light-bulbs, seeds, mousetraps, small toys, cards, string, sealing-wax, school exercise books and straw hats. No poisoned wheat for the rodent population, however. That, in deference to the ancient practice of the miller stocking all the grains, is sold at the bakery. And no paper hankies ('not much call for them here') but good-quality cloth ones along with equally traditional towelling napkins for both infant and female use. In addition, almost anything could be ordered on request from a large catalogue, and Madame Démeure would also take orders for clogs to be made by her husband.

All monies received from any source seemed to be dropped straight through the inconspicuous slot in the shop counter into the drawer that served as an all-purpose till. We never dared reflect on how the VAT inspector would tackle the Démeure establishment. Perhaps the inspector did not dare either, or perhaps Madame Démeure did occasionally do frenetic, summary paperwork behind the scenes. Certainly Monsieur Démeure did not. In the rural tradition from which they sprang, husband and wife each have their own sphere, and his lay out of doors. He always seemed busy there, though one could not quite say what he did. He was a trundler of barrows, a feeder of chickens, a grafter of fruit trees of which he was particularly fond. Some people said:

'It was the war – being a prisoner those five years. He wasn't the same, after. Affects a person, you see.'

'Monsieur Pissavy was a prisoner for all that time too.'

'With Monsieur Pissavy, it's not the same.'

'I reckon it was Maxime finding, when he did get out, that a ten-franc note he'd been keeping stitched in his clothes all that time wouldn't buy so much as a meal.'

'That famous note.'

Others simply said: 'Well, he's a clog-maker by trade, what do you expect? There isn't the same call for clogs today.'

The first time I heard this remark I took it lightly, as it was spoken, almost as a joke. Only later did I come to some understanding of the significance of obsolete skills or outdated experiences lying inert across lives, weighing down what they should have sustained. A larger and more personal capital than ten-franc notes has been devalued in French villages by social changes. And the very idea that a trade, once learnt, is fixed for life, becoming the state of being to which one has been appointed (*état* in old-fashioned French usage) forms in itself part of this antique capital. Until well into the present century clog-making was the trade for which Chassignolles was renowned; the village once had a score of men producing the handy, protective wooden footwear that everyone in the country wore for work and the children wore to school. Business contracted between the wars but showed no sign of actually disappearing, and took on a new lease of life between 1940 and 1945 when shoes became hard to buy. That, however, was its Indian summer. In the 1950s the wooden shoe industry began its terminal decline. Today bunches of them still hang, like fruits harvested and since forgotten, in dusty barns and disused workshops, and in the village street a silence has fallen. No clattering *sabots*, after hundreds of years of them. And no hooves either.

Chassignolles was a local centre for wooden shoes because, in the past, it was surrounded by forests of oak, ash and Spanish chestnut, a vast world unpopulated except by woodcutters, charcoal-burners, and isolated peasants gathering dead wood for fires or minding the hairy pigs that snuffled for acorns in great troops. The very name Chassignolles derives from the old French for oak, *chesne*. Only gradually over the centuries, as the demand for agricultural land increased, was the forest cut back into separate woods and coppices. From locally cut trees there came, as well as clogs, the roof timbers of every house, every stick of furniture, every farm implement, every barrow and cart. A trade in timber also developed. From the seventeenth century on, whole trunks were transported laboriously to the Indre and sent down-river into the Loire and so to the shipyards in Nantes. Thence, as the components of ships, they eventually made their way to India, the Far East and across the Atlantic to the New World.

But as well as being the all-purpose material on which life ran, wood was the only fuel, industrial as well as domestic. Till the mid-nineteenth century, when railways began bringing in coal, it was wood that powered the local iron forges and the workshops making glass and pottery. The importance of the forest as a source of livelihood crops up again and again in the history of the Lower Berry. Still today, viewed from a vantage-point on the edge of the higher, barer Champagne Berrichon to the north, the Indre valley seems hidden in folds of dense vegetation – actually the hedges of the small fields. It is the country which George Sand christened for the purposes of her novels the 'Vallée Noire'.

Chassignolles began life as a fortified medieval priory, an outpost of the great abbey of Déols by what is now Châteauroux. In the

17

classic way, the monks were driven out and their property sold by the State at the Revolution. The existing small houses round Chassignolles' church form a protective curve that follows the line of the one-time wall, and the largest of them incorporates a defensive turret on one side of its miniature courtyard. The place was fortified because central France had long been accustomed to troubles. In the fourteenth century the English presence induced the state of endemic civil strife now known as the Hundred Years War, and for a while, a rival royal capital to Paris was set up in Bourges, on the other side of the Berry, in what is now the Department of the Cher. The Black Prince passed that way, taking the key towns of Châteauroux and Issoudun before retreating again to Poitiers. On Chassignolles' doorstep, the town of La Châtre was attacked by English troops occupying the nearby village of Briantes, and defended by the Barbançois family who, on the strength of this success, got money from the French king to build a fortress. Fifty years later the war was over and the fortress had been made obsolete by the invention of gunpowder, but its great towers and story-book keep still stand among the quiet fields.

The sixteenth century brought more troubles to the Berry. The Wars of Religion devastated Bourges, where an intellectual Protestantism had begun to flourish, and left much lasting bitterness in other progressive towns such as Vierzon and Issoudun. Fortunately the Lower Berry was insufficiently progressive, even then, to find itself at the heart of the strife, though when an exhausted truce was finally called in 1594 it was under the government of a certain Claude de La Châtre.

After that the focus of French political action moved definitively north to the Parisian basin, leaving the Berry to cultivate habits of peace. In the seventeenth and eighteenth centuries outsiders stigmatized the region as 'backward', even 'poor', but these things are relative: the Berry may have lost its position as the wealthy heart of France, but it was still much more fertile and quietly prosperous than the vast, mountainous regions directly to the south. Its population remained stable, with almost as many 'hearths' (households) recorded near the end of the Wars of Religion as there were two hundred years later shortly before the Revolution.

The national events of 1789–94, with their permanent, emblematic effect on French consciousness, seem to have had remarkably few immediate repercussions in the area except for the departure of the monks. No heads rolled. A few aristocratic landowners were chased away too, or thought it prudent to retreat, but a number of them insinuated themselves back fifteen or twenty years later by repurchasing confiscated property through proxy names. Some, adopting semi-rustic clothing, even took up farming themselves, inconspicuous and scattered versions of the gentleman-farmer on the English model. Other holdings were acquired by the tenant farmers on the spot, whose social aspirations were rising to meet the standards prevailing among the newly impoverished gentry. So, one way and another, most of the fields remained in the charge of those who had always looked after them and certainly had no desire to see them 'redistributed to the people'. In any case, that part of France always had a large number of small farmers, *petits propriétaires*, scratching a living. The theory that the Revolution gave the land for the first time to those who laboured on it hardly applies in the Berry. But it is a potent idea, here as elsewhere in France, and has encouraged a peculiarly French and literally grass-roots form of Communism.

More than in any other European country, perhaps, notional political orientation in France continues to follow the lines traced by history and now mossy with age: peasants against nobles, teachers against priests, regions against central government. The basic historical myth in the Berry is of a people rejecting outside interference ('outside' being anywhere beyond the confines of the old province) – yet, paradoxically, priding themselves on a back-ground of cosmopolitanism due to the waves of different people that have passed by.

'So the English have come back to claim their own?' a neighbour suggested mockingly to us in the first year, when we were still objects of mild interest and surmise. (This unspectacular country-side is far from the touristic circuits of the Loire, Lot and Dordogne and Provence: a foreign house owner was, and is, a rarity.) To my look of enquiry, he explained: 'The English were here before, you know. Your kings were kings of Aquitaine too, in the olden days. There's a draper in La Châtre called Langlois – well, he's retired now, the old man has, but do you know you can still see he's an Englishman? The dead spit of your Winston Churchill.'

The English were driven out of La Châtre in 1360.

Bernardet, too, had a story of a tall, fair family called Langlois living in the next house to his when he was a child – one of the group of houses across the way from ours. 'And you see the house after, the one that's falling down now? Well it seems that belonged at one time to some people called Sarassy and they were dark as gypsies. Perfectly respectable people, but – it was in their blood. The Saracens were hereabouts. In the olden days. Think of Sarzay – yes, the castle. Well, that's a Saracen castle, I reckon.'

'Saracen', in French parlance, used to denote all Muslims and Arabs, rather as the English used the term 'Moors'. The last and most northerly battle with the Moors took place near Poitiers in 732, and by the tenth century they had retreated again to Spain. The name Sarzay may indeed be some far echo of their presence, but the fortress there is the one built by the Barbançois four centuries later to intimidate the English. In myth, 'the olden days' tend to form one condensed period, situated at some date remote, but not too remote, from living memory.

In France this period falls naturally before the Revolution, where it is conflated with the Ancien Régime and conceived of as a timeless, seamless epoch. It is also, in spite of traditions about Wicked Lords and folk memories of serfs eating frozen grass by the winter roads, perceived as a golden era, the location of fairy tales. It is the pristine land seen in the miniatures of the *Très Riches Heures du Duc de Berry* and on the flower-sprinkled tapestry landscapes of the Lady with the Unicorn, which were woven at Aubusson a little way to the south. It is a world full of dangers – huge, trackless forests, outlaws and brigands, cruel blows of fate, parents forced by necessity to cast out their children, wicked step-parents, stolen children being eaten in castles – yet it is also a fundamentally moral and democratic world. The beautiful daughter of the poor woodcutter really does end up marrying the Prince who has seen her while out hunting. The little drummer boy with the merchant father has the confidence to cock a snook at the King who, having first scorned him, has now heard about the richly laden ships and is trying to marry off his daughter:

> *Petit tambour, je te donnerai ma fille*
>
> (Little drummer, you can have my daughter)

To which the drummer replies in the same tone of egalitarian intimacy:

> *Sire le Roi, tu peux garder ta fille,*
> *Dans mon pays 'y en a de plus jolies*

(You, your Majesty, can keep your lass;
Where I come from, we have prettier by the mass)

These kings and princes of folk-song don't sound quite like Charles Sept or Louis Quatorze. They seem more like landed gentry or even just prosperous farmers, rich and powerful only by the standards of the closed societies in which they lived. In the same perspective Bernardet had a story that the house where the 'Saracens' lived, which had an imposing barn, had earlier housed a *maréchal de France*, a Field Marshal, and that his fine chargers had had the barn as their stable.

I gazed over the peaceful, semi-derelict scene. Barbary ducks, belonging to Monsieur Chezaubernard, the retired hedger-and-ditcher in the end house, waddled and fussed on a patch of waste pasture.

'You don't actually remember that time yourself do you, Monsieur Bernardet?'

'Not myself, no. But my grandfather did.'

In his mind there existed, only just beyond his own experience, a Chassignolles as busy and populous as in his childhood but a more glorious and self-contained microcosm of the world elsewhere. It was a place where a military chief stabled his horses and falcons were reared for hawking parties, where monks held court in the church as in a palace and where the house with a miniature tower and courtyard was home, not to a man who repaired bicycles, but to a nobleman with gold in his coffers.

Where La Châtre is concerned this vision may once have had a basis in reality. La Châtre is the small town seven kilometres from Chassignolles, the place where for centuries the village has gone to market, or for a day out, or to seek a situation or an education, to plead a cause or to shelter in the hospital as a last resort. In the fifteenth and sixteenth centuries, when the draining of the marshes and the cutting back of the forests was ensuring the Berry's continued, if quiet, prosperity, the walled town of La Châtre had its own might and self-sufficiency. No modern communications sucked its power away to distant administrations. Real noblemen built grand houses there founded on the wool of the Berrichon sheep that ranged the partly tamed heaths and moors to the north of the town. There was a dungeon tower high above the Indre where soldiers were garrisoned and political prisoners were kept, and a chain of water-mills and tanneries along the river's edge.

Today tanneries and mills are silent and no modern manufactories have replaced them. The dungeon-tower is a museum full of lace caps and stuffed birds – the birds being the unfortunate bequest of a leading citizen of a hundred years ago. The modern military installations, like the industries, are thirty kilometres away in Châteauroux, and so is the prison, the Assize Court and, now, the nearest railway station. La Châtre is still a shopping and service centre, packed with people from the country round about for the Saturday outdoor market, but the great houses with high gables, flights of stone steps or courtyards behind elegant gates, are lived in by local attorneys, general practitioners and insurance agents.

The very lack of twentieth-century sprawl, and therefore of twentieth-century social and architectural pressures, has, superficially, made La Châtre seem unchanging. Her population, at around five thousand, is much the same as it was in the middle of the last century. It has merely shaken itself out a little from the narrow lanes and medieval tenements of the old town into a sprinkling of suburban villas on the western side; and these have not altered the basic appearance or street patterns of the town any more than the stuccoed residences did in the Avenue de la Gare when they were added in the 1880s. You can still set out on foot from the market square and be in the fields within a few minutes, with no sound but larks and the running river.

La Châtre has also managed to cling on to the physical trappings of power, even though much of the reality has moved to Châteauroux, Limoges or indeed Paris: no doubt this is because the other market towns of the Lower Berry are even smaller. The town is a Sous-Préfecture – a ceremonial cog in the centralized administrative wheel. It has a Town Hall whose eighteenth-century façade hides the vestiges of a one-time convent: the town cinema is alongside it in what was, before the Revolution, the convent chapel. It has an income tax office (Hôtel des Impôts) and a Law Court (Palais de Justice), used now for small claims: the imposing front steps of the Court are speckled with moss. It has a Gendarmerie, various modern hospital buildings as well as the ancient one, a local high school, a sports centre, a swimming pool, a tourist office and a municipal library established in the grandest old private house of all – the austere Hôtel de Villaines, whose owners once ruled the town with all the majesty of *noblesse* being obliging.

It also has a Famous Literary Figure. George Sand (1804–76) did not live in the town itself but in the pretty, turreted manor house known grandly as her 'château' two or three miles up the road, at Nohant. It is La Châtre that figures, street for street, in several of her novels, and the surrounding countryside was the inspiration of much of her writing.

In her lifetime many of her country neighbours were wary of her, regarding her as an eccentric woman with an immoral personal life and given to dangerous idealistic enthusiasms – an upper-class type that was by then well established. Her father was an officer in Napoleon's Grand Army, her mother had been a camp-follower and was the child of a man who sold birds on the streets of Paris. Her paternal grandmother, who largely brought her up, was herself the child of an illegitimate son of the King of Poland. Present-day Anglo-Saxon attempts to set George Sand up as a feminist icon, an original rebel against 'bourgeois morality', are misconceived. But it must be said that the twentieth-century French tendency to canonize her not only as a Great Writer but as *la Bonne Dame de Nohant*, as if she had been some kind of country saint ministering to the poor and beloved by all, is equally wide of the mark. In life, George Sand had local enemies as well as admirers; her numerous novels are variable in quality and hardly qualify as 'great'. What matters most about her today is that she was the first person in France to write about the rural and artisan classes with personal knowledge and sympathy. Unlike her contemporary Balzac, who made his own contribution to the enduring French urban idea of the brutal peasantry, and Zola, who added to it later in the century from a position of metropolitan ignorance, George Sand regarded the country people as individuals like herself. Her stories such as *La Mare au Diable*, *François le Champi* and *Le Meunier d'Angibault*, are a fount of incidental local information concerning the world we have lost – and which was being lost even as she was depicting it.

Her early works were more conventionally literary and worldly. It was not till the 1840s, when the first passable road had at last been constructed between La Châtre and Châteauroux and the new railway from Paris had got as far as Orléans, that she turned her imagination back towards her own youth. The customs, language, dress and beliefs of the Berrichon countryside, which for more than a century had seemed to travellers so timeless, were suddenly revealed to be vulnerable to change after all. Progress showed signs of coming, even in this quiet heart of France. George Sand, with her trousers, her cigars and her romantic Republicanism, was no enemy to progress in theory, but the same sense of the romantic made her wary of how far-reaching the results of progress might be.

> The young people of today no longer see wandering, on a misty autumn evening, goblins, fairies or wills o' the wisp ... Within my own lifetime, my village has seen more changes in its ideas and customs than for centuries before the Revolution ... In only a year or two from now the railways will have levelled out the floors of our deepest valleys, carrying away with them as swiftly as thunder our time-honoured traditions and our wonderful legends.

She wrote that in 1845. That, as it happened, was the year after Célestine Chaumette was born in the untouched rusticity of Chassignolles, still almost inaccessible along mud tracks through the oak woods.

Chapter 4

We set out seeing the lives of those who have gone before from a distorted perspective. I became half aware of Célestine Chaumette (a name redolent of both rusticism and genteel nineteenth-century piety) before I had ever been in her house or found her cache of letters. She had been Zénaïde's grandmother, and Zénaïde, through her romantic association with the painter, was a colourful but indistinct figure and many years dead herself. Célestine had been, I was told, one of the last old ladies in the region to wear as part of her everyday dress a white goffered cap with a bow under the chin, like the ones in the museum. She had been a nice person with a presence of her own, evoked with respect but also with a degree of sadness, constraint, perhaps guilt. No one could recall just when she had died, but that event had not taken place in the village nor yet in La Châtre. She had been in Châteauroux, all of twenty miles away, in the care of the Little Sisters of the Poor. In French rural terms to end up with the Sisters, however devoted they might be, signifies some sort of social or family failure.

I had had one or two other things intimated to me about Célestine's later life, but once her letters were in my care I did not want to ask any more about that for the moment. I did not want to see her as a stooped old woman in black and a cap to whom life had not always been kind. I wanted to push aside the webs of time and change that separated us and rediscover her as she must have been when those letters were written to her: a quintessentially pretty, vital, sought-after girl.

However, I guessed that she had come back in the end to join her contemporaries in the village cemetery, so there I went first to look for her.

The cemetery is a friendly place. Even after a mere twenty years of coming to Chassignolles I recognize most of the family names. To wander round it is also to appreciate the cat's-cradle of marriages that bind the members of the Commune together. A middle-aged woman told me she had worked out, on a recent stroll among defunct neighbours, that she was in some measure related to over half the population, living and dead. In a burst of confidence she suggested to me that I might consider getting buried in the cemetery myself, 'near me, then we could chat. That would help pass the time!' Behind the joke lay the country assumption that the dead do not at once become physically remote and other as they do in cities. The transition from working the land to lying beneath it is natural, almost matter of fact, and there is a corresponding aversion to the idea of being buried far off in alien soil. In the days before the funeral the person continues to lie on his own bed – though in his best suit – and is brought to the burial ground on a hand-wheeled bier with a great, placid crowd of known people, in their own best suits and coats, following behind.

Yet the realities of physical change and decay too are inescapable in the country. At some point the imagination has to relinquish the person, to consign him to a different dimension. Is this why rural French cemeteries are so oddly formal and, to English eyes, grace-less compared with what lies all around them? The English notion of the graveyard itself as a place where sheep may safely graze, derived from centuries of Protestant psalm-singing, does not appeal to the Latin tradition. Chassignolles' cemetery has a fine view down a small valley, across a rivulet, towards the setting sun, but it is an enclosure of dust, neatly raked, of stone chippings, polished slabs, dirty glass and rusting iron. Not only grass but free-growing plants and trees are taboo.

Perhaps, simply, those who work close to nature all their lives do not prize it: for their memorials they want something more deliberate, some artefact. It has been explained to me that a sheaf of wild flowers, however exquisite, will not do to lay on the grave of old Madame Chose. The Chose family, if they are not to feel slighted, will expect a formal sheaf from the florist in La Châtre or, better, a plant in a pot. Or, better still, a brightly coloured artificial bloom that does not fade: the immortality of the spirit tastefully symbolized by cerise and viridian plastic. One may also contribute to a stone plaque, with a strut like a framed photograph, saying 'To our beloved Aunt', 'To a much regretted Neighbour', 'In memory of a dear Godmother', or whatever sentiment is appropriate. Some graves have a permanent array of these plaques as on a dressing-table and this has inevitably become a worldly status symbol of the respect and affection the defunct commanded in life.

But some do not. *'There is no name, with whatever emphasis of passionate love repeated, of which the echo is not faint at the last.'* It took me a long time to find the Chaumette family vault, mainly because the black granite slab with the names had become detached from its cross and was lying in pieces in the eroded, flowerless dust. Laboriously I reassembled most of the bits.

Célestine was there. And Charles her son. And Charles's daughter Zénaïde. Also mentioned were Célestine's father and mother.

Zénaïde was born in 1895 and died in 1954. So, as I had been told, she was not quite sixty when her Australian painter lost her. I remembered Bernardet saying to us with one of his elegant turns of phrase, when the old painter was still alive but becoming forgetful, 'It would be best if he were to die here, really. The one who was his companion is in the cemetery' – *'Celle qui était sa compagne est dans le cimetière'*. But chance fell otherwise, and the old man died at last a long way from the patch of French earth he had made his own.

Zénaïde's father was born in 1865 and died in 1934, so he too did not make really old bones. He survived his mother, but only just. For Célestine, I saw, almost reached ninety. Born in 1844, she lived on until 1933.

It is a vertiginous stretch of time. Célestine entered a world where not even cart tracks but just narrow footpaths linked villages like Chassignolles to the outside world, and measures of distance were expressed in terms of how far you could walk in a given time or how much of a field a man could plough in a day. She was born into a France in which the inhabitants of each region and sub-region considered themselves essentially people of that *pays*, with their own dialects and customs, and French citizens only in a theoretical, remote way that did not affect their daily lives. In the 1840s the great mass of the people had no formal education at all and, more fundamentally, had no notion as yet that progress and change were elsewhere becoming regarded as part of the natural order of existence.

Wolves still roamed the woods and forests, seized lambs on the misty edges of fields and were even seen in hard winters to enter farmyards. But wolves were not the only dangers at large. In the imagination of the people, especially in the Berry, which was a country famed for the supernatural, the hills and valleys were crowded with spirits. The dead and the fairies (often mingled) hung around at crossroads. In the moonlight, Midnight Washer-women washed the souls of unbaptized babies, while on windy nights in the racing clouds whole trains of unearthly huntsmen crossed the sky. Round La Châtre, a being resembling a man but larger, known as Le Grand Bissetre, was sighted hovering over pools in certain years. He was a bad omen – but then so was the familiar screech owl, whose mournful cry, when heard at a distance, sounds like heavy breathing and whose feet on the roof overhead are like human steps. Marsh gas, a light in the wood, a beast snuffling in a dark field, the buzzing of insects – any of these could be a portent of some alarming event.

As for an unfamiliar face encountered on a path, a pedlar with books of printed words in his pack – one never knew what such meetings might signify. Even the known might turn out to be sinister: who could tell but that the woodcutters and the charcoal-burners, who passed their time in the forests, might not be *meneurs de loups*, secretly in league with wolves? The peasant novelist Émile Guillaumin, writing in 1904 of the world his grandparents had known, evokes the horror of the little swineherd on a heathland when he is accosted by one of these strangers, even though the man is only an itinerant tree-feller looking for a spring to fill his flask. 'When I saw the big, dark person who was not from any of the three neighbouring farms, I was so terror-struck I could not move.' Elsewhere Guillaumin writes: 'The peasants were always afraid. They didn't know just what they were afraid of, but they were always afraid of something.'

'That 'something', conceived of as the visitation of a spirit or a neighbour's evil spell, was in reality famine, sickness, absolute want, recurrent realities still for those who worked the soil. Until well into the second half of the nineteenth century, most of those who dwelt in the countryside were on the perpetual edge of poverty, entirely vulnerable to a bad harvest, an extra-cold winter, a chance stroke of personal misfortune. The awareness of this is enshrined in songs:

> *Dansons la capucine, i'a 'pas de pain chez nous,*
> *'Y en a chez la voisine, mais ce n'est pas pour nous –*
> *Ahr-rr . . .*
> (We dance the beggars' dance, there's nay bread in our house,
> There's plenty at our neighbours' but it's not for us)

Many people still, in the time of Célestine's birth, fed and clothed themselves entirely on what they produced or made or could barter locally. Nothing was bought for money but iron and salt, solemn purchases made once a year in November, on St Martin's Day. (It is perhaps significant that iron and salt, coming by way of the alien towns, were the two things that malevolent country fairies were thought to fear.) Till the late 1840s salt was expensive on account of the notorious Salt Tax which also made its purchase obligatory, but it was nevertheless essential to every household for pickling and preserving food for the winter. Iron was also expensive, and might be thought of as equally essential for farm implements, but even in regions like the Berry, where there were forges, it was something of a rare, special commodity to the ordinary smallholder. Still, in the mid-nineteenth century, the wooden plough on the medieval model, made for and by the hands that would drive it, was in common use, with the addition only of an iron tip. The odd cooking pot, knife blade and needle was bought at long intervals. But sugar, coffee, lamp oil, wax candles, bought furniture or cloth – in the country, even to the relatively prosperous family, these things were exotic luxuries and would be for another twenty years. The long winter nights, sometimes passed in the stables along with the animals for warmth, were lit, at best, by spluttering smelly, home-made tallow candles, more often by scraps of wick floating in pans of nut oil or by the even more primitive *pétrelles* – slivers of wood dipped in resin to emit a tiny sparkle. Matches were unknown. Fires were laboriously struck with tinder and flint, or reignited with a borrowed clog-full of smouldering cinders:

> *Va chez la voisine,*
> *Je crois qu'elle y est*

29

Car danš sa cuisine
On bat le briquet

(Go to the neighbour,
I think she's there all right,
For I hear in her kitchen
Someone striking a light)

England, on a different timetable with different historical milestones, had evolved considerably in the seventeenth century and still more in the eighteenth. Adam Smith, in *The Wealth of Nations* (1776), pointed out that the English agricultural worker commonly had in his lowly cottage all sorts of products from distant countries that had been through many hands. Not so in France, where distances were so much greater and local cultures much more distinct. There the industrial revolution began to transform life for most people much later and in a much more piecemeal way; the difference is still apparent today. Even when it had wrought its transformation in parts of France in the early nineteenth century, the banker Jacques Lafitte complained that these areas were trying to sell their products to consumers who were stuck in the fourteenth century and seemed content there. Moreover, these non-consumers, the rural masses of France, were then the great majority of the population.

But George Sand had glimpsed the future and spoken presciently, even though the railways took longer to arrive in the Lower Berry than she predicted. When Célestine made her inconspicuous entry into the world, stealthy changes were just beginning to be felt which, over her lifetime, would sweep the fourteenth century away – and the fifteenth, sixteenth, seventeenth, eighteenth and even the nineteenth. She and her contemporaries would experience the quiet, irresistible revolution brought about by what a senior French civil servant called 'the two great motors of civilization', the spread of roads and railway lines and the coming of education for all. But beyond this, she herself lived on to see the telegraph, the bicycle, the camera, the telephone, the internal-combustion engine, even the cinema and the aeroplane. She saw the occasional car vibrating in the village square and the mechanical reaper clattering in the fields. She heard wireless sets burbling in the cafés. She lived to see her grandchildren's generation dancing in short skirts to the alien music of a wind-up gramophone. Before this, she had seen that generation forcibly involved in a war of hitherto unthinkable proportions from which many never returned.

Much of France changed more in the years between 1840 and 1930, or even 1914, than it did during the five centuries before. In our own late-twentieth-century world it has become commonplace to emphasize the speed of social and technological development and to speak as if this were in itself a unique and stressful experience. We are greatly mistaken. The transformation of the world around her that someone like Célestine had to absorb between childhood and age makes our adjustments seem relatively insignificant. A more apt comparison might be between nineteenth-century France and many parts of twentieth-century Asia. The historian Eugen Weber makes the point that, in the years before the Franco-Prussian war and the Paris Commune of 1870–71, much of central and southern France was at the stage of development that we now associate with the Third World – with Paris in the role of distant, colonizing power. Perhaps, therefore, the experience of Célestine's generation in Chassignolles can be perceived now by looking at rural India, where local famines have faded away only in the last twenty years, superstitions and customs remain powerful, but roads, electricity, tractors, modern medicine and, above all, radio and television, are at last modifying an immemorial way of life for ever.

The story of Célestine's life, therefore – which is hardly a story in any intricate sense, just an outline in pencil with details noted in faded ink – is the story of an epic period in recent French history. Uncovering facts about her to add substance to the letters, I realized that what I was also discovering was a social drama of evolution: not so much the story of a woman but of a place and thus of ten thousand other places like it.

Even confining myself to one village, I have only been able to present in the light of a retrospective day a few individuals among hundreds of possible ones. Their particular, obscure destinies reflect great events or movements that were taking place far beyond their own circuits or conscious experiences: the making of a whole French culture and way of thought that still – just – endures.

Chapter 5

When I first began to find out about Célestine's life I was accustomed to the more centralized record-keeping methods of Great Britain. It did not initially occur to me that the dates I had hunted down among broken shards in the cemetery might be more conveniently available in the village Mairie. I was aware that all births, marriages and deaths in France are registered in this very local way; but I assumed that the town hall registers of fifty years ago, let alone a hundred and fifty, would long since have been sucked into the maw of French bureaucracy. I thought that I would have to go to the county town of Châteauroux to consult them, probably travestied on to faint and unconvincing microfilm like a dialogue with ectoplasm, on which it is impossible to keep track of more than one page at a time.

I did know, however, that the Mairie possessed a fine map of the Commune dating from 1843, drawn by hand. It is coloured in delicate washes of ochre, pink and green, with the names of fields and outlying hamlets in a flowing script. It is inscribed: *'Terminé sur le terrain sous l'Administration de Mr. Bonnet, Préfet, Mr. Pirot, Maire, Mr. de Boureulle, Directeur des Contributions directes, Mr. Colsen, Géomètre en Chef du Cadastre.'* So careful and complete was the work of these gentlemen that the present-day map, which shows the dimensions of every parcel of land for legal purposes, is still based upon it and drawn to the same scale. Happily, the

Lower Berry has not suffered the *remembrement* (regrouping of land) in the name of efficiency that has swept away field patterns, and with them memories and history, in much of France nearer to the Loire. In fact there are, if anything, more subdivisions of land now in Chassignolles than there were several generations ago, as a result of the legal Code that obliges families to divide up an inheritance into equal shares.

The present mayor is also Monsieur Pirot. He is related to the earlier one: all the numerous Pirots in the district are said to be descended from two Serbian brothers who came to France as soldiers of fortune during the Wars of Religion. He had shown us the old map years before, in response to a query regarding our own house and land. Now, realizing that it documented Chassignolles in the very year of Célestine's birth, I went to study it again with more minute interest.

Although the speckled woods were then more extensive than they are now, you could still use this map to find your way to almost any corner of the Commune. And yet it is another place that it depicts. The village of 1843 had the same basic shape, clustered round the meeting point of several roads, that it has today, but there was then no Mairie and no buildings on the site of the present café, the baker's or the post office. Fenced vegetable gardens occupied the place of the cemetery: the crosses of graves filled the space round the church where the road now runs. The small, old houses along the line of the medieval fortifications and the house with the tower were there. But a close examination of most of the other buildings on the map suggested that even though they occupied the same spaces as the present-day houses they were not necessarily these houses. Today the village as a whole looks just old, in a generalized, settled way. But between Célestine's childhood and the First World War, much rebuilding must have taken place.

Our own house, for example, is built of local rough stone, rendered, and its pinky-brown floor tiles of fired clay are laid straight over the earth and participate in the changing damp or dryness of the seasons. The walls are very thick, the oak and elm timbers that support the tiled roof were hewn by hand and raised in the same pattern that you find in buildings hundreds of years older. But the fireplace is small and the one main window is a conventionally sized casement with factory-made fastenings. These last details speak of a building not constructed till the latter half of the nine-teenth century. On the old map the rectangle marking a house on the site coincides with the position of ours, once you allow for the widening of the footpath into a road. However the fireplace, as shown by the bulge of a bread oven, is at the other end. I think that at some time in the 1870s or '80s the building that was here was demolished and the materials were used to raise a new house on the same foundations.

Modest as our house is, I can imagine that when it was rebuilt it represented a distinct advance in comfort and modernity compared with the dwelling it replaced – huge old hearth, small, glassless window or perhaps just the hatched upper half of the door, like a stable door, to let in the light, beaten earth floor, animals stabled behind a flimsy partition so that their warmth might penetrate the human living space. There are still houses like this in the Commune. But most have today been relegated to farm use, and many more have evidently gone.

The process continues. The Monsieur Pirot of today pointed out to me that even since I had known the village myself at least three houses on its outskirts had been allowed to fall down and disappear, while others scarcely larger, in carefully 'traditional' design with rustic shutters to please the planning authorities, had risen nearby.

'People would rather have a home with a proper damp course and modern conveniences. It's only natural. And it's cheaper to build again from scratch, out of the pattern-book. The old materials aren't wasted, though. They're sold for what they'll fetch. Or people just take them, if they're left lying around, to patch up their own houses.'

I thought momentarily about the indestructibility of matter – the likelihood that some of the stones the thirteenth-century monks built into their fortifications are dispersed to this day round houses elsewhere in the village. I remembered an abandoned house near our own which had looked solid enough until one year its roof had become a skeleton, stripped of tiles, open to wind and rain. Now, ten years later, all trace of it had gone and the site had been incorporated into next door's vegetable patch.

'Once the roof's gone on these old properties the walls just go back to the soil,' said Pirot equably. 'They're just earth and stones.' The centre of Chassignolles, these days, is 'classified as a monument', which is to say Listed, but I discovered soon after this that the municipal council was in a dispute with the Beaux-Arts, the listing authority, about the garage proprietor's right to demolish one of the last pre-Revolutionary cottages in the street.

Pirot, the owner of many cows, was less interested in old houses than in the shapes of the parcels of lands in 1843. Casting a practised eye over them, he was able to point out which segments are now in what use. The average land holding in the Commune today is forty to fifty hectares (about a hundred acres) either owned or rented, with many proprietors holding less. Many of the old field names are still current. With some of them – La Grande Salle, Le Champ Rouge – the origin of the name is obvious: the latter pasture still has a vein of iron-red soil across it. Other names speak of uses now forgotten except in this survival: La Forge, La Gitte (the animals' lair), Le Bute (archery butts), Le Champ Galland (the tournament field). Others again suggest lost history: was buried gold once unearthed in Le Champ de l'Or? What was the Roc au Sourd (Deaf Man's Stone) in the field of that name? And does the name 'Pendu' (hanged) attached to both a field and a crossroads indicate the one-time presence of a gibbet?

Pirot could not tell me. But he remarked that there was a Chêne Pendu (literally, 'hanged oak', but perhaps once the Oak of the Hanged) in a wood on the edge of the Commune.

'In the Bois de Villemort?' I asked. We had sought it out one unnaturally still, balmy day in the dead of winter, when a luminous blue light had shone through the bare branches and crows had clattered among the dead leaves. The tree is so huge that an adult photographed standing beside its trunk appears in the picture as small as a doll. It had not been hard to believe that unpleasant retributions had once gone on in that isolated spot, though it is true that malefactors were not normally strung up in the depths of woods but by roads where passers-by could be impressed by this demonstration of justice received. I discovered later that the only record of bodies on the great oak is of those of eighteen wolves, strung up there after a wolf hunt organized in 1849 when strenuous efforts were being made to drive man's traditional enemy out of the Berry. The wolves remained unimpressed, for near the end of the century the Bois de Villemort was one of the last places where they were sighted or heard in the area.

Villemort – 'dead town' – must indicate an abandoned settlement, but Pirot knew of no story connected with the name. The only human habitation near that place on the old map and still the only one today is a late-medieval gentleman's residence: one of those 'castles' with a turret or two, an ancient chapel and an external staircase. Here is another hint of past greatness in this quiet place: huntsmen, hawks, hounds – all the vanished pageant.

On the old map the property at Villemort looks rather more extensive than it is today, with outbuildings that are now only shadows under an adjacent field when the light falls the right way. Similar ghosts of buildings appear round the Bernardets' farm-hamlet (Les Béjauds – 'the falcon nursery') about half a kilometre from the village, and at other outlying farms. It has been suggested by the French historian Braudel that the sites of these well-established hamlets may go back to prehistory; that they are possibly older, in many cases, than the villages which developed later round crossroads and fords. Still, in the first half of the nineteenth century relatively more people lived in the settlements among the fields where they worked and fewer *au bourg*. There were not so many reasons, in the 1840s, to settle in a village that as yet had no shops, few artisans, no administrative centre but the church, and no school. What turned out to be the golden age of village life lay in the future – in Célestine's adulthood.

The tracks leading to these far settlements were as large as, or larger than, those leading in the direction of the next village and on to La Châtre. Evidently, in the 1840s, most paths were for short journeys within the Commune, from one field or neighbour to another, not for travelling from place to place in the modern sense. Indeed, in many parts of France at that time, including the Lower Berry, a general network of routes was entirely lacking. Some good long-distance highways had existed since Roman times, and others had been constructed, usually for military purposes, in the last half of the eighteenth century or during the Napoleonic wars, but these left much of the country untouched. The British traveller Arthur Young, in his enthusiastic *Journals*, put forward the idea that French roads were superior to English ones, but the maps of the time show this to be based on some highly selective travelling. As George Sand wrote in *Le Meunier d'Angibault*:

> In the centre of France, in spite of all the new main roads that have been opened in recent years, country districts still have

such poor communications that it is difficult to get from the local people exact directions to another place even a short distance away ... Try asking in a hamlet the way to a farm a league distant [*circa* two and a half miles] and you'll be lucky if you get a clear answer. There are so many little paths, all much alike.

I have seen it suggested elsewhere that some of these supposed paths were, in any case, not paths at all but strips of outgrown woodland between the fields, going nowhere, a snare and delusion for the wheeled traveller. They even had their own local name: 'Mysterious retreating perspectives beneath thick shade, *traînes* of emerald green leading to dead ends or to stagnant pools, twisting abruptly down slopes that you can't get up again in a carriage ...'

Today some of these old paths and false paths round Chassignolles remain as they always were, deep, green veins running between old hedges, well preserved but little used. Others have arbitrarily disappeared into the fields, while the same operation of chance has turned others again into tarmacked roads. Three proper roads lead from Chassignolles in the general direction of La Châtre, while a fourth, probably the oldest of all, descending a valley to ford a tributary of the Indre, is today almost forgotten and in places impassable with saplings and brambles.

Each time I looked at the old map I felt myself being drawn into it, possessed by the feeling that if I studied it hard enough it would, like a photograph gradually enlarging and enlarging under my gaze, carry me deeper into those narrow lanes, allow me to see the small oblongs transformed into the shapes of roofs and doors, eventually revealing the trellises of vines, the tracery of the plough, every tree, every stone, every dung-heap ...

'Was it something particular you wanted to find out?' said Monsieur Pirot.

I did not want to appear intrusive and in any case I did not yet have a formulated plan. I murmured that I wanted to check up on one or two things. Only then did it occur to me to ask how far back his other records went.

'Oh, to the Revolution.' That magic date between Then and Now.

'What – all here in the Mairie?'

'Certainly. All the Birth, Death and Marriage registers going way back. They're in that cupboard there. And we've got the records of Council meetings too.'

'Not back to the Revolution as well?'

'Well, back a long way. As long as they had Council meetings, I suppose. They're very old books.'

'That's wonderful. May *I* consult them?'

'Of course,' he said, surprised that I should even ask. 'Anyone can. But' – he added quickly – 'it's Silvie the Secretary you want to see. That's her department. I don't know much about them. Yes, Silvie my niece. She's a Pirot too.'

Silvie, young and pretty and soon to be the mother of a baby girl, was already showing signs of being one of those linchpins on which village life has always depended: the person of some education and energy who is nevertheless happy to remain in a deeply rural society and help it to function. There are not enough Silvies in rural France today: this lament is heard on every side. And yet there are rather more now in Chassignolles than there were in the previous generation. They, in the 1960s, were tempted away to the towns, to the shops and businesses of La Châtre or the factories of Châteauroux or yet to the more visionary possibilities of Tours, Orléans or Paris itself. Today unemployment in the towns is perhaps making the remote countryside seem more attractive again – even with omnipresent fears about the future of the traditional French agriculture on which this part of the Berry has always depended.

Silvie was used to a trickle of enquiries about distant births, deaths and marriages. For people intent of proving that Great Aunt Marthe had been born an Aladenise and that *her* mother had been an Ageorges and that therefore a certain orchard should still be in the family, Silvie would copy out declarations of ancient life-events in her own French school handwriting. It was rare, however, that anyone came asking for the Minute books of the Municipal meetings, which were stacked on top of each other in the far recesses of the cupboard. She got the books out for me, blowing dust from hand-sewn covers, and seemed happy that someone should be interested enough to turn the long-unread pages. We were a long way here from microfiche readers and bar codes. By and by, when she saw that my interest in the books was not going to be assuaged in a mere hour or two's work, she let me look at them whenever I wanted, whether the Mairie was officially open or not. She also, with patience and good humour, helped me to reconstruct several family-trees by reference to the Birth and Marriage registers. I was lucky to find Silvie, though just how lucky I only realized when I tried to consult similar documents in a much larger urban Mairie and was met by a bland refusal even to let me have the books in my own hands. Only specifically requested entries, I was told, could be delivered in photocopy form.

'Why?'

'Because otherwise you might see something relating to someone else.'

'But there are no rules about what I may specifically request, are there?'

'No, no.'

'Well, then . . .?'

But evidently rules, however illogical, were rules. The cause of disinterested historical research was not going to be furthered in that town hall.

In Chassignolles, the very early 'Deliberations of the Municipal Council', as they are collectively called, consist of disparate sheets of hand-made paper roughly sewn together and put between covers at a later date. The pages start in the year 1810, by which point the immediate traumas of the Revolution had passed. The calendar had reverted from the single figures of the New Era to its traditional form; the Napoleonic Code was attempting to spread a homogenizing blanket over the enormously varied territories that made up France. The entries for these early years tend to be brief, the records of men with a respect both for the written word and for the expensive material on which it was set down.

An exception to this occurred after Napoleon's defeat and his replacement by the Bourbon monarchy, when, for a few years, the records seem to have been kept by one Louis Vallet or Vaillet or Vallete who was also the mayor. This man, alone among his fellow-citizens then and for several decades, wrote a fluent, hurried, almost modern hand in correct French. When I first identified him I guessed (what I later found to be the case) that he, or rather his father, was one of those upper-class landowners who made themselves scarce during and after the Revolution but returned at the Restoration to resume something of their old place in society. Vallet may in the long run have profited from the turmoil, for he acquired a lot of land, some of which had previously belonged to the Church; in fact he became the largest landowner in the Commune. He seems to have been inclined to treat the place as his own fief and to have had little respect for new authority. He got into trouble with the Préfet (the figure of national command in distant Châteauroux) for cutting down trees on the highway and building his own watercourse without regard for others. After he ceased to be mayor in 1825 it was stated by the new mayor (Pirot) that *le Sieur Vaillet* was known to have made off at an earlier date with the silver vessels from the church; the Council ventured the opinion that he should be invited to return them. Vallet no doubt answered that he had taken the silver into protective keeping at the time when the Church was being dispossessed by the newly formed state and its priests driven into hiding. By the 1820s Chassignolles' church was being repaired after years of neglect: rain and bird droppings had been coming through gaps in the wooden tiles of the roof.

Vallet must have made his peace with the others or simply been too prominent a person to ignore, for after a few years he was back again as a member of the Council. He continued, though, to cause occasional trouble. As late as 1845, when he was well into his fifties but apparently no more circumspect in his behaviour, the exasperated Council even took him to court in La Châtre *'pour avoir fait enlever les terres provenant de la fosse publique appartenant à la Commune'*. The public ditch was a remnant of moat from the medieval church fortifications. Presumably the soil in it was valuable manure and he had refused to apologize. There is no mention in the Minutes of the time he pulled down an old farm building and discovered in its foundations a hoard of eighth-century silver and gold coins: I found that reference elsewhere, in the notes on the La Châtre region of a nineteenth-century antiquary. The village must have thought that was just Vallet's kind of luck. I wonder where those coins are now?

For many years, both before and after Vallet's reign, the Minutes seem not to have been kept by any formally appointed Secretary but by one or other of the handful of men in the Commune who could actually write. There was an Aussourd who filled this role at an early date. (Names beginning with 'Ala' or 'Au', meaning 'son of' – son of the deaf man, son of Georges, son of Our Denise – are very common in the Black Valley.) Later the books were kept by a François Charbonnier, born in 1799 – *L'An VIII*. He was one of a proliferating Chassignolles family of Charbonniers ('charcoal-burner') all called François or Jean or Denis through several generations. By the time I reached the Minute books of the later nineteenth century I needed to remind myself that the Jean Charbonnier then signing as a councillor could hardly be the one who was already there by 1810. But literacy clearly ran in this able family; I was slightly disappointed when I established that the Charbonnier who was the first effective schoolmaster *circa* 1860 was not one of its members and came from a different village. There are Charbonniers in Chassignolles to this day who appear, from their land holdings, to be descended from the original family; they are know collectively as the *Tourangeaux* because they are supposed to have come from the Touraine. Since when? The Revolution?

The village was lucky to have the likes of the Aussourds and the Charbonniers; many Communes did not, even town ones that headed Cantons. Balzac wrote in *Les Paysans*, which was published in the year of Célestine's birth: 'Many mayors of Cantons turn the copies of the Rules and Regulations that are issued to them into bags for holding raisins or seeds. As for the mere mayors of Communes, you would be shocked by the number who cannot read or write and by the way in which the civil registers are kept.' A modern perspective on the matter might be that it was excessively ambitious of the French government at that period to have set up all over that deeply rural land such an urban concept of local government that it required unlettered men to take time off from their land to keep civil registers at all. Why, one might wonder, have such civil and municipal responsibilities been scissored into such small parcels? Why not a more centralized system? The traditional answer to this refers to the grassroot and egalitarian basis of French democracy, but there is another answer which is probably even more relevant. For all its conviction of profound change, the Revolution simply took on the existing parish system and the secular mayors inherited exactly those duties of ceremony and record which had previously fallen to the village priests. For the first few decades of the nineteenth century there was not even a change of setting; the church continued to be, as ever, the place where assemblies took place and where the records were kept.

Although Pirot, who succeeded Vallet, was mayor for many years till 1846, I do not think he himself could write. His careful signature is that of someone who has learnt to do it as a trick and does not otherwise employ a pen. He could probably read a little. During his time, with the exception of the Charbonniers and of Vallet when he was there, the other nine or ten councillors all 'declared themselves unable to sign' and continued to do so for much of the century. This was no fiction: when the occasional councillor did decide to try his hand at a signature he did so in toppling, unformed letters – a Chaumette appears early on in this form. The cast evolves and changes over the course of time; by 1855, when this Minute book ends, several family names had appeared which are still found in the village, but non-literacy continued to be the prevailing style. These men, as municipal councillors, were the élite of the village; several of them owned substantial amounts of land for that time and place; others were millers or smith-farriers whose occupations placed them distinctly above the ordinary peasantry; all would have been accustomed to buy and sell in the local markets and keep accounts. They were no doubt skilled in twenty different ways that we have now lost and shrewd enough at deciding whether or not the cost to the Commune of replacing a ford with a bridge, widening a path or building a new house to attract a schoolmaster, would pay off in benefits. But reading and writing they did not undertake.

In the early Minutes there are many gaps, but from 1839 the record was kept fairly regularly in a book provided for the purpose. The second book begins in 1855 and runs till 1880, the third from 1880 till 1905. Versions of schoolmasterly copperplate succeed each other, some clearer than most modern hands, some so ornate as to be semi-impenetrable. If you sit and turn the pages by the hour it can seem as if village life went round in perpetual circles. The budget for the school is regularly disputed, concern is expressed that the church tower needs repairs yet again, and the widening of this or that essential path by the purchase of strips of land from adjoining holdings seems to have got little further forward than it had seven years before. A recurrent phrase in the description of Council meetings and eventual decisions (often of a procrastinating nature) is *ayant mûrement délibéré*. This is best translated in English as 'after much discussion', but *mûrement* strictly speaking means 'ripely'. It reflects the self-image of Chassignolles' leading citizens. *Pères de famille* in good, locally woven woollen trousers and waist-coats, oak-green in colour, and shirts or smocks of home-grown

42

linen, they sat round in a state of congenital Berrichon caution and hard-headedness, refusing to let themselves be hustled into anything, mature deliberation personified.

And yet, cumulatively, as you read on page by page and year by year, the cycles modify: changes are taking place after all. The constant minor dramas about the enlargement of paths or the creation of new ones are local evidence of much more widely spreading communications and burgeoning trade. After the mid-century, demands to the Préfet to authorize the establishment of new 'fairs', which were regularly held cattle and grain markets, begin to appear; these demands were passed from Commune to Commune so that all parties could endorse them. Business was steadily increasing, more produce was being bought and sold instead of just consumed on the spot. And then, at the same period, there comes one entry (summer 1855) like a sudden hail from the future, or a distant whistle heard across the fields – the first excited mention of railways.

Of the cataclysmic national events of the nineteenth century – the successive uprisings, the overthrow of king or emperor, *coups*, the Franco-Prussian war, the Paris Commune and its bloody repression, then the final establishment of France as a republic – hardly a direct mention reaches the Minute books. And yet hints of these events are there, like distant thunder below the horizon.

For example, among some loose, undated papers slipped into the 1839–55 volume is the draft of a formula for swearing grovelling obedience to the French Constitution and the Emperor. This must date from January 1852, when the hopefully entitled Prince-President, Louis-Napoleon, had managed to transform himself into the much more autocratic figure of Emperor in the tradition of his more famous ancestor. One must assume that in Chassignolles the swearing-in ceremony did dutifully take place, though on this the Minutes are silent. What is significant in the Minutes is that in 1852 the mayor changed, and the new incumbent was not, judging by his name, a villager but an old-style aristocrat: Léon Geoffrenet de Champdavid. The idealistic Second Republic from 1848 to 1851 had brought in the vote for all male householders, which was a step well in advance of other European nations. In keeping with this spirit, mayors were to be elected by the Commune. But by

43

1852 this had changed again and new mayors were appointed by the local Préfet.

No sooner was he installed, than Monsieur Geoffrenet de Champdavid insisted on repairs being done to the church and to the presbytery, in order to attract a priest. Chassignolles had had no resident Curé since the Revolution, but a return to old ways was now evidently to be the order of the day and what was happening in Chassignolles was just one example of a general shift. The Revolutionary, anti-clerical spirit that had flourished briefly in the area three years before, encouraged by George Sand and her progressive friends, was now very much out of fashion. The new widespread vote, far from ensuring the Republican reformers victory, had worked against them: in the Berry, in January 1852 twenty times more votes were cast for Louis-Napoleon as Emperor than for the Republican cause. Republicanism, it was now felt, was for townspeople. The word doing the rounds in the countryside was that the Republicans would force down the price of wheat, and therefore the peasants' profit margin, in order to gain cheap bread for the big cities. La Châtre had turned temporarily against the Bonne Dame de Nohant, even demonstrating the fact noisily at the gates of her manor. It was being said that she had got local people into trouble with the authorities, and to no purpose. As a Préfet of the Indre (D'Alphonse) wrote earlier in the century:

> Placidity [*douceur*] is the distinctive characteristic of the inhabitants of this Department. They appreciate it when good is done to them; they complain little when ills are caused but support them calmly and resignedly ... The Berrichon respects and looks up to the Government not because he finds it so admirable but because the Government leaves him in peace, and peace is for him the most natural and best of states.

Or, as Émile Guillaumin put it in *La Vie d'un Simple*, which is set in the next Department, towards the Loire: 'In the country, we trouble our heads very little about what Government get up to. Come Peter, come Paul, it isn't our affair. What is, is the routine drudgery of work, and that does not change.'

Guillaumin's writing has become something of an early socialist text, with its insistent theme of the harshness of the more fortunate towards the less. Other people's reminiscences strike a less brood-

44

ing note, but there is no doubt that Guillaumin does capture the obsessive hopes and anxieties of those working on the land. The French peasant with his few hectares might seem to have been more independent than the farm labourer across the Channel working for a large landowner, but in practice he was perpetually in thrall to the vagaries of the seasons and to events in the world beyond his horizon. The egalitarian principles of citizenhood – free and fraternal – were imposed on top of older and tougher imperatives, and do not quite sit easily there to this day.

During the more violent political spasm of 1870–71 it was remarked by another observer that the Berrichon peasant showed a new tendency to keep his hat on and offer his hand to a social superior as to an equal, but that, come King, Emperor or Republic, he would still vote for the person who simply seemed likely to procure him the best deal.

True to form, the Minute books of Chassignolles entirely ignore the events that had brought about the fall of the Second Empire by September 1870. No hint of the drama going on elsewhere surfaces till two months later. Then, Paris was entering its long winter under siege by the Prussians. Since a detachment of Prussians was also much nearer at hand, on the Cher at Vierzon, one might think that the inhabitants of the Lower Berry would have had qualms about their own safety and the need for military protection. Certainly in La Châtre, where troops of newly conscripted soldiers passed through singing songs to the local bagpipes, people were conscious of being in a country at war. There were rumours of cannon fire being heard; men ostentatiously carried around with them the old-fashioned carbines they used to shoot game, and women started knitting woollen waistcoats for *nos p'tits gars* in a way that prefigured the great, sad working parties during the next round of hostilities in 1914–18. However, a testy entry in the Chassignolles Minutes for November merely notes that the governmental demand for 3238 francs to be voted from Communal funds for the National Guard was 'quite impossible'. All that was in the Commune kitty at that moment was 989 francs, 29 centimes. The Government could have that, if it wanted. The lively topic of debate that autumn was not the invasion and social unrest in the north, but the construction of the first properly made road between Chassignolles and La Châtre.

With the hindsight of history, one might argue that this road was a more truly significant and representative event than the replacement of the Second Empire by the Third Republic. Whether the other changes at village level that the 1870s and '80s were to bring would have come in any case, even without a Republic to orchestrate them, remains a matter of debate. The democratic spirit of Republicanism did, however, lay an obligation on all its male citizens that, under older regimes, had been largely avoided: in the last quarter of the century the Minutes of Municipal meetings in Chassignolles fill up with requests – to be forwarded to the military authorities – that this or that young man should be excused from military service since he was needed down on the farm. So the most obvious sign of the distant events that were shaping France's history was the desire on the part of the village to keep their boys away from them.

In the local newspapers, revolutions in Paris surface a little more, since they were written for and by townspeople. Their circulations were counted in hundreds only, and till near the end of the century they hardly penetrated the villages. So, for instance, *L'Écho de l'Indre* (later *L'Écho du Berry*), which was published in La Châtre, represented exclusively the preoccupations of the *bonne société* of that small town or, if we are to believe George Sand, the six or seven *sociétés* that did not necessarily consort with each other, let alone vote the same way. These social divisions, in practice, operated more along political lines than along lines of class. In essential terms the small towns in the first half of the nineteenth century seem to have been as close-knit as the present villages. In addition, whatever urban airs they might have given themselves, the townspeople lived so close to the countryside that their interests were more or less identified with it. The figures usually given for percentages of urban as opposed to rural populations in France are therefore misleading. For the entire nineteenth century, the 'urban' population of the Indre hovered around twenty-eight per cent as opposed to seventy-two per cent 'rural', but the urban were hardly so in the way we would use the word today. Most La Châtre families owned fields or orchards or a vineyard outside the city; many of them supplied some of the made goods or skills that country people were now beginning to purchase.

The cultural gulf between town and country in France, which existed then and still exists to a large extent today, has more to do with social manner and self-image than with any deep-seated material differences. French class fantasies are not the same as those that are current across the Channel. The better-off inhabitants of English country towns have for a long time cultivated that peculiarly British rural inverted snobbery, innocent yet tenacious, which expresses itself in old trousers, darned sweaters, dogs, guns and *Country Life*. In contrast, the inhabitants of provincial French towns like La Châtre and Châteauroux have traditionally turned their eyes towards Paris. They adopt a *tenue de ville*, all neat suits and shoes, carefully styled hair and ceremonial greetings. But in reality Paris is far away from La Châtre even today, and was a great deal farther for much of the nineteenth century, when it took from nine to twelve hours in a coach before you got even as far as Châteauroux.

The name of the main street in La Châtre was obediently changed over the years from Rue Nationale to Rue Royale, then Rue Égalité, then Rue Impériale and then back again to Nationale, as great events demanded. There were occasional eruptions of patriotic fervour over such manufactured 'events' as the Emperor's birthday – and, indeed, the occasional demonstration, from one of the *sociétés*, of anti-Royalist emotion. But the real concerns of La Châtre were much the same as those of the surrounding villages: the state of the roads, visionary schemes for railway lines which more often than not failed to materialize, the weather, the harvest, the floods, the drought, the insatiable needs of the poor and the disgraceful misbehaviour of young males – and occasionally young females too, how shocking – after the local fairs.

Because of the extensive and unique record available to me in the cupboard of our own Mairie, it was some time before I sought out the official Archives in Châteauroux. With a car, forty kilometres is nothing. Without one, however, as I have often been in France, the journey abruptly expands to the dimensions it must have had at the turn of the century. It begins with seven kilometres into La Châtre on foot or by bicycle to catch one of the infrequent buses that run to Châteauroux today from the moribund railway station. The bus does not take the direct route but, impersonating the branch-line train that it has replaced, it makes its way circuitously for an hour or so through half a dozen villages in the valley of the Indre before finally surfacing on to the modernity of the main road into Châteauroux. There it gets up a sudden speed, past the new sheet-metal hangars called Mammouth and Bricomarché and Jardiland, graceless as pink elephants, before its triumphant arrival at the station with minutes to spare to catch a train to Paris or Toulouse. The same gathering crescendo has to be executed in reverse for the return journey, driving back into the past with diminuendo effects as the sun goes down over the pastures of the Black Valley and the mist begins to rise.

But even in Châteauroux, when I finally began to go there to absorb the census records, the *Écho de l'Indre* and other sources of urgent news from another time, I found that no modern techniques stood between me and this material. The grandly named Salle des Archives behind the enormous, classical Prefecture turned out to be domestic in scale: it must have been the dining-room of a middle-class family house of the last century. I would sit there in company with a maximum of a dozen other readers, most of whom seemed to be rustling the papers of the Services de Cadastres (land registry), no doubt checking up as ever on Great Aunt Marthe's legacy. Huge, battered volumes of bound broadsheets or census returns were brought to me after only a brief wait. Obsolete dust escaped in little puffs as I opened them.

The sheer wealth of cumulative minor facts available in these pages seemed immeasurable, vertiginous. The nineteenth century was the first period in history when, all over Europe, the lives of all individuals began to be recorded in a systematic way at regular intervals: thus the potential of the census returns is almost limitless, or limited only by the time and intentions of the researcher. An entire present existence could be spent summoning people from the lists and tracing their interlocking destinies. But this vast information bank remains schematic and confined to certain circumstances: only by interpretation, conjecture and additional knowledge is life breathed into it. Whereas the pages of old newspapers, some of them yellowed and flaking, others as white as if they had hardly been glanced at since the day they were printed, rich in discursive detail, sometimes maddeningly inconsequential, always full of more submerged content than could ever be systematically tabulated – these are the very breath of vanished lives.

The Salle des Archives seems in itself to belong with those lives. The pattern of the floor tiles evokes all the large, traditionally patterned meals that must once have been consumed there, with vegetables following the meat rather than accompanying it and table-napkins the size of sheets. The façade of the building is in neat grey stucco with Second Empire ironwork on the door and windows like hundreds of other unremarkable houses that arrived in Châteauroux along with the railway after the middle of the last century. But the street where it stands is the Rue Vieille du Prison, the Old Street of the Prison, and runs down to a tower and portcullis and the huddle of narrow lanes that once made up the entire town. Châteauroux, which today numbers some twenty thousand people, is, like La Châtre, a medieval walled city; it has merely been more drastically transformed.

From the front windows of the Salle des Archives, across the street, is visible a house with a sun dial on its pointed gable bearing the words *Il est toujours temps de bien faire* – 'It is always time to do good.' That cannot have been much consolation to the prisoner brought in chains that way towards the tower. The back windows of the Salle, however, offer a gentler view. Grass and municipal dahlias disguise a one-time farmyard, but behind them is an unmistakable barn. The house's urban façade and nineteenth-century interior are camouflaging a building that is actually far older and originally sheltered a very different way of life. Even here in Châteauroux France's essential rurality is not far below the skin.

Chapter 6

But what of Célestine and her family?

I am particularly fond of the early Registers of Birth in Chassig-nolles. Well thumbed over the years to provide evidence for all the other documents French citizens have traditionally been required to carry, some of the pages are edged with real thumb-marks, the insignia of people whose hands were permanently impregnated with wood ash and cow dung because opportunities for effective washing were so few. In these pages the birth of Célestine Chau-mette was listed in 1844. But there were a great many other Chaumettes born at that period. In the same decade came a Silvain Chaumette, an Ursin, a Félix, a Françoise, a Marie, a Maurice and an Auguste. In 1850 came a Solange, while in the 1830s there had been a Gilbert, a Louis and another Félix, this one with 'nt' noted after his name – 'naturel', illegitimate.

When I checked this list against their full birth entries, they did seem to be all the same family: the same paternal Christian name kept reappearing. By and by, however, I established that there was a Silvain-Germain and a Silvain-Bazille, classic Berrichon names, and that each of these men sometimes dropped the second part of their name in statutory declarations, which made them indis-tinguishable. Célestine was the daughter of Silvain-Germain, born in 1816 (or 1817, if you prefer the mention of him on his daughter's grave). But most of the others of her generation were the progeny of one or other of Silvain-Germain's first cousins: Silvain-Bazille (born 1811), his younger brothers Maurice and Louis and his sister Marie, who was the person unlucky enough to produce the natural-born Félix twenty years later.

Silvain-Germain was the son of a François Chaumette. Silvain-Bazille and the others were the children of a Pierre Chaumette. François and Pierre were brothers. They were born in the years immediately after the Revolution, when time ran differently. François' birth was declared on the twenty-first day of Germinal in Year III of the French Republic (early April 1794) before Aussourd, who described himself in the new politically correct style simply as 'citizen of Chassignolles' – '*élu le trente Floréal l'an Second aussi de la république françoise pour dresser les actes de naissance, Mariage et décès des citoyins*'. The declaration was made at the *maison commune*, which till four years earlier had been known as the church, by the father of the baby, a male friend and the baby's maternal grandmother, Jeanne Merlin. The baby, who had been born at five o'clock the previous afternoon, was produced in person, as was the custom at that time, but no one but Aussourd was able to sign the entry in the register.

It was this François Chaumette, Célestine's grandfather, who signed his name in the early Minute books forty years later in a toppling, painstaking hand. As a young man he usually styled himself *journalier* – day-labourer – but by the 1840s he and his son Silvain-Germain had together opened the inn at the village; like his aspirations to literacy, this suggests a degree of enterprise. He lived on till 1861, when he would have been sixty-six or sixty-seven, a fair age for that period, but his own father had done better. Célestine's great-grandfather, yet another Silvain, was born long before the obligatory keeping of records; his brief baptismal mention might still be quarried out of the parish register. He was stated to be eighty-eight years old when he died in July 1844 two months after Célestine was born. All the large mid-nineteenth-century Chaumette clan are therefore descended from this Ancien Régime figure. Late in life, according to mentions of him on various birth and marriage registers, he was sacristan to the church, which had by then been rescued from its temporary secular disguise. Sacristan was a position usually reserved for someone of standing in the community who was felt to need a respectable job to bring in a salary, however tiny, but by the standards of his time Silvain

Chaumette was not poverty-stricken. He owned a well-built house and a garden in the centre of the village – a property that was to become highly significant to the family fortunes when it was inherited, in the fullness of time, by François.

In earlier days, Silvain the sacristan styled himself *tisserand* – weaver. His sons François and Pierre sometimes did also, though later François called himself a day-labourer and then, having inherited a piece of land, a 'smallholder', before finally becoming an innkeeper. These shifts in occupation and status tell their own tale. For centuries, the area had been one in which handloom weaving was done in the cottages. (Tisserand and Tissand are common local surnames, along with variants such as Tissier and Tixier). Hemp and flax were grown and harvested as a family enterprise – an important one, in which rituals and dances were employed to make the stuff flourish. Once it was safely harvested, it was left to soak in the Black Valley's numerous streams, spread out to dry again in the sun and then cooked slowly in the big bread ovens that were a regular feature of most dwellings built before the mid-nineteenth century. After that, though the stuff could be trodden underfoot like grapes, it was usually a local specialist, the *chanvreur*, with his own particular implement, who was called in to mash the baked fibres expertly so that they did not break up.

The *chanvreur* had a certain mystique attached to him, like a miller or a farrier: a man who was local but who went about the countryside and got to hear things. Sometimes special knowledge of herbs and healing was attributed to him (as it was to George Eliot's Silas Marner) and he might be feared. Elsewhere, and particularly in the Lower Berry, he was seen as a jolly, benign fellow, a teller of yarns, and it is in this role that he presides over George Sand's pastoral stories.

After all that laborious work, crowned by the *chanvreur*'s visit, the magic stuff still had to be spun into a continuous thread – hours and hours of female work in the firelight – before it finally reached the loom. No wonder the eventual bolt of cloth was valuable either to use or to sell, and clothes made from it were worn for decades, passed on from one member of the family to another, patched and turned and cut down at last into frocks and pinafores for the smallest children.

I have seen the last vestige of a weaver's loom, still clinging to the low ceiling between the beams of the house once occupied by Pierre Chaumette and his descendants. And I have been shown pieces of linen and jute woven in the Commune that are still, after more than a hundred years, surviving as useful cloths in houses in the village. But they date from the time when the cottage industry had declined into a minor one with few commercial outlets. Once, almost every sheet, shirt, smock or coat that was worn, bought, sold or bartered in the Berry would have been made there, but already by the early nineteenth century the strategic improvements in France's main-road network, and the coming of the first steam-powered mills, were putting the hordes of cottage weavers out of business. An enquiry into their trade in 1840 revealed that the weaver 'can no longer be rewarded as he was formerly, since mechanical spinning and weaving now creates cloth at too low a price for hand weavers to be able to compete'. Sure enough, by that time a wholesale linen sheet merchant had set up in business in La Châtre. He imported his goods by packhorse from the mountains of the Auvergne, where the rivers were strong enough to power the new mills and life had always been hard enough to make labour very cheap indeed. Of the family who started this business, prospered and so gained entry through marriage into the world of the local gentry, we shall hear again.

It was the same story with wool. Since the end of the Middle Ages, sheep had been one of the major products of the Berry. Once the Hundred Years War was over, great flocks of them used to drift on the uncultivated uplands between La Châtre and Châteauroux; they were cared for by young *pastoures*, boys and girls who led a life there in summer isolated from their families sometimes for weeks at a time. Each autumn most of the rams were slaughtered for meat, because of the difficulty of keeping beasts alive in the byres through the winter in the days before fodder crops were known. But the main point of the Berrichon sheep was the fleece, and this the villagers of the Lower Berry combed and carded, spun and then wove. But here, too, by the nineteenth century progress had begun to disrupt the ancient patterns of production. The industry continued, but it became concentrated in a few centres. A factory had been set up in Châteauroux specifically to process local wool. It dealt with linen as well, prospered in the Napoleonic wars and continued to do so, with a few setbacks and changes of ownership, for the next hundred years. It was the chief manufacturer of army uniforms in the 1914–18 war, providing employment for half the country round about and sending men to die in the mud with good felted Berrichon wool on their backs. By that time the home-weaving industry of the area had been moribund for sixty years.

So it was, I surmise, that the generation of men born around the time of the Revolution, the generation of Pierre and François Chaumette, grew up styling themselves weavers like their ancestors before them, only to find in middle life that the trade would no longer earn them or their sons a living. Most of them, as skilled artisans, possessed no land to speak of; they therefore had no resource but to hire themselves out as labourers to neighbours who, in most cases, were only peasant farmers themselves. This was a possible way of earning a living from the spring through to the autumn harvests, though it was well recognized that, even so, wages were barely enough to feed a growing family. But in the dead of winter, when the fields were bare and still, crows pecked in the snow and the owner and his family had themselves retreated to the farmhouse kitchen on a diet of stale bread, chestnut soup and hoarded potatoes, what was the landless labourer to do?

The plight of this or that one occasionally crops up in the Minute books as someone 'really indigent', possibly ailing as well, and needing a hand-out to survive. Silvain-Bazille Chaumette, Pierre's son, appears in this guise after the middle of the century, and so do more than one of *his* sons. '*Le sieur Chaumette*' – another Silvain, Célestine's second cousin – 'day-labourer, is the father of five children, of whom two are still very young ... He is poverty-stricken, without any resource but his own labour. His only son, whose work is indispensable to help raise the rest of the family, is likely to be called up soon into the Army ...' That dates from 1883. Four years later it was the turn of Silvain's brother, Félix, born the same year as Célestine: '. . . he has asthma and a weak constitution which prevents heavy work. He has four children including two young daughters and also has to help his father, aged seventy-five, who is too infirm to work.' The father in question was Silvain-Bazille. The very next entry mentions another of this numerous family, Louis, then fifty, a weaver with rheumatism, obliged to come to the help of the same old father and also his father-in-law. Apparently the more prosperous branch of the family, Silvain-Germain's, was either unable or unwilling to help support these poverty-haunted cousins as they proliferated down the generations.

The more intelligent or fortunate ex-weavers were able to turn to good account the very conditions that had destroyed the weaving business. The improvement of a few roads and tracks which made it possible, for example, for alien cloth to be imported into the Berry from the Auvergne, also created new rural openings and occupations. Commerce was at last beginning to impinge on the subsistence-based rhythms of country life, and with it would come a new race of *commerçants*, tradesmen-villagers with special roles who borrowed a tinge of bourgeois character and practice from the local town. People began to set up as carters, as wheelwrights to service the vehicles that could now lumber along the widened tracks, as smiths to shoe the horses that were gradually becoming more numerous: till then, the work animal of central France had always been the slow-moving ox. Others opened village inns, places where travellers could find sustenance and a bed of sorts, just as in a town. The inn was also somewhere for a villager to get a drink if he possessed no vineyard of his own. The consumption of wine, which had traditionally been for feast days only, was gradually increasing in France, though the time was still far off when it would become the standard drink of the masses, automatically supplied even in the poorest restaurants. In La Châtre, by 1847, there were a score of cafés and drink shops when thirty years before there had been only one. Now the villages were beginning to follow the same trend. In Chassignolles, it was François Chaumette and his son, who were possessed of a well-situated village house and some spirit of ambition and foresight, who started the first inn.

The Chassignolles peasant did not necessarily pay in cash for his glass of the local *vin gris*, any more than he paid in ready money for his ploughshare or other up-to-date farm implement now being forged for him in the new smithy. Bills were normally settled once a year, and often not in coin but in potatoes, wheat or other grains: the tradesman, since he was not a producer himself, would need these. Day-labourers were also paid in kind. Right up to 1914, country people did not handle money much. They trusted each other, with credit that sometimes ran on from one generation to another, but they did not trust, for a long time, the cash economy of the towns.

One should not imagine either that this first Chaumette tavern was like the café of a later date, complete with bar-counter and an array of bottles, a price list and a yellow varnished notice about the suppression of drunkenness in public places. Not till later in the century were *cabarets* licensed and regulated by the local Préfet and his police. (*Cabaret*, the official designation, was then applied to any drink shop, however informal and rural. The non-French reader should suppress the inappropriate mental picture of a small nightspot, with literal *folies bergères* perhaps being enacted by the local shepherdesses!) Informally, the Chaumettes referred to themselves not as *cabaretiers* but as *aubergistes*, innkeepers, and their trade would have been carried on in their own kitchen with the addition of just an extra bench or two round the oak table. A traveller of the period complained that a rural inn might consist of no more than one room beneath a loft, plus a lean-to at the side as minimal guest accommodation furnished with straw palliasses and mice.

Another description occurs in George Sand's novel *André* (published in 1851 but set some fifteen years earlier). It is about a maker of artificial flowers in La Châtre – a provincial Mimi – who falls in love with the son of a local landowner impoverished by the Revolution. They frequent the same dances and fêtes, but he is far removed from her in education and prospects. She honourably decides to resolve this situation by removing herself to the house of a kinswoman all of thirty miles distant. André, accompanied by a male friend, pursues her in the best romantic tradition and catches up with her some way along the road in a small village:

> They found the hire-carriage propped on its shafts at the door of an inn ... Dawn had not yet broken. The driver was partaking of a pitcher of the vinegary local wine which he much preferred to better vintages. Joseph and André cast a hasty look round the room, which was feebly lit by the light of the fire in the grate. They saw Geneviève sitting in a corner, head in hands, bent over a table ... Succumbing to the exhaustion of a night being shaken about over the stones, the poor girl was asleep.

Such was the nature of travel when it still took a whole day to get from La Châtre to Châteauroux, with the ever-present risk of the carriage straying from the path and overturning in a bog. Most of the poorer people never travelled at all, except on foot or, by a chance lift, up behind a wealthier neighbour on his horse. Once in their teens, a boy or girl would walk into the nearest market town for the seasonal hiring fair, where they would find themselves a situation, but before that day came a child reared in the depths of the country may never even have seen a highway, let alone used it. When Sand's François le Champi, aged ten, first sights the lumbering La Châtre–Châteauroux coach, he thinks it is some strange beast and runs from it in terror.

A similar coach, unheated, drawn by six or even eight horses, took three or four days to reach Paris. Not surprisingly, the English tradition of coaching as a dashing and even jolly experience, over a good network of gravelled turnpikes in a smaller country, finds little echo in French social mythology. Even the bourgeoisie of the country towns visited Paris only once in a lifetime, in order to say they had been, with much discussion about it both before and after. (The same is, however, still true today of many of the elderly in the villages.) In central France, journeys farther afield than Paris, Bordeaux or Lyons were simply not believed in; people who claimed to have been in Flanders, Italy or the Rhineland, let alone England, were hardly questioned at all, no one having any idea what to ask them.

The Chaumette inn, in its early days, would not have seen strangers from a distance, except insofar as the double word *étranger* (stranger/foreigner) was then applied to people living in another *pays* a mere twenty kilometres away. It catered for passing *chanvreurs*, pedlars and stonemasons, those useful but slightly suspect itinerants who roamed France more and more easily as the nineteenth century got into its stride. For local people, the inn took messages and packages to pass on, probably transmitted money on account and made small loans. They may have stocked a few dry groceries as well. Before village shops, post offices and savings banks arrived, the Auberge was the first village link with the world beyond its borders.

When I first got to know Chassignolles in the 1970s, two of these old-style inns were still in existence, besides the modern Café-Restaurant-Hôtel directed with entrepreneurial zeal by Madame Calvet (*'Lunchs de Noces! Déjeuners d'Affaires! Eau Courante dans les Chambres'*). They were on opposite sides of the church: one was run by Madame Aussir, whose husband was a carpenter, and the other by Madame Chauvet, whose husband had been a tailor. In this, they followed the tradition that family innkeeping was usually combined with another trade, sometimes in the past a seasonal one such as butchery or oil-pressing.

Madame Aussir's husband once made us an oak stool, and I used to visit her in her spacious, warm kitchen where the elderly farm-workers of Chassignolles would sit imbibing in a row. In its grander days the café, under the name Hôtel de France, had developed a formal front room for customers, but the old men preferred the warm kitchen. 'They just pick their chairs up and bring them in here,' said Madame Aussir in tolerant despair. Afterwards they would line up in the dark outside to relieve themselves against a stone cornice so encrusted with greenish lichen that it must have served this same purpose for generations. There was a public lavatory just on the far side of the war memorial, built by the Commune in an access of Socialist hygiene about 1968, but the old men preferred the traditional spot.

Some used to frequent the establishment round the back of the church also, along with schoolboys with money for lemonade and table-football in their pockets, but it was clear that this Chauvet café was running itself down, subsisting quietly until its proprietors could take their formal retirement. About 1980 it closed its doors. I rarely went in there, for in those days I had no idea that this was the one-time Chaumette inn.

It is built so close to the church that there is barely room to drive a car in between: I have been told that there was once – 'Oh, long ago. I've only heard tell' – a stone archway at that point connecting the two buildings. The inn is the obviously ancient, irregularly shaped house that appears on the map of 1843, but it has been enlarged and altered several times since. Not till I got inside it again, which was years after it stopped functioning as an inn though its bar still stood ghostly in the front room complete with ageing liqueur bottles, did I learn from Monsieur Chauvet that the house had been there 'in the time of the monks'.

From him I also heard that it had had a vaulted outside staircase of fine stone, roofed with tiles, leading to a large attic room where wedding receptions and the like were held. This distinctive feature, known locally with an impressive disregard for chronology as a 'Saracen staircase', allies the building with the fifteenth-century private mansions in La Châtre and with the 'castle' of Villemort. The attic, converted to bedrooms, is still there. The staircase, however, was pulled down by Chauvet in 1946 when he wanted to renovate the place.

'I was rebuilding the main café-room entirely then, you see,' he explained with a hint of apology which suggested that he might, today, have spared the staircase. 'The ceiling was so low – great, black old beams. Made the place so dark.' He is a small, stocky man but he raised a hand to indicate a height barely above his own head. There, under that vanished low ceiling, several generations of Chaumettes ministered to the needs of the village. I also, for a reason that will become apparent, believe that for many years before the Mairie was built the Council held their meetings in the attic up the stair.

The whole house is roofed today with the neat slates of the late nineteenth century, but at Célestine's birth it had wooden shingles or thatch. A great many of Chassignolles' houses and barns would originally have been thatched, but so many fires started in their roofs and went on to consume entire properties that a series of prefectural regulations were passed which gradually excluded the use of thatch. So, in an uncharacteristic quirk of modernity, the thatched cottage passed away from central France where it had once been as common as in rural England.

The Chaumettes also owned property in the run of smaller houses and one-time workshops on the far side of the church, the buildings that follow most clearly the curve of the original monastery-fortifications. Here, by one of these mouselike dwellings whose floors lie well below the level of the present roadway, is another outside staircase – a modest wooden one this time. In this house, Célestine's mother died.

She was an Anne Laurent. She came from Nohant, George Sand's village, and her occupation in the Marriage Register of 1838 is given as *'bergère'*, shepherdess, thereby completing the fleeting mental image of her and Silvain-Germain as characters in one of George Sand's rustic idylls. I know that she eventually died in that house rather than in the inn across the way because I was told so by the present occupant. Mademoiselle Pagnard has been for many years the chief repository of Chassignolles lore. In childhood she was an admiring younger-sister figure to Zénaïde Robin, Célestine's granddaughter, and she liked to talk about Zénaïde, whom she felt had had a more adventurous life than she herself had.

'Zénaïde's great-grandmother died in this very room we're sitting in,' she remarked to me conversationally one day. 'Of cancer of the breast, poor woman. She tried to treat it by putting a slice of best raw steak on it that she got from the butcher. People believed, in those days, that that was what you did to draw a cancer out; it would feed on the steak so not on you. They didn't go in for doctors much, then.'

She spoke with such authority that at first I assumed she had seen with her own eyes the desperate lady in an unbuttoned linen camisole, applying the unaccustomed luxury of butcher's meat to a white bosom defaced by an ulcer.

'I don't know,' Mademoiselle Pagnard continued, musing, 'how long the meat was supposed to stay there. It would have Turned, of course ... Perhaps it had to be renewed regularly? Expensive, if so.'

'And it couldn't have worked.'

'Of course not. Made things worse, if anything. Maggots and so on.' ('*Les vers se sont installés.*')

'How simply awful.'

'Yes. Well.' Herself a brisk survivor of one modern operation for cancer, Mademoiselle Pagnard explained with an echo of horror in her voice from another time: 'They thought so too. They called it the Evil Sickness.' ('*Le mauvais mal.*')

Only later did I realize that the death of Zénaïde's great-grandmother, even if it took place at an advanced age, must date back well before Mademoiselle Pagnard's birth. In fact it occurred in 1884. But to Jeanne Pagnard the personalities and actions of those who inhabited her world before she did, walking on the same stones, sleeping under the same rafters, have always been as real as the events of her own long life. Another of those she cannot have known in person, but presented to me just as if she had, was her own great grandfather on the maternal side, François Chartier, who was Chassignolles' earliest shopkeeper. If, as she agreed with me once we got down to dates, her own parents were born in the 1870s and her grandparents (roughly the same generation as Célestine) around the middle of the century, then the entrepreneurial Chartier was, like Silvain-Germain, born during or just after the

Napoleonic wars and, like the innkeeper, made the most of what the time might offer.

In the 1850s he set up as a travelling grocer, the forerunner of the modern vans. That is to say, he used to walk into La Châtre to buy his stock and then trudge with it in a pack round the country-side. As this was the period when such extras as sugar, spices, candles and even chocolate and coffee were beginning to be appreciated on the more prosperous farms, his enterprise was opportune. Later – I afterwards confirmed from the census records that this was in the early 1860s, just as Célestine had grown to womanhood – he opened his village shop.

'See that little place at the end of the run that's empty now and got a great big poster on it for a supermarket? Yes, beside where the elm used to stand before it was cut down . . .' It was here, in this miniature, dimly lit dwelling more like a stable than a house, that he carried on a business that thrived and continued to do so even when competition came. Although he was illiterate, he kept accounts in picture code, thus reinventing writing from first prin-ciples. 'He was canny,' said Mademoiselle Pagnard. 'Sugar came in triangular loaves in those days, like small pyramids – you had to break bits off. Well, often people couldn't afford a whole loaf, they just wanted a little. So my great-grandfather used to break it up, and he charged a little less for the bits from the bottom of the loaf because they weren't quite so sweet. People knew and they came to him for that. 'Course, he charged other customers a bit more than the standard price for the pointed bits that were the sweetest.'

The progression from itinerant packman to shopkeeper typifies what was then happening for the first time all over rural France. The trade of pedlar went back hundreds of years. In the centuries of little or no communication between one *pays* and another the pedlar was the only source of news, a breath from elsewhere. A sighting of the solitary figure, bent under his pack, moving at the field's edge against a line of trees, brought the children of the farm running and the women from kitchen and cow-shed. It has been suggested that much of the peddling that went on was not especially lucrative, but it gave the chance to see the world to men too restive by nature to be content with the deadening rhythm of the fields. It might also provide a boy from a poor home with a pretext to seek his fortune, leaving the family with one less mouth to feed. But peddling, like all adventures, could be hazardous. Some men became victims of criminal assault on lonely roads, or were attacked by wolves or drowned in flooding rivers or were found dead of exposure in the winter snows. Others drifted into crime themselves or descended to begging. Begging was long a feature of the French countryside, and sometimes it took on a menacing aspect.

The poorer peasants, locked in the struggle for sheer survival with their annual purchases of iron and preserving salt, may not have had much use for the pedlar's wares, but there were always more prosperous families to be tempted. By the nineteenth century, in spite of Jacques Lafitte's discouraged remark about half of France still being stuck in the fourteenth century, the demand for made goods was inconspicuously growing. A description of the contents of one pedlar's pack at the time of Célestine's birth lists thread, cotton, quantities of needles, pins and buttons, thimbles, scissors, hooks-and-eyes (a newfangled extravagance), ready-made braces (ditto), knives and combs. There were also more frivolous items such as snuffboxes and 'Limoges ware' (small, decorative china boxes given as keepsakes), and cakes of soap. Other records mention pencils, penknives, quills and notebooks, for those whose skills now extended to the keeping of accounts, in pictures or otherwise.

Reading matter and religious pictures were also staples of the early-nineteenth-century pedlar's trade, along with religious medals and chaplets. The books were usually little 'Almanachs' bound in blue paper: they contained a mixture of religious and folk aphorisms, home remedies, hints on etiquette of the Don't-belch-at-table variety, potted histories, descriptions of famous trials and fairy tales. It was from such books that people like Pirot the Mayor and François Chaumette became acquainted with the alphabet. (France being a Roman Catholic country, there was never the encouragement to Bible reading that characterized Protestant rural life in England.) Earlier, the Almanachs were called *grimoires* (grammars) and contained both prayers and spells: they seem to have been acquired as talismans even by households where there was no one who could decipher them.

The construction of some new main routes in the later eighteenth century and under Napoleon was done for nationalistic reasons, not with the aim of benefiting the regions through which they passed. They did, however, make it possible for pedlars to go further afield more safely and to get their goods from more widespread sources. Troops of pedlars were organized by masters in the towns. By the 1840s it had even become possible for them to deposit their takings safely in savings banks in the main towns on their route, rather than running the perpetual risk of being robbed for the cash they carried.

But that was the Indian summer of peddling. The same advances that made life easier for the solitary trader with his pack ended by making him obsolete. Country footpaths were widened into tracks for carts which could carry more goods more easily. Shops multiplied in the towns. In La Châtre, the Pissavy family, who had set up to sell cloth from the Auvergne after the Napoleonic wars, and who at first sent pedlars with bolts of it all over the Berry and the Touraine, found by the mid-century that they could deal more profitably by acting as wholesalers selling to traders in fixed premises. By the later part of the century the men on the country roads with packs or baskets were still selling their wares, but those from afar were now more marginal, gypsy-style figures – chair-caners, china-menders, illicit sellers of non-Government-manufactured matches done up to look like cheeses. The more regular and respectable sellers on the road were now, like Mademoiselle Pagnard's great-grandfather, local tradesmen making deliveries: the village shop had been born.

Jeanne Pagnard was described to me by a contemporary as 'the daughter of peasants – but rich peasants'. The family had been in the wheelwright and saddlery business. When I first got to know her I called her 'Madame', assuming that the elderly man I saw coming and going from her house, wearing clogs and accompanied by the last working horse in the village, was her husband. In fact he was her brother. Another brother had died before we came to the village, and this younger one was to drop dead of a heart attack in her kitchen a few years later. The three Pagnards had all been born between 1906 and 1910 and none had ever married. Perhaps they had seen enough of the financial and physical burdens of large families in their youth to be wary of marriage, or perhaps the three of them simply felt complete in themselves: they lived together all their lives. After her second brother's death, Mademoiselle Pagnard (as I now knew her to be) became more confiding. She has always had the capacity to make friends, and now she missed her lifetime's companion.

'People say, "After all, losing a brother isn't quite like losing your husband," but for me, at my age, it has been exactly like. Being alone . . . From time to time an idea passes through your mind and you want to share it. But you can't go knocking on someone else's door just with an idea, so if there isn't anyone on hand it just goes away again and is lost . . .'

Ideas figure distinctly in Jeanne Pagnard's mental landscape. She told me another time that she did well at school and was particularly good at maths: no doubt the account-keeping great-grandfather's genes making their appearance. After completing the village school course and attaining her certificate by the age of twelve, she would have liked to go on to some further education and there was talk of her doing so, but 'our father had had bad luck during the War. We owned a plantation, and he'd just cut down a lot of wood to sell when war broke out and he was called up. He was away four years and by the time he came back the wood had rotted where it lay and was unsaleable.'

This, at any rate, was the story. The First World War is commonly credited with having ruined even more lives and institutions than it did in practice: it has become the new divide between the chronologically moving Now and the static Olden Days. Nevertheless it is literally true that conscription in France was implemented in 1914 in such a summary and dramatic way that the men who were carried off to war were forced to leave all manner of unfinished business behind them. Even the harvest had not been got in – a mistake that all parties concerned were careful not to repeat the second time round, in 1939.

Baulked of the course in bookkeeping in La Châtre or Châteauroux which might have carried her, as it did Zénaïde, into a different way of life, Mademoiselle Pagnard settled for becoming a dressmaker – a *couturière*, in the rather grand French term that is employed even at village level. In this she was following her father's mother, the daughter of the grocer and the person who became a model for her. Her own intimate knowledge of village events that had taken place well before her birth derives from a childhood spent largely in her grandmother's workshop. 'There were always several girls there sewing, employed by her. It was jolly.' (*C'était gai.*) 'More fun than my own home. And Grandmother loved to recount things.'

This grandmother, Catherine Chartier, had also achieved an education ending in a school-leaving certificate, a rare thing for a girl born in the 1850s. 'She could write a really good letter. And she could add up and subtract. But I don't think anyone had ever shown her how to multiply. Because when she wanted to work out how many metres of cloth were needed for something, she used to put the price of each metre down in a column and add them up like that. When I got big I tried to tell her the proper way to do it, but she just laughed and did it her way.'

The man Catherine married, Charles Pagnard, was a gardener who worked for several local notables, including the engineer who owned the stone quarries in the next Commune. These quarries employed thirty or more men from Chassignolles, according to the census, and were worked with the latest machinery. It did not take long for young Madame Pagnard to make herself indispensable to this family. 'The lady of the house was a Creole, from Dominique, very beautiful, and she used to get my grandmother to make copies of the latest Paris fashions from magazines for herself and her two daughters. There was one muslin dress I always heard about, with silk and lace rosebuds all around the skirt. Pastoral style, it was called. Pastoral!'

Madame Pagnard's grandmother, who had not at that time acquired one of the new sewing-machines, stitched away at this fabled dress while clad herself in a genuine Berrichonne peasant's cap. Her devotion paid off, for the family spent two to three months every year in Paris. This was 'for the Season' and to allow its head to pursue Parisian engineering interests, including assistance to Monsieur Eiffel in designing the Tower that was raised for the first centenary of the Revolution. Their Chassignolles' dressmaker used to accompany them there, having become an indispensable, unofficial ladies' maid: in this way she experienced the Paris of Zola, of Haussmann, of *opéra bouffe* and sensational posters by Toulouse-Lautrec. It was a remarkable journey from one world to another at a time when, out of the thousand-odd population of Chassignolles, only ten had been born outside the Department of the Indre and most of these had come from the Creuse only a dozen or so miles distant.

'What about her own children?' I wondered.

'Oh, she left them with her mother,' said Mademoiselle Pagnard with a note of admiration in her voice. 'You understand, she was much more advanced (*beaucoup plus évoluée*) than the typical country women of that time. She really made the most of herself.'

So, in her own way, did Jeanne Pagnard. Grandfather Pagnard also gardened for the family at the Chassignolles *domaine*, the Big House set in its own grounds to one side of the village. Young Jeanne Pagnard began sewing for them and formed a relationship with the family that has lasted a lifetime.

The Domaine is owned, and has been since the 1860s, by successive descendants of the Pissavys, who set up as linen-merchants in La Châtre. (By the inter-war period the ramifications of this traditional, Mass-going family had spread all over the Berry. Today they are proudly said to number 450 'if you count all the attachments' – one of whom is the local MP.) Mademoiselle Pagnard has been called on by the occupants of the Domaine over the years not only to sew for them but on occasions to act as responsible overseer for children and servants. She has a detailed knowledge of several generations of the family and speaks of them in the intimate and slightly possessive way of a retired nanny. They have become her own people, as significant to her as her cousins and their progeny and somewhat more special. Both her vocabulary and her rolling local accent have been modified by decades of educated conversation. She and old Madame L (née Pissavy-Yvernault) have spent their lives observing discreet but fixed lines of social demarcation, but today, hearing them talk together, the impression is of two old ladies who can speak more frankly to one another than to almost anyone else – two survivors of a world that is now disappearing in its turn over the horizon of history.

Chapter 7

In her stories, George Sand had to make her peasants speak more or less standard French to be understood by her readers. She explained in a preface that their real speech would have been impenetrable to an unaccustomed ear. For the remarkable thing about early-nineteenth-century France, compared with a more compact and unified country such as England, was that most of the population did not speak recognizable French. The Bourgogne, the Auvergne, the Cévennes, the Limousin, the Guyenne, Provence, the Berry and numerous other smaller areas each had its own language, which might be incomprehensible to the people of the next *pays* only twenty or thirty miles off. Just before the Revolution, an investigation revealed thirty distinct different *patois* in France plus many more local variants, and an encyclopedia of the period roundly declared: '*Patois* – a corrupted tongue spoken all over the provinces. The true language is spoken only in the capital.'

That is a nationalist and Paris-centred view. *Patois* was not a faulty version of 'real' French; it had its own genesis. Medieval France had had two equally important tongues, both descended from soldiers' Latin: the *langue d'oc* and the *langue d'oïl*. The *langue d'oïl* was the language of northern France, from the wealthy plains south of the Loire up through Paris and Reims till it petered out in Flanders. Once the centre of power was concentrated in Paris, this tongue therefore became the basis of standard French. The *langue d'oc*, which was spoken over most of central and south-western France and gave its name to a substantial area, lost status and, without any cohesive force, fragmented into numerous versions. It was, however, extremely long in dying, as were the other local languages of entirely separate origin such as Breton and Basque. In Eugène Le Roy's famous novel about a Périgordine peasant, *Jaquou le Croquant*, a Gendarme comes to interview a little boy and does so in the local tongue. The child's comment is that the man 'spoke the *patois* like the people do in Sarlat' – not as in his home village. That employé of the State may not have spoken French at all at that early-nineteenth-century date, or, if he did, he would not have spoken it as his first language. The historian Weber calculates that even late in the century, when improved communications and the reforms of the Third Republic were between them revolutionizing country life, French was still a foreign language to a good half of France's citizens. Many would say this situation continued to a much later date.

The Lower Berry lies just, though only just, within the area where the prevailing tongue belonged to the same family as standard French – the *langue d'oïl*. This meant that the *patois*, in all its variants, died out earlier there as a separate language, merging more easily into the mainstream language than the distinct southern dialects would do. In 1835 the newly formed Ministry of Public Instruction, whose great mission was to make the disparate citizens of France all speak one tongue, published a report. This noted that the Department of the Indre was French-speaking, but the other part of the Berry – the Department of the Cher – was less so and that in the Creuse immediately to the south hardly any French was spoken at all. The term 'French-speaking' should, in any case, be treated with more caution than the optimistic Ministry inspectors may have applied. Understanding questions in French and producing a few adequate answers for the alien gentleman in the black jacket and riding boots is one thing; talking the language round your own fireside is another.

The fact that early minute-takers such as Aussourd or Vallet or Charbonnier recorded Council business in French does not necessarily tell us about the actual words used round the table, for there was then no set formula for writing *patois*. Any written record had to be in French, more or less, and this applied also to private correspondence. What, then, did the Chaumettes and their neighbours speak among themselves? I think it was recognizably French of a sort and could be turned into 'proper' French by education; but in everyday conversation it would probably have been so peppered with local words as to puzzle a listener from Châteauroux or Bourges, let alone from Paris. Even today I notice people in Chassignolles, those born in the first three decades of the present century, taking care in conversation with me to select the standard words for 'beans' or 'barrel' or 'wasp' or whatever; talking to one another they will use a country term. Or a child, whose everyday talk is of international *futbol* matches and video games, will unselfconsciously use an archaic term in some such sentence as 'The cow's had her calf.'

If *patois* survives even today, then how large a part of speech it must have been a hundred and fifty years ago. But the Chaumettes, father and son, with their ambitions and their inn in the centre of the village, were probably among the more competent speakers of regular French. The reason I know they were ambitious (apart from the evidence of the inn itself) is that Silvain-Germain, the son, learnt to read and write fluently. This was at a time when fewer than one person in twenty in the Indre could read, and since this figure included townspeople the proportion of those literate in the country must have been far smaller. But it was beginning to be seen as a desirable skill: George Sand was sometimes asked for reading lessons by the individual workers on her estate, and found many of them quick to learn.

I do not know for certain how Silvain-Germain acquired his skill, though I can make a guess (see below). He was born in 1816 or 1817 and was therefore in his teens already and past the usual age of education in 1833, when the Government passed the 'Guizot Law' with the intention that each Commune should set up and maintain a primary school. Till then, only sixty-two Indre Communes out of 247 had any sort of school at all, and these accounted for only about three thousand pupils. Unsurprisingly, no mention of any Chassignolles school appears in the Council Minutes at that date.

Yet the population of the Commune, like that of most of rural France, had grown since the beginning of the century, from 673 in 1801 to 984 thirty-five years later, and much of this growth was post-Napoleonic war. In the census of 1836 over half the population were described as *garçons* or *filles*, and although these were the terms then applied to unmarried persons of any age the great majority of them were in fact young. There was no longer the high infant mortality that had kept populations down under the Ancien Régime. A run-through of the registers in the Mairie for that year (a typical one) reveals thirty-two births, six of them 'natural' children, as against seventeen deaths, and nine of these were those of adults well on in life. The prevalent modern idea – much pushed by at least one populist French writer – that in the past child death was a commonplace against which parents simply hardened their hearts, is not borne out by such figures. Of the eight child deaths, five were those of babies or young children from elsewhere who had been put out to nurse in Chassignolles by the orphanage-hospital in Châteauroux, and such deaths tell their own tale. Only three 'own' infants died in Chassignolles families that year. A fever, probably malarial, still made itself felt in the watery Berry then and severe local shortages were still occurring – the last major one in the area was in 1847 – but widespread plague and starvation were slipping into history. The young generation were surviving and multiplying and needed educating.

But new Law or not, it does not seem that Chassignolles organized itself a school after 1833. Not till late 1841, when Silvain-Germain was a married man in his twenties, did the Council begin to deliberate the step of acquiring a schoolmaster. The inhabitants, apparently, had been 'manifesting a desire' for one.

At this date teaching was miserably paid; the village schoolmaster could be anyone, including indeed the local innkeeper. Fourchon, in Balzac's novel *Les Paysans* (1844), is just such a man, a jack of all trades who has learnt a thing or two while on the road or in the army, and takes to schoolmastering as another seasonal job along with rope-making. Other schoolmasters of the period doubled as cobblers or gravediggers or, more respectably, the sacristan would take on the role. In the Berry, with its strong traditions of 'the world behind', the mysteries beneath the surface of life, the position might be filled by someone known as a local healer and spell-caster. Evidently the concept of basic literacy as a tool of national enlightenment, in opposition to old superstitions, had not yet impinged on much of France. This was in the days when print itself was potentially suspect, or at any rate deserving of a wary respect. In Balzac's *Le Curé du Village* (1839) the carefully brought-up daughter of a tradesman in what is actually La Châtre has a book bought for her, *Paul et Virginie*, a classic pious tale for the young. Her semi-literate mother is worried by it and suggests that it should be shown to the priest, since for her 'any printed book appeared in the guise of a *grimoire*' – the old pedlars' chapbook. But among the more forward-looking literacy was now being seen as a tool worth having. 'Writing bureaux' were being set up in the towns, as they are today in Indian towns, where those who could not do it for themselves could get letters written and also forms filled in for that French bureaucracy whose wheels were beginning to turn. One advertised in a La Châtre newspaper in the 1840s was run by a local aristocrat whose family had been impoverished by the Revolution. (He is also, incidentally, thought to have been George Sand's first lover.)

Things did not move fast in Chassignolles. Two years after the subject of the school had first been mooted, and Célestine was on the way, Mayor Pirot was still suggesting that 'the need for primary education makes itself felt more every day – that it is urgent that we provide it – that the best way would be to build a schoolhouse and that till the Commune has such a lodging to offer it will not be able to find a teacher'. It was agreed that the schoolhouse must be central and that the parents must help pay for it. However, just where this was to be and how it was to be financed was still being discussed four years later.

By the following year, February 1848, a row had developed centering – once again – on the egregious Louis Vallet. The site that had finally been chosen did not please him and, having failed to engage public sympathy on the matter, he offered to pay the expenses that would now be incurred in changing to another site. The Council, *ayant mûrement délibéré*, decided by a majority of five to four to stick to the site already decided. The Minutes do not reveal where this was: they have a tantalizing tendency not to record such central facts, presumably because these were known to all already. I eventually discovered this first school's position from a very elderly retired teacher, who had it from his grandfather who had been a pupil there. Sure enough the building there, which was later a café and is now a private dwelling, has the date '1848' on its lintel.

In May 1850 the new Government of the Second Republic had passed a law obliging each Department to help financially with the setting up of rural schools. It is probably no coincidence that by May the Chassignolles schoolhouse had finally got itself plastered and furnished and the Council was now discussing ways of paying a teacher. By October they had found themselves one, Albert Hénouville, who sounds as if he came from nothern France and was thus a complete foreigner in Berrichon terms. He acquired eight pupils, all boys of course, whose parents each contributed a franc a month – which I calculate to have been roughly the same at that date as the cost of the bread a growing child would consume. As an extra sum, it was hard for the most ordinary peasant families to find, even had they desired schooling for their children as the mayor kept on insisting they did. In fact there is ample evidence that in the Berry, as throughout rural France, most parents did not. As a disapproving member of the Indre Regional Council remarked a few years later: 'Very little improvement in the rural Communes. Poor families are indifferent to the thought of education and are more concerned to send their children out to work.' Most of the population were then poor.

A different teacher was there by 1852 and another again by 1856, when the census records as *instituteur* a Guillaume Poissonier, another outsider, aged twenty-seven, with a wife and three small daughters, one new-born. He apparently was not successful in attracting custom either; not till 1862 does cautious satisfaction begin to be expressed. The mayor (by then a local man again, Noel Yvernault, replacing the extravagantly named Geoffrenet de Champdavid) remarked that 'since September 1859, the time when Monsieur Charbonnier was appointed teacher in Chassignolles, he has always been of exemplary and irreproachable conduct, from every point of view'. One wonders what unexemplary conduct the previous incumbents had displayed. 'By his zeal and devotion he has been able to make the school flourish . . . The number of pupils, which on his arrival was reduced to 6, has now risen to 46.'

It was suggested, and agreed, that Monsieur Charbonnier should receive directly from Communal funds a hundred francs annually 'by way of encouragement', but a cautious rider was added to the effect that no promises would be made about this to any successor 'in case he should not deserve it'. Jacques Charbonnier, who was only twenty-one when he took the post, in fact stayed for over thirty years, acquiring a wife and children in his turn. In later censuses he drops the Jacques and calls himself Auguste, perhaps his second name which he regarded as more fitting to his position in the community. Although not one of the Chassignolles Charbonniers, he came from a village only a few miles away: no doubt, as a local lad with an accent to match, he was much more acceptable than his predecessors. But finding the money to subsidize the school and fixing its budget remained an annual preoccupation for the Commune, and continued to be so till the coming of the free and compulsory national education system in the 1880s.

The time had not quite arrived when a country *instituteur* automatically took on the job of Secretary to the Mairie as well. The whole saga of the school's establishment was in fact recorded by the busy pen, with its emphatic down-strokes, of Célestine's father, Silvain-Germain Chaumette. He is identifiable by his signature, which is in the same hand. He had already replaced François Charbonnier as keeper of the Birth, Marriage and Death Registers for a while around 1840, and the handwriting reappears in the Minute book in 1848, when he had become a member of the Council. He did not remain a councillor after the upheaval of 1852. The oath of allegiance to the new Emperor is not made out in his hand, nor is the rough draft of a sycophantic letter congratulating His Highness and wishing him a long life. From this I conclude that Silvain-Germain had Republican sympathies, that he had come to the fore in 1848 (when George Sand and her friends were trying to rally the conservative Berry to the cause) and that he retreated again when reaction and the Second Empire set in and Geoffrenet de Champdavid was put in charge of the Commune. But he did not retreat far. Clearly a man who wrote with such ease was too useful to lose. The Minutes resume in his hand, for it seems to have been that same year that he moved into a new role as Chassignolles' first paid Secretary. This no doubt provides a useful secondary activity to subsidize that of innkeeping, and where in any case would the Council meetings have been held but in the inn's large upper room? He remained in the job till his death.

As to where he learnt his skill, I came across a possible answer in the first census, that of 1836. The family were living in the house that had not yet become the inn: François, then down as a smallholder, his wife Marie Petitpez ('smallfoot', a name still current in the Commune), Silvain-Germain, who was then aged about twenty, a young sister apparently known as 'Felissé', and a lodger. This was François Hélion, aged sixty-six, styled *ancien militaire de marine*

73

retraité – 'retired from the fighting navy'. The name first struck me as implausibly Greekish for central France until I noticed that, in that census, Elizabeth is commonly written 'Hélizabette' and Étienne 'Hétienne' and I saw from a later census that the Commune also contained an ordinary farming family called Elion. So this old sailor of Copenhagen and Trafalgar was a local man, come home after many years of bachelor existence to finish his days in the village. This is just the sort of person who, at that period, had acquired literacy on his travels as well as much other general knowledge. In view of his age in 1836 he must have been there for most of Silvain-Germain's childhood, and it does not seem fanciful to suppose that he may have been the boy's teacher and mentor.

Apart from the tributes to the Emperor, the other odd papers that are slipped between the pages of the Minute book for 1839–55 are in Silvain-Germain's writing. In April 1849 he certified that one Jean Moulin had that spring destroyed two litters of wolf cubs in the woods of the Commune and was owed the monetary reward the Préfet then offered. Jean Moulin (a name with a dramatic but irrelevant twentieth-century echo) was the local man charged with wolf-hunting under the direction of the Lieutenant de la Louverie in La Châtre, who was a swashbuckling but ageing local notable. Moulin's exploit dated from the same year as the celebrated hanging of wolf carcasses on the oak in the Bois de Villemort. The drive to eradicate the wolf from the Berry had begun. The creatures were said to have increased in the Indre and to have become more 'bold and desperate' during a couple of bad winters in the mid-1840s, but the symbolism and passion with which the hunt was pursued seems to indicate a wolf phobia going beyond the rational, with its roots in tales of werewolves and diabolic pacts between man and beast.

There is also a paper by Silvain-Germain dated 1850 which sets out a formal complaint about the *garde-champêtre*, the local gamekeeper cum village constable who was paid by the Commune: he was said not to be doing his job properly and to be taking – or extorting – bribes from malefactors. He was also said to be an habitual haunter of *cabarets* (in the plural, so presumably the reference was not so much to Chaumette's own inn as to the cafés in La Châtre) and a scrounger of drinks. The Commune proposed to remove this gentleman and replace him with another, a retired soldier who was generally respected ('*lequel jouit de l'estime général des habitants'*). But, frustratingly, both the name of the disgraced guard and that of his successor are left blank.

Another paper is more remarkable for the light it sheds both on village life and on Silvain-Germain's own capacity to express views in writing. It is the undated rough draft of an impassioned appeal destined to be sent all the way to Paris:

To the Minister of justice –
Monsieur le Ministre,

The undersigned inhabitants and members of the municipal councils of the communes of Chassignolles and la châtre beg you, on behalf of a certain pirot [*un nommé pirot*] to grant him pardon or at least to mitigate the life sentence to which he has been condemned in the recent session of the Assize court of the Indre. In support of their request they have the honour to present to you the following considerations: Pirot belongs to an honest family of the commune of Chassignolles of which his father was for a long time the mayor. He has exercised the trade of locksmith with a certain skill [*avec assez d'habilité*] and has even invented a new design of plough which has been favourably received by the Agricultural Committee of the Indre. He has been generally liked and esteemed in his village and the municipal council have set forth the proof of this in a certificate which is here enclosed along with that relating to his criminal conviction. Pirot has thus lived quite peacefully till the age of over 45 when following a discussion on monetary affairs [*à la suite d'une discussion pour des affaires d'intérêts*] after several attempts to bring back to his house his wife who had left him, he was led to commit the action for which he has been condemned and which has been punished as attempted murder.

The circumstances are set fourth in the court's papers: it is therefore useless to reproduce them. It is simply necessary to state that no one has been injured or killed by him. We the undersigned know what respect is due to the Justice of the country but beg to say that his condemnation has produced a painful effect on the entire neighbourhood where he is known [*une impression douloureuse dans le canton où il est connu*] and that many persons still doubt whether Pirot had any other intention than to frighten his wife's family who seem to have been encouraging her not to return to the marital home.

Whatsoever the truth of the matter [*Quoi qu'il en soit*] we the undersigned invoke as reasons to your good will and your sense of justice a peaceful and honest life of 45 years, a gentle and affectionate character, a habit of sober work [*un caractère doux et inoffensif, des habitudes laborieuses*] which has inspired feelings in others in a way a violent or dangerous man could not do . . .

The letter continues in this vein. When I discovered it, I longed to know just what had taken place and when. I had not at that point come to recognize Silvain-Germain's handwriting, but by chance soon after I came upon what seemed to be an echo of the drama in the local paper of that name. In August 1850 it was announced, among brief legal items, that a *séparation de biens* (separation of property) had been pronounced at the request of a Marguerite Charbonnier from her husband Antoine Pirot, both of Chassignolles. A formal separation was the only divorce then available to the ordinary person, but it was quite an effective one. I assumed at first that this would have been a sequel to the attempted murder and the court case, perhaps taking place some time later, but at least I now had a full name for Pirot under which to seek further details.

Taking his stated age, forty-five, as a clue, and assuming that the events referred to in the paper dated, like most of the Minute book, from the 1840s, I was looking for a birth some time around the turn of the century. Sure enough, in the register for autumn 1803 (7 *Brumaire l'An XII*), Antoine Pirot made his appearance. His father was Silvain Pirot, '*Propriétaire et maréchal*' of Le Flets, one of the Commune's outlying hamlets. So Silvain, like François and Denis Charbonnier, owned enough to qualify as a landowner and was also a blacksmith – a person of some substance, as you would expect of a future mayor. At Antoine's birth Silvain was stated to be 'at the wars', a sign that the Napoleonic *levée* of young men to fight battles such as Austerlitz and Jena was making a sweep even in this remote countryside. The birth was announced, and the baby presented in person, by his maternal uncle and by the midwife Marie Chaumard, whose name often appears at this time.

'Over 45 years' on from 1803 takes us to 1849 or 1850. So the gentle and inoffensive Antoine had evidently committed his unprecedented act just when France herself was passing through one of those periodic re-enactments of revolutionary emotion and countermeasure which are the chief milestones of her nineteenth-century history. It was also just at the time when the active Silvain-Germain Chaumette, then in his early thirties, had become a councillor.

To discover something about Antoine Pirot's problematic marriage I had to search through more of the registers than I had expected. Most couples married young. Public assumptions pushed them along ('Dancing together again, I see: that'll make a marriage') or there might be a child on the way to precipitate matters. By the age of twenty or so a boy had usually developed his skills, was doing a man's work and could not expect any particular increase in his fortunes. There was no point in waiting longer in a society where everyone held much the same ideas on the conduct of life, and individual fulfilment was not ordinarily considered. Silvain-Germain was twenty-one, give or take a few months, when he married Anne Laurent, who was to become Célestine's mother. *His* father, François, was only twenty-one at his birth. The men of the Charbonnier family, from which Antoine's wife came, show a similarly rapid turnover of generations.

But Antoine took his time, not marrying till he was thirty-three, an exceptionally late age for a countryman at that period. In George Sand's *La Mare au Diable*, Germain, who is approaching thirty and is already a widower with several children, is kindly warned by the father of his dead wife that he really should find himself a new one, 'or you will have left it too late'. Love, it was felt, was something for the period of brief physical flowering only, and it was assumed that no young girl would find a man of Germain's age attractive, even though George Sand described him as handsome and not yet 'worn by labour'. Instead, it is suggested that he marry a woman who, though still comely, is already a widow herself and a 'good prospect'.

A similar suggestion was perhaps made to Antoine Pirot. The wife we find him marrying in 1836 was not only a widow – she was seven years older than he was. The François Charbonnier who was keeping the registers at the time of her second marriage was her uncle and the Charbonnier family occupied a farm next door to the Pirots. It looks as if the main purpose of the marriage was to unite two properties into a more profitable one. If so, it was destined to fail spectacularly, resulting not only in domestic unhappiness but a crisis in the fortunes of both families. When I managed to date more accurately the event that led to the charge of attempted murder, I realized that the *séparation de biens* pronounced in favour of Marguerite was not the consequence of her crisis with her husband but the final action that provoked his violent attempt to drag her home. It is clear from the appeal to the Minister of Justice that she had already left him by then. What had raised such hostility against him in her? One is tempted to wonder what inadequacy of nature, tacitly recognized by the community, may be cloaked in the description of Antoine as a 'gentle and inoffensive' person.

I wrote to the Ministry of Justice myself some hundred and forty years after the event, hoping for further information. After the usual delay, they referred me to the location of their nineteenth-century archives and supplied a reference number. I wrote then to the appropriate department of the Bibliothèque Nationale and eventually got a helpful letter admitting to the case of Pirot, Antoine, in the records but regretting 'the file relating to a possible pardon in this case no longer exists. The fact is, many files were destroyed near the beginning of the present century . . .' The writer told me, however, that the conviction appeared to date from July 1851, and suggested that I might find an annotation on the records of the Assize Court – which were kept in Châteauroux.

Another trip to the quiet house in the Rue Vieille Prison: was that prison, which was part of the ancient fortifications of Châteauroux, the place where Antoine was held before his trial and pending his assignment to a long-stay institution? The infamous seaport forced-labour prisons, the *bagnes* with chained prisoners that were run by the Navy as the successors to the hulks of the Ancien Régime, were abolished that same year, 1851; Antoine had a lucky escape. But the Houses of Correction on the British model, which were then rising in the Assize Court cities and populated by the dregs of those cities, were hardly suitable places either for a peace-loving forty-five-year-old peasant. The last paragraph of Chassignolles' appeal on his behalf reads: 'In prison his good conduct has led the administration to decide that he merits special treatment: he has in fact been separated from the other prisoners and placed in a room by himself where he can devote himself to the work in which he is a specialist.'

Just what call there might be in prison for the speciality of locksmith gives pause for thought. The letter ends, with a final flow of Silvain-Germain's eloquence and knowledge of the circumstances. 'Doubtless Justice has its rights, but when Justice has been satisfied it cannot be of any use to exclude from society [*rejeter hors des voies sociales*] a man who has only weakened in a moment of confusion or drunkenness and to make an outcast of him.'

The census shows that the Pirot ménage had moved, after marriage, to a house in the centre of the village where Antoine had his metal workshop. By 1850, evidently, Marguerite had deserted him and returned to Le Flets, which was a mile or more distant. Was it alone at home or was it perhaps in the nearby Chaumette inn that Antoine indulged in the drinking session that was to have such terrible consequences for him? I see him in my mind's eye setting out with furious intention, probably by night, maybe with some lethal tool of his trade in his hand, down the muddy path past the Croix Pendue in the direction of his in-laws' farm.

Since a Charbonnier was still a member of the Chassignolles Council at this time, it must be assumed that even the family of the aggrieved Marguerite felt that the affair had been blown up by Justice out of all proportion. A generation earlier, when there were fewer organized brigades of Gendarmerie in the countryside to call upon, the whole business would probably have remained between villagers.

Silvain-Germain had said that the circumstances were laid out in the Court papers. When I followed the recommendation to explore the Assize records in Châteauroux I had hopes that I might turn up the whole story. In the catalogue I found reference to the criminal dossiers for cases relating to the late 1840s and some from 1852, not only for Châteauroux but also for the Lower Court in La Châtre. For 1850–51, however, there was nothing listed. When the short-lived Second Republic foundered in November 1851 and the Prince-President assumed his role as Emperor, repercussions were felt at the local level and those who had recently been running the Courts were summarily swept from office. As is traditional in such circumstances, some hasty burning of papers probably took place to avoid subsequent account-settling.

In my disappointment, I tried calling up the scrappy files for 1852, made hopeful by a reference to a Perrot. But he turned out to be one of half a dozen men from a village just outside La Châtre topically accused of 'exciting the hatred of citizens one against another' at the time of the November plebiscite. His sentence was three months in prison and a hundred francs fine, which was the equivalent of about four months of a labourer's earnings, but Perrot may have been of skilled artisan class. Other Republican spirits about the same time got a straight six months for *rébellion*, and I assume that the scattered charges of spreading false news, 'outraging the Mayor' and 'defaming a magistrate' are signs of the same repressive zeal on the part of the newly installed Imperial establishment.

Otherwise, the Châteauroux and La Châtre Courts at that period could produce nothing but a trickle of assaults (*coups et blessures*) usually punished with a few days in prison, disturbing the peace at night (*tapage nocturne* – idem), minor thefts, a deception (*escroquerie*) and a good deal of persistent vagabondage, sometimes aggravated by begging with menaces. On the whole, robbery was punished more seriously than physical violence, but two men found guilty of violent robbery on the highway each got five years' hard labour, and a would-be rapist (*attentat à la pudeur*) was sent for fifteen months to Châteauroux's new House of Correction. An *outrage à la morale publique* (indecent exposure?) earned a month inside.

What strikes one today is the relatively tiny number of cases and the relative severity of the judgements. This was a fundamentally peaceful and law-abiding society; the crime rate for the Indre was then, as now, well below the average for France as a whole. The region had evidently come some way since the eighteenth century: then, gangs of *chauffeurs* ('heaters', not drivers) had roamed the countryside, torturing peasant landowners by heating up their feet to get them to reveal where they hid their savings.

In 1852 there were no murders reported, not even an attempted murder. No Antoine Pirot. Yet domestic murders were apparently not unusual, for a few years earlier the Châteauroux paper *Le Journal de l'Indre* had suggested that the sale of arsenic should be banned, and it seems that each time a case of poisoning occurred the spouse fell under suspicion. Perhaps this was why the local authorities had been so ready to assume that Pirot's wild foray to scare the Charbonnier family was a premeditated attempt at murder.

You might have expected the *Journal de l'Indre* to carry the Pirot story, but in July 1851 this intensely urban, royalist, Catholic, bourgeois organ evidently had other matters on its mind. As for the more local *Écho de l'Indre*, that summer it seems to have been chiefly preoccupied with odd wolf sightings and bankruptcies; also with the buying and selling of vineyards, including one adjoining the Charbonnier land at Le Flets which may have been part of the property Marguerite Pirot had taken back from the wreck of her marriage.

Otherwise, its few pages are filled with Sirop Laroze for stomach complaints and 'choleric influences'; and with invitations placed by a shipping company in La Rochelle for men to join a voyage to *les mines d'or de la Californie*. The Gold Rush of '49 was having its repercussions even here. In response, an editorial at the same time complained that the sons of peasants were leaving the land for the towns, a refrain we shall hear again and again. The conclusion was that they should stay in their villages and continue the occupations of their fathers at the station in life where Providence had been pleased to place them. Poor Antoine Pirot cannot be accused of having wanted anything but this.

I felt that now I would never know if Pirot had been pardoned or not. But when I returned to the census records in Châteauroux I came across an answer of a sort. In 1856, five years after the court case, Marguerite Charbonnier was back at Le Flets, living on her own. She had a brother and a cousin living nearby but she was sixty now (though she gave her age as fifty-eight), her parents were presumably dead, and she does not appear to have had children by either of her husbands. Maybe, also, she was not a particularly popular woman. In the margin by her entry is written '*son mari est absent − détenu*' − detained in prison. So Silvain-Germain's eloquence did not, after all, soften the hearts of the black-robed gentlemen in Paris.

By 1861, although the rest of the Charbonnier clan were still around Le Flets, Marguerite had gone.

On a pristine morning in early spring, when points of white fruit blossom are precariously appearing against the sky above the newly dug earth of the vegetable gardens, I watch the Monsieur Pirot of today walk through the centre of the village towards his Mairie wearing his mayoral sash. It is Sunday, but the doors stand open. There is a General Election, another sub-chapter in the great wrangle between the Republican ideal and the forces of tradition and conservatism which has been the history of France for the last two hundred years. It is said – correctly, as it turns out – that the Left are due to suffer a landslide defeat. Monsieur Pirot is a lifelong Communist supporter, following in the steps of an admired uncle who died in the Resistance. (There was a good deal of Resistance activity during the Occupation in the Indre, since it was just south of the Line of Demarcation.) How Monsieur Pirot reconciled his politics with his position as a prominent Chassignolles landowner puzzled me a little, till it was explained to me by another that in central France Communism is equated with the triumph of the small man over the large absentee landlord. Hadn't the Communist Party earlier this century stated clearly that when it came to power it would abide by the land revisions made under the Revolution and not embark on another round of expropriation? To cling tenaciously to one's own few hectares, resisting Government interference, is therefore, by a rural logic, to be a good Communist.

Monsieur Pirot looks quite stoical, even cheerful, at the prospect of a left-wing rout. Like every farmer today he is certainly more deeply worried about the long-term implications of the Common Market and the 'crisis of overproduction' than he is about political labels. He is a heavy, compact man and his rolling walk is the kind which, like a laugh or a facial expression, is inherited down the generations. If we had film footage of our own great-great-grandparents, as one day some of our great-grandchildren will of us, we would rediscover not only our own chins and eyes but our gestures, our voices, our way of moving.

Monsieur Pirot is descended from one of Antoine Pirot's uncles. But when I asked him tentatively if he had ever heard of a Court case he was at a loss. He had never seen the draft letter asking for pardon. When I told him about it, he remarked gently that it was a good long time ago, wasn't it, and that in those days people were different. Weren't they?

II

The Cheerful Day

Chapter 8

The Pirot drama occurred when Célestine was between six and seven years old. Let us return to the year of her birth, 1844.

Thirty-two babies were born in Chassignolles that year, the same birth rate as in the previous decade. Only one of these infants died, though three older children succumbed.

That same year, General Bertrand, Maréchal du Palais, died in his great house in Châteauroux on the edge of the ramparts overlooking the river. He had been one of the handful of obstinately faithful generals who accompanied Napoleon into exile in St Helena. Several years after his own death his remains (always euphemistically referred to in French as 'ashes' in spite of the Church's dislike of cremation) went to Paris to lie beside those of his Emperor in the Invalides: they travelled on the brand-new railway line.

In 1844 Clemenceau, who was to lead France out of another great war a hundred years after the Napoleonic campaigns, and whose life span was to be very close to Célestine's, was three years old. Émile Zola, whose novels were to document so many aspects of the rapidly evolving nineteenth-century society, was four. In that year too Louis-Napoleon, the future Second Emperor, whose name was eventually to become synonymous with a cynical and materialistic regime, published a work which, for the time being, endeared him to George Sand's socialist friends – *The Extinction of*

Pauperism, containing suggestions for interventionist welfare policies. He was also by training an engineer, a man looking towards the future.

In the *Journal de l'Indre*, the Châteauroux newspaper that liked to keep up with metropolitan affairs and published a *roman feuilleton* about an aristocratic family living in the Faubourg St Germain, there was a news item about Red Indians from America being paraded in Paris like exotic animals. There were also rumours that an invention called 'the electric telegraph' was being tried out between Paris and Versailles. (It did not work.)

On the edge of the Commune of Chassignolles in full summer the month after Célestine's birth, a wolf appeared from a small wood out of the mist that preceded a hot day and carried off first one lamb and then another without the shepherd girl being able to stop it.

Few of the local footpaths had yet been widened enough to take a cart. But in the last few years the Chaumette family, in their old house with the outside stair, had opened their inn. It was chiefly the enterprise of the twenty-eight-year-old Silvain-Germain and his wife, but François Chaumette, then in his late forties and living nearby with his own wife, daughter and carpenter son-in-law, also began styling himself *cabaretier*. The family owned a little land too; it was François who had apparently seen to that. Except for the unfortunates who had failed to acquire any, like cousin Silvain-Bazille the weaver and his brothers, anyone of any standing in the Commune had his one field, his cow or a couple of goats, a pig, perhaps a mule or a donkey for haulage. (Only the larger landowners had their own plough-oxen, so a good deal of borrowing and work trading went on.) In many areas still, at that period and for long after, the tenant farmer struggling to meet both his own needs and the landlord's and having nothing to show at the end for all the labour invested, was a common figure, but Chassignolles never had very many of these. However, those with no land still tried to rent a patch to grow one crop, or reared goats or geese by pasturing them on common land and chivvying them for walks along the grassy paths: the basic occupation in the Commune, then and for the next hundred years, was subsistence farming. The gradually evolving trades of smith, farrier, wheelwright, sadler, carpenter, innkeeper, trader, builder and so on, started as part-time occupations, bringing in extra money to a life which, till then, had been almost universally precarious, in thrall to the vagaries of chance and the seasons.

The Chaumettes and their neighbours and customers lived mainly on bread, cheese, vegetables and potato-cakes, with a dish of *fromentée* (frumenty – cracked wheat boiled in milk) as a special treat. After Célestine's birth Anne Laurent would have been given a bowl of hot, sugared milk to drink; had the baby been a boy it would have been mulled wine. In the inn, eggs and butter may sometimes have been consumed, if they were kept on offer for passing customers, but the poorest peasants still took most of these products into La Châtre to sell in the market. The market was where all beef and mutton went as well. The diet of the wooded Lower Berry was recognized as being more varied than that of the sheep-runs of the plains, but the only meat regularly eaten by the ordinary people, and that only on Sundays, was home-cured pork, or the occasional chicken for a celebration. 'Butcher's meat' was even a faintly suspect commodity. The folk-song about three small children who meet a butcher in the fields at night, and are invited into his isolated hut, reflects a rooted fear centring on an urban and upper-class luxury and the dubious trade of those supplying it. (The children have their throats cut and are laid out, like pigs, for salting, but St Nicholas appears and magically restores them to life.) In fact Chassignolles, even in its commercial heyday of five grocers and two bakers, never ran to a butcher's shop. Horse-meat, which became part of the staple diet of the urban working class in the late nineteenth and early twentieth centuries, complete with special shops advertised by wooden horses' heads, was never much eaten in the countryside. The horse had become the peasant farmer's work companion; people said it would be like eating a fellow human being.

In the mid-nineteenth century bread was still by far the most important item of diet. It was rye bread – white flour was another luxury that was only grown to be sold to the wealthier towns-people. Home-grown grain was ground in one of the Commune's three water-mills; one was near Le Flets and was kept by a Char-bonnier, and another was owned by the Mercier family, who still live there today. Bread was baked at home, but only at long inter-vals. The batches of heavy, ring-shaped loaves were hung up to keep, safe from rats and mice and picking fingers. They continued to provide the daily ration even when stale and dry. The ceremonial, almost sacramental cult of fresh bread, the *pain quotidien* that today sends customers on daily or even twice-daily excursions to the baker's for long loaves crackling with warmth in their rack, had not yet been born. Commercial baking had only reached the towns.

Those who had insufficient land to grow their own grain had to buy it, and after a bad season the prices rose and went on rising because hoarding began. This operation of market forces was not perhaps as hard on the poor as the artificially raised prices imposed by the English Corn Laws, but it could still have a devastating effect on the peasant budget and on that of town dwellers who bought bakers' bread. Even when grain was plentiful the cost of this for a family of six accounted for about half the earnings of a labouring man.

Célestine was born in May and that summer was an unusually parched one. Some village wells ran dry and women washed linen at the rivers in a trickle of brown water that could not clean it and left a tainted scent of its own. Then the following winter was particularly hard. The temperature went down to nine and then twelve below zero (centigrade); rain turned to ice where it fell. The Mayor of La Châtre (then, as for many decades, George Sand's Vicar-of-Bray friend, Delavau) had forbidden the trapping of larks, but the Préfet of the Indre overruled him, inviting the Gendarmerie to take no action 'since it constitutes the only resource available to the labouring classes without work'. The larks, incidentally, were not eaten by the trappers, but sold for a pittance in the markets – to buy bread.

The following summer was wet. The Indre broke its banks at La Châtre, carrying away two houses and flooding the Rue Royale. The waters, according to the *Écho du Berry*, 'rose to a height that the oldest inhabitants in the area [*les plus anciens du pays*] cannot recall ever having seen before'. Riverside vegetable gardens became lakes, mills up and down the river's length were damaged. Between La Châtre and Chassignolles the stone bridge over a tributary stream (the Couarde), which had only been built the year before after much discussion, was swept away. (It was replaced by a wooden one, which collapsed ten years later under the weight of a heavy peasant woman with a basket of grapes.) Crops standing in the fields were spoiled. The harvest was poor and was made worse by storms that broke over the harvesters' heads.

The next summer, once again, was dry. By the end of the year, the price of bread had risen from twenty-four centimes a kilo to forty-two. During the same period the wages of casual labourers in the towns had been reduced by almost a third. George Sand, at Nohant, carried a pistol in her pocket at night, and for the first time in her sturdy life she took a man servant to accompany her when she went walking in the countryside, for fear of being attacked by one of the starving vagrants who were known to be roaming about. By recent legislation, vagrancy was a criminal offence, and in an attempt to discourage begging 'charity offices' and workshops had been established in the main towns. La Châtre did not yet have one, but the indefatigable Delavau had plans for one. It had been noted, however, in Châteauroux, where one had been set up for several years, that its existence made citizens less inclined to give personally to the poor: the long saga of public aid to those in need, which has had such a profound and equivocal effect on all developed societies, was just at its inconspicuous beginning.

In Chassignolles, those landowners who grew enough grain to sell on the open market presumably benefited from the rise in prices, but there must have been many affected by the general, absolute dearth. Fortunately, among the woods of the Black Valley were – and are – plantations of Spanish chestnuts, and the harvest of these had always been important as an alternative basic food-stuff. But even in a small town like La Châtre troubles and confrontations were occurring. Already, earlier in the year, the real miller from the mill at Angibault a few miles away (who should not be confused with the one in George Sand's story or yet with an earlier one who was a personal friend of hers) had been convicted of abstracting another miller's bags of grain in the market-place. In the Berry millers were paid not in cash but in kind – a proportion of what was given to them to grind – and it was by selling their percentage in the towns that they made their money. Though peasants, they tended to be richer and more worldly-wise than their neighbours; in time of shortage they became natural targets for resentment and were suspected of taking more than their share and of hoarding. This miller was imprisoned for a year. In the autumn, when the harvest had now been inadequate for three years, another resented figure in La Châtre, a grain merchant called Gaultier, said to the would-be customer who complained to him of his rising prices, 'You haven't seen anything yet, you'll find yourselves eating grass' (*'Vous n'avez pas fini; on vous fera manger de l'herbe'*) – a direct reference to the traditional bogey of starving Ancien Régime serfs from which the spirit of the Revolution had been created. This was in late 1846; within fifteen months the collapse of the July monarchy was to take place in the 'Revolution of '48', followed by the short-lived Second Republic. Gaultier's words nearly produced a riot on the spot.

An actual, more serious grain riot occurred in 1847 in the small town of Buzançais in the northern Berry. There, women selling produce in the market were said to have worked on a group of day-labourers and incited them to stop a cartload of wheat that was setting off to Issoudun, the nearest town of any size. Issoudun was then one of France's smallest Préfectures: Balzac wrote that its drowsy airs would have turned even a Napoleon fat and lazy. But in Buzançais the cry went up that the sharp townsfolk were taking the bread from the mouths of the country people who had grown it. This was the age-old peasant fear, but it may have been exacerbated by the fact that Issoudun had recently acquired a railway station. Was the wheat going to be sent to the undeserving, alien people of Paris?

The affair escalated. The men raided the grain stores and houses of several well-to-do local landowners. Hostages were taken. One of these shot at rioters with his carbine and was in turn set upon and killed. At the noisy trial that followed, three of the rioters were condemned to death and twenty given life sentences. This was considered excessive even at that time, and was evidently an attempt to impose exemplary order in a situation that was, in any case, to be the last of its kind. Only the exceptional string of bad harvests could have produced this crisis at a time when local famines, let alone widespread ones, were becoming a thing of the past.

In a country as large and variegated as France, food lacking in one area could nearly always be supplied from another one if only it could be transported, and transport was slowly improving. Bad and rough as the cart roads were in the 1840s, there were simply many more of them, at least from one town to another, than there had been a hundred, fifty or even thirty years before. There was now, along the valley of the Indre between La Châtre and Châteauroux, a road of sorts and a stagecoach service, whereas in George

Sand's childhood there had been 'no road, or rather there were a hundred ... a labyrinth of twisting tracks, of marshy ponds and great heathlands ... people continually got lost'. The plots of two of her stories involve the extensive night wanderings of strayed travellers in this will-o'-the-wisp landscape. (Much of it today is a terrain of intensive cultivation, shorn of its old hedgerows, along the straight, modern Departmental road.)

The old rural idea had been that roads from one *pays* to another were unnecessary and even undesirable: they might bring strangers in who would eat up your food. There was clearly a final echo of this paranoia in Buzançais. Even in the well-established rural towns the belief was that the coming of a main road would bring higher prices for basic commodities, though, if anything, the opposite was the case. Before the railway had linked it with the world, Issoudun itself had been resistant to invasion. Indeed its bourgeoisie were so determined about this, according to Balzac (in *La Rabouilleuse*), that they actually succeeded in getting the chief road from Vierzon to Châteauroux, which should logically have gone via Issoudun, diverted through Vatan – where it remains to this day.

But once a few more routes had been constructed country people discovered that they could use them to take their own produce to markets farther afield, and the notion of the desirability of communications was gradually born. In 1817 the Council in Chassignolles had refused, to a man, to contribute towards the cost of building a stone bridge over the large River Creuse twenty miles to the south-west, on the circular argument that there was 'no trade with those parts'. (This is one of the oldest Minute records.) By 1836, however, when a new law provided for subsidies to enlarge paths that linked one Commune to adjoining ones, they were keenly in favour of this, and contributed to the building of the ill-fated stone bridge over the Couarde in the early 1840s even though it was outside the Commune.

The hunger experienced in the Berry between 1846 and 1848 was not a matter of absolute lack of food but of the number of people who, always near the breadline, slipped below it in times of shortage and raised prices. The new administration of the Second Republic, bent on humanitarian reform, including the creation of work schemes, did a survey of the poor: it found that the Indre alone had over five thousand 'absolutely destitute' people out of a population of about two hundred and seventy thousand, which is approaching two in every hundred. Only half of these were considered fit to work, always supposing they could find work. Many of the rest were probably old, or very young. In its numbers of abandoned babies and small children (always a good index of general poverty and of particular years of crisis) the Indre was the third-worst Department in France.

But at the same time the very fact that the destitute could now be counted and, presumably, helped by the new charity offices, shows what a long way central France had come since the starving serfs and brigands of a hundred years earlier. By the same token, the unmarried girls who abandoned their babies did so knowing that they would probably be found and taken off to the local hospital run by the Sisters. If the infant perished before being found and the mother was officially identified, she might be charged with infanticide. If it were retrieved dead from a place where it was never meant to be found, such as under a pile of straw or in a stream, she could be punished with half a dozen years in prison. The fact that such cases were now brought to Court is itself an indication of the way society was evolving and becoming more 'civilized'. In the Berry there had always been a popular horror of the crime of child-slaughter, but that was probably because it had also been rather common. The 'midnight washerwomen', whom the late-night traveller was apt to see as he weaved his way home from a celebration, were authoritatively stated by some to be 'the souls of mothers who have killed . . . They incessantly beat and wring what looks like wet linen but which, seen close up, is revealed as a dead baby . . . They are condemned to wash the corpse of their child until the Last Judgement.'

Those unwanted infants who escaped this apocalyptic fate and survived to reach the hospital were presently put out to nurse. The census for 1846 shows quite a few of these foundlings placed in Chassignolles households. They were known locally as *champis*, children found in the *champs*, the fields, and though they seem to have died off rather more than legitimate children, many did live and flourish. One of George Sand's novellas is a sentimental but well-documented tale of such a foundling making good. A real-life example appears in the Chassignolles census for 1846, having already grown to manhood. The seductive name of Valentin Aimable had been bestowed on him. He worked as a labourer and, at twenty-three, was married and already had two small children.

There are also examples of much more recent date, including the father of the present baker. A foundling in the streets of Paris *circa* 1900, fostered in the Black Valley and later apprenticed to a miller, he saved up to buy the goodwill of the Chassignolles bakery, and became a linchpin of the village. His son (the devoted Monsieur Meyer) took on the business after him.

By the middle of the nineteenth century France had the means for relieving absolute want and suffering, but the memory of death by starvation continued for a long time in popular myth and political propaganda. In a paradox which is not uncommon, the symbolic figure of an emaciated peasant driving his worn plough team, silently attended by a still more skeletal being with a scythe, received fresh currency in the 1840s in a popular print after Holbein, just at the time when the reality was passing into history. But not till the generation that had known real hunger at first hand had died off, around the end of the century, did the fear of it die out also. It is customary to speak and write as if, in any one era, the population expressed homogeneously the attitudes and expectations relevant to that era, whereas in practice the world is always well supplied with people and prejudices of the time that is past and with half-formed expectations of a world yet to come.

When Célestine appeared she was no doubt placed ceremonially in the arms of her great-grandfather, Silvain. His birth, counting back from his declared age on his death registration, took place in 1756. All his ideas and assumptions were therefore formed in the feudal, pre-Revolutionary era when the monks were still occupying the church and the houses round it. After the changes that came, even in the conservative Berry, in the wake of the Revolution, the Directoire and the Napoleonic wars, this lost era must have seemed as quaintly antique as the time before the First World War now seems to us. I see Silvain Chaumette in my mind's eye clad to the last in the wool-and-goat-hair breeches that were by then obsolete wear and with his thin old hair in an eighteenth-century pigtail under his round black Berrichon hat.

In contrast, the next generation, that of Célestine's grandfather François, of Antoine Pirot and also of Louis Vallet, grew up in a time of unprecedented change and this too must have gone on informing their hopes, expectations and fears throughout life. The anti-monarchist *coup* of 1848 took place, it has been said, essentially because people still living remembered 1791. By the same token, that brief Republic failed and was replaced by a more autocratic, Bonapartist regime because people also harked back to the days of Napoleon.

What did François wear when his granddaughter was a child? (He died when she was seventeen.) Almost certainly, the dark-blue linen smock of the region and, by this date, dark woollen trousers, all woven in the family. Clogs on his feet, inside them thick wool *chaussons*, half socks and half slipper, dyed brown with walnut juice. He probably never owned a pair of boots though he, like his father, would have had the round hat and a brightly coloured cravat for Sundays. Waistcoats in quilting or sheepskin, extra shirts and the like, even extra pairs of trousers, were piled not over but under the smock in cold weather.

With Silvain-Germain, however, we move into a different era. Born just as the destructive wars had come to an end and a monarchy had been restored, he seems like a harbinger of the future, an example of the kind of man who was then rather rare in a village but who, by the end of the century, would be found on every corner. Even if he wore the standard smock and clogs during his working day, his status as an innkeeper, man of letters and presently Secretary to the Mairie is likely to have been reflected in a set of more bourgeois clothing for best, in the factory-made cloth that was now obtainable locally. These could have been made up in the village, where someone who styled himself tailor (son of the Garde-Champêtre) had set up by 1846. With the new cloth came more closely fitted town styles; dark cutaway coats were being seen in the countryside, along with gaily checked or striped materials worn for stylish contrast. A young master blacksmith who, like Antoine Pirot, was admitted to Châteauroux prison in the early 1850s, was brought there from the Court in what were evidently his best clothes, including a black suit, leather boots, a black cloth cap and a waistcoat striped black, violet, blue and white. Another skilled man arrived with proper shoes, an assortment of colours in his trousers and waistcoat, and a cravat in 'brown cotton with flowers' – this at a time when the more ordinary inmate appeared in much-mended wool and goatskin.

The difference from one generation and/or social class to another was still more marked in the women. The girl from a neighbouring village, working as a servant in Chassignolles, who was sent to prison for theft and took her illegitimate baby in with her, entered gaol in standard peasant garb: a 'coarse' chemise, a blue cotton dress, a grey checked apron, a linen underskirt, a cloak, a black fichu and white cap, blue wool stockings and clogs. This outfit, plus some swaddling clothes for the baby, was all she possessed in the world.

In *Le Meunier d'Angibault*, the miller's old mother wears on Sundays a small apron of Indian-printed calico 'which she had looked after carefully ever since she was young, valuing it greatly because in those days it had cost four times as much as finer stuff would have cost today'. In the same book, the social and chronological evolution of another family, the on-the-make Bricolins, is indicated by the way the women of the family dress. The grandmother appears 'as a peasant' and is illiterate; the mother is dressed 'like a priest's housekeeper' – that is to say, in a dark dress of bought stuff, made up with some regard to the prevailing style, and probably worn over the stays (corsets) that were unknown to the peasantry but obligatory among genteelly bred women. 'She knew how to sign her own name legibly, and could find the time of sunrise and the moon's phases in the pedlar's Almanach.' Meanwhile her daughter Rose, in keeping with her modish name, reads novels from the same source, does the housekeeping accounts for her father, and has learnt new dances such as the polka as well as traditional folk ones. For dancing and for church she wears a pink muslin dress copied from a fashion plate. She probably, though George Sand does not say, wears several layers of petticoats under this and even drawers – also unknown in traditional peasant society.

Just so, a few years later, when Célestine was in her teens, would her wardrobe and accomplishments have been different from those of her mother, who grew up as a shepherdess and at the time of her marriage could not write, and her grandmother Marie Petitpez, wife of François. For Célestine, too, was reared as a literate, refined girl, destined in hope for a wider life.

It must be said, however, that by modern standards no one, refined or lowly, rich or poor, dressed in hemp or dressed in silk, was then particularly clean. Most French people of all classes never, in their whole lives, submerged themselves in water, or even stripped to wash except at long intervals. Many peasants never washed at all, even after the labours of a summer's day – a good sweat was held to be cleansing in itself. It is true that in a life of incessant toil fetching water for one's personal toilette might seem just another tedious chore, but even those villagers who had servants to go to the well for them did not indulge in much cleanliness beyond cosmetic attention to face, neck and hands. Nor did they wash their personal linen often. Laundry was done in great loads that were allowed to accumulate for months, and of course the heavier garments were never washed at all. The schoolmaster's or Secretary's black coat was almost as impregnated with its owner's odour as was the shepherd's smock, and even the muslin dress worn for strenuous dancing at a festival may have been carefully hung back in the wardrobe with its lingering human scent undisturbed. Till the end of the century no one in France, even in the towns, began to suggest there was anything wrong with smelling of oneself. When the first bath was installed in Chassignolles (in the Domaine, in the 1920s) the village wondered with amusement why the wealthy Pissavys were so dirty as to need it.

The people of Chassignolles were all rather short by today's standards, and even by the standards then prevailing in France. In the year of Célestine's birth, the contingent of young men sent by the Department for military service ended up sixteen men below strength because many of those originally summoned were later rejected as 'too small'. Even a generation later, in 1870, a number of Berrichon conscripts were rejected for this reason, from a cohort whose average height was no more than 1.64 metres (five foot five inches). I have reason to believe that the Chaumettes were on the tall side for their time and place, but this is not to say a great deal; George Sand's miller of Angibault, known as *le beau farinier*, is particularly admired for his unusual size, which is given as five foot, eight *pouces* (thumb-tops – inches).

Le Meunier d'Angibault appeared in 1845 but seems, like many nineteenth-century novels, to be set in a timeless zone a few years earlier. In it, the impoverished noblewoman arriving in the Berry to visit her mortgaged castle, Blanchemont (actually Sarzay), reaches Châteauroux by coach. The railway is not mentioned. Its much-heralded arrival was, however, the preoccupation of the 1840s, and was the great chronological marker which, in retrospect, can be seen to have divided the old world from the new.

Rumours about the prospect of railways began in the late 1830s when the first line opened between Paris and nearby St Germain-en-Laye, but that was more of a toy than a serious venture and the commercial implications of railway transport were not at once seen. It was known, however, that in England railways were already proliferating, and it was with English engineering advice and investment that the first proper lines were planned: Paris to Rouen (opened 1843) and Paris to Orléans (1845). Orléans lies midway between Paris and the Berry, so once it was pencilled on the maps the local administration did not waste any time in suggesting that it might usefully be extended southwards through their area.

Not everyone was happy at the prospect. Carters, owners of livery stables and post houses, coach drivers and innkeepers all complained that the iron way would destroy their trade: they seemed to have imagined the railway to be all-penetrating. A condescending editorial in the *Journal de l'Indre* remarked that in spite of the much advertised spread of enlightenment among the people – a sprinkling of schools? more pedlars? more pink silk dresses? – they did not know what they were talking about. Railways, the editorial explained, did not destroy trade but increased it. The writer then rather spoilt his case by saying that it was quite likely, in any case, that the new invention would never actually reach the Department of the Indre.

Railway fever had, however, arrived in Châteauroux in advance of the trains. Large schemes were envisaged. Concessions were sold and share offers were floated. By the middle of the decade the Orléans line was working its way, via Vierzon and Issoudun, to Châteauroux with more than a thousand navvies. These were given free evening classes in reading, writing and arithmetic: more enlightenment, and perhaps an attempt to keep them out of the trouble that gangs of single men usually found. The newspaper published an encouraging article about how the railway was really not more dangerous than other forms of transport but less – even in England, that byword for modernity, though there, of course, the trains ran too fast . . .

Châteauroux station was opened in November 1847 on what was then an open field site just outside the town; the town soon stretched out to meet it. Each old town, many of them still partly walled at that date, went through the same metamorphosis as the railway reached it with its transforming breath. The station spawned a new suburb, while the 'old town', with its narrow streets tumbling towards a river that had once been all-important, declined into a purely working-class quarter. La Châtre went through the same evolution a generation later, though it was never transformed in the way the county town was.

Châteauroux opinion was divided between those who insisted that the line must not be allowed to stop there and those who, on the contrary, said that it should remain the railhead. In the same way Argenton, an ancient town on the River Creuse and the next place of any consequence to the south, insisted that they too wanted the railway to reach them, but that it should stop there. Traditional fears and jealousies had evolved but not disappeared. The inhabitants of both the Indre and the Creuse saw the advantages of sending their wine and mutton to towns in the north, but were much less enthusiastic about the possible arrival of cattle from the Limousin to the south. Needless to say, by the time the unstoppable railway reached Argenton (where the station opened in 1854) there were already plans to extend it to Toulouse.

But the Châteauroux to Argenton stretch, roughly following the route of a Roman road, ran through a wild, poor lakeland section of the Berry, far from La Châtre and Chassignolles. Regret at this state of affairs found expression in the Chassignolles Council the following year. With unusual fluency, the Council declared that since the Indre had only achieved one railway line which completely bypassed a large part of it, the Department was missing out on 'a national movement that is important for agriculture, commerce and industry'. What was needed was an east-west line, coming down from Tours, linking Châteauroux with La Châtre and on to Montluçon and then Clermont-Ferrand in the Massif Central. Such a link, the Council said, would effectively bring the Lower Berry into a network of communication with the Atlantic ocean on one side and Switzerland and Germany on the other.

I assume that this untypically progressive and cosmopolitan call, which reflected the visions of Louis-Napoleon himself, was passed on to the Préfet in Châteauroux. As a matter of fact, since Chassignolles' mayor, Geoffrenet de Champdavid, was a friend of the Préfet, it was probably instigated by the Préfecture. As to the supposed heady advantages of eventual communication with Switzerland and Germany, at that point Chassignolles could hardly be expected to foresee (Châteauroux did not) that ten years later the iron-smelting industry of the Berry would be abruptly killed off by products arriving by rail from the more up-to-date foundries of the Loire, followed by imports from Germany and Scandinavia.

The idea that railways were an excellent thing, or at any rate something they could not afford to miss, had now implanted itself in the Berrichon mind. For the next forty years, the long-delayed but enticing prospect of the Tours–La Châtre–Montluçon line and, later still, the building of branch lines through other neighbouring towns and villages, provided a constant theme of expectation in the Council meetings. There was even an exciting moment in 1900 when Chassignolles thought it might acquire a station of its own.

In Célestine's childhood, however, the prospect of local trains and indeed the very sight of a train lay in the future. Life was still bounded by the village and wherever else could be reached on foot. Who were the Chaumettes' neighbours?

The most prominent one was the maverick gentleman Louis Vallet, who has already surfaced several times in this chronicle. According to the tables that accompany the map of that period, by then he owned more land in the Commune than anyone else. I imagine him dressed, like the badly behaved Gros Propriétaire in George Sand's *La Mare au Diable*, in 'half-bourgeois clothes' with a black cutaway above ordinary country riding-breeches. If he consorted as a social equal with anyone in the Commune, it would have been with the Geofrillon-Simon family who appeared from nowhere on the census in the 1840s as the occupants of isolated, ancient Villemort. They consisted of an elderly married couple, a son and two daughters in middle life and a retinue of servants. None of the younger generation had apparently married, but one of the daughters had a six-year-old son called Hubert. Dilapidated aristocrats they may have been, but they must have had Republican sympathies for, in late 1848, after the *coup*, one of them took over as mayor for two and a half years. Vallet also rejoined the Council at this time. Ten years later they were all gone and Villemort was in the charge of a tenant farmer.

Vallet lived, like the Chaumettes, in the centre of the village. Through the land-registry tables I traced him to the old house with the tower and gated courtyard, the only gentleman's residence available. It stands immediately opposite the house that was built as a school in 1848, which explains his objection to that project. I had long been interested in this miniature and forlorn grand house, which was occupied in the middle decades of the twentieth century by a cycle-repair shop and before that by a grocery business. One old lady told me that, as children, they had believed the tower to have been a dungeon where prisoners had starved to death, 'because we'd peeped in and seen skulls there'. Probably it had been used as an ossuary for the bones that surfaced every time one of the buildings near the church was extended or restored. (Some human teeth from the same source ended up as a lucky charm and *memento mori* in the Pagnard sewing basket.) Other delights of the house include original wooden tiles round the dormer windows at the back of the courtyard and, at right angles to this building, a later one reached by an airy double flight of steps: a charming eighteenth-century pavilion with a whiff of Fragonard and *fêtes champêtres*.

So the house contained several separate quarters, and there Louis Vallet led his idiosyncratic existence. He never seems to have married. The first census, that of 1836, lists him as a 'landowner', with several other members of his household down as 'servants', including a Jeanne Aussourd, who varied the age she gave over the years but was actually born in 1798, down as his servant. She was a niece of the Aussourd who had kept the registers in the Revolutionary days of Vallet's father, and this man's sons, her cousins, still lived nearby. They were a family above the social level from which servants usually came and it might seem strange that Jeanne was performing this function – but significantly the census lists in Vallet's house two more Aussourds, Colette aged eleven and Françoise aged five, both Jeanne's daughters.

Ten years later Louis Vallet and Jeanne were still together. There is no sign of Françoise at this point (away at convent school?) but Colette was now inhabiting another part of the house with a young husband, and both of them were listed as being on Vallet's staff. As if to throw a genteel disguise over Colette's origins, her *husband's* family name is given as Aussourd, though he may of course have been her cousin.

By 1856 Louis, who would by then have been nearly seventy, had gone, presumably into the earth between his house and the church, but Jeanne was still ensconced in his property and was now styling herself *propriétaire faisant cultiver* – an owner with others working her land, successfully it would seem since she now had five servants. Also living with her was her younger daughter, now calling herself Marie and married to a man much older than herself, surnamed Choppy. Colette and her husband and children lived in another house nearby.

It would seem that Jeanne's inherited property, however interesting its origins, now ensured that she moved in the most genteel circles of village society. For also in part of the tower-house, perhaps in the eighteenth-century pavilion, was a separate establishment consisting of an elderly priest and his even more elderly housekeeper. The census-taker's description of him as *desservant*, mass-server, suggests that he was not the official Curé. Geoffrenet de Champdavid, on his appointment as mayor four years earlier, was keen that the dilapidated presbytery should be put in good order, but evidently this had not yet happened.

The priest and his old lady were still keeping Jeanne Aussourd company ten years later, but by 1872 they were both gone and a very young Curé had come to occupy the now-renovated presbytery (where he soon made himself unpopular). Jeanne remained, withdrawn into a smaller portion of the house, with one middle-aged servant. She was still there fourteen years later in 1886, rising eighty-eight, an independent survivor of a lost age.

I had thought that the picture of her life I had put together would remain supposition, but when I mentioned the tower-house one day to Mademoiselle Pagnard she replied at once.

'In my grandmother's day it was lived in by a woman who'd had children by a gentleman . . . A lawyer from the Creuse who came here at the time of the Revolution.'

I told her how pleased I was to hear this, but suggested: 'Actually I think it must have been his father who came here at the Revolution. Otherwise, he'd have been over a hundred.'

'If you say so . . . Anyway, the family came from there.' *Étrangers*, said her tone. 'I don't recall his name, though.'

'Vallet?'

'That's it! Fancy you knowing. Vallete.' She solved the variant spellings by sounding the t. 'The woman was supposed to be his housekeeper but he left everything to her. She was very well off then. People gossiped, but that's because they were jealous . . . She had a daughter called Frauzine.'

'Frauzine? But that's not a name.' In France, then and till very recently, a name had to come from a State-approved list.

'No, it's not a name! I think she called herself something else later, to be more like everyone else.' So 'Françoise' was the census-taker's compromise. Elsewhere in the Aussourd family at that time appeared an Angélique, a name that (like Célestine) spoke of social aspiration, and Colette Aussourd's son was called Prosper after the writer and statesman of the period, Prosper Mérimée.

'I remember being told that Frauzine got most of the money in the end. And as she'd married a gentleman [*un monsieur*] name of Choppy, who was in business and who died and left her all his money too, she did very well. She wasn't, you know, like a village woman at all.'

The name Choppy had been saying something to me. By and by I remembered a saga from a Council Minute book:

'When they were building the Mairie they needed to buy the site from a Madame Choppy and she made difficulties about it.'

'Oh yes?' said Jeanne Pagnard, as if she had known all the protagonists and was not going to be surprised by anything. 'Well that would have been her mother again, you see. She ran every-body. You couldn't tell her anything.' She added after a moment: 'Everyone knew that Frauzine and the other daughter were from him, the old man, but you couldn't say so. It would have been a scandal.'

We sat there in the autumn sunshine of 1992, contemplating the gossip of some hundred and twenty years earlier.

'The schoolmaster lived there too, in the tower-house, at one time,' added Jeanne Pagnard presently.

'Monsieur Charbonnier? Yes, I noticed that.' In the 1870s, Au-guste Charbonnier, with wife and baby daughter, had moved into the accommodation vacated by the old mass-server. More genteel company for Jeanne Aussourd, from a time before national edu-cation was formally pronounced 'secular' and a priest and a teacher did not necessarily represent opposed worlds. Both elderly priest and young teacher are in fact mentioned affectionately in the same sentence in a manuscript memoir, written *circa* 1880 about the 1860s, that came into my hands only as this book was going to press (but see Afterword).

'Yes, Charbonnier *was* his name. But you know how I know? Because my great-grandmother, my grandmother's mother that is, learnt to cook in his house. No, not from his wife – from his mother, who came to live with them. Apparently she was very interested in cooking, and that was in the days before most people were bothered with it. I mean, they just ate whatever was there. Beans in the bean-harvest season, chestnuts all winter . . . But Monsieur Charbonnier's mother, she was skilled at it and taught my great-grandmother a lot of dishes. Goat-cheese cakes . . . and special *galettes de pommes de terre* . . . with cream and herbs.'

And I too tasted in my imagination the creamy potato-cakes of a woman born around the time of the Battle of Waterloo.

I had another reason for being interested in the Aussourd family. An Aussourd was among the young men who wanted to marry Célestine.

Chapter 9

'*Ma chère*,' he called her at the head of his letter. 'My dear.' Or rather '*Macher*'. His written French, though fluent, shows an innocence of the correct agreement of tenses and genders. It reproduces the spoken word in such a way that some phrases are impenetrable on the page but yield their meaning when they are put back again into the human voice – of which the English version below can only be an approximate echo:

La Loge, 19 April 1863

My dear,

I venture to write 2 little words to let you know my intentions [or 'my attentions to you', *mes attensions*] for my idea is to come and see you.

For if I were to suit you as you suit me I think we could make a match of it together. Before anything else I would like to know if I suit you, before speaking to your parents that is, for I know that they have the right to decide your Destiny.

Youve known me so long that you must know what I am like. As for yourself [*temps qu'a toie*] I have always known you to be a good girl [*une honnaite filles*] and I would do it without fear with you. And I have a feeling it might be the same way with you about me.

[Phrase illegible from split in paper] . . . to accept me to wed if that suits you Ill talk to you and to your parents about it as soon as possible. If I write you these few words now, it is because I know you can read my writing. And I think you might like [*sapoura te faire un plaisir*] to get a letter from me, which comes to you by way of one of my good friends. If my letter makes its mark with you, you will be kind enough to write and say so. I'm just writing from warmth of feeling [*amitié* – the word had, like *ami*, a stronger and more intimate sense then than it does now]. If that doesn't work, at least I will know. I'm doing this from the bottom of my heart and I would like it very much, when you have got this letter, if you would send me your answer at once. You dont need to be afraid that anyone but me will see your reply for theres no one else in my house who knows how to read, and you can trust me: Im not one to play tricks on you [*Je suis pas pour te trempé*].

Ill close now, as I dont have anything else to note for you today.

Except I am hoping to be your dear one for life.

Baptiste Aussourd

The letter is folded several times, as if to make an inconspicuous package to be slipped from one hand to another, and addressed on the outside of the sheet: '*Amademoiselle Salestine Chaumette aubergiste a Chassignolles.*' The idea seems to have been for the friend to carry Célestine's reply back with him, so that Baptiste would know if he should make his ceremonial visit or not – clearly 'my idea is to come and see you' implies more than just the suggestion that an old acquaintance should look her up next time he is in the village. The use of the intimate form *tu* indicates that he was a childhood friend. In the country at that date, and long after, it was common for young men and women to marry having known each other all their lives and many of the marriages within the Commune were made for material reasons – 'Your parents . . . have the right to decide your Destiny' – but this is hardly the letter of a young man who has been pushed into proposing by his family.

Just who Baptiste's parents were proved more difficult to discover than I expected. In the first half of the nineteenth century Aussourds were plentiful all over the Commune. In addition to Jeanne reigning with her natural daughters in the tower-house, there was her brother and two male cousins, one of whom, André, was born in the same year as Célestine's grandfather. Though he does not himself seem to have gone in for writing, André followed his father, the register keeper, on to the Council, where he remained for decades. He came to possess a large quantity of land around a hamlet called La Loge (now on the map as La Loge Brûlée – the Burnt House). He seems to have had only one surviving daughter himself – Angélique – but by the 1840s his extended family at La Loge consisted of nephews and their wives and children. When one nephew died, another quickly married his widow and was producing twins with her within a year. By the next decade there was also an Aussourd widow there called Agathe. Like Jeanne Aussourd in the tower-house, she was one of the very few people in the Commune living on the proceeds of land worked by others. The resemblance does not end there. In 1856, Agathe, then apparently thirty-six, had one daughter. In 1861, still a widow and claiming to be only thirty-seven, she had two daughters, one three years old.

Although no Baptiste Aussourd of suitable age to be courting Célestine figures in the Birth Registers, I first assumed, because of his letter-heading, that this suitor belonged somewhere in André's clan. The young men of that family would not have needed to hire themselves out to strangers as teenage boys and girls from the poorer families routinely did. As Baptiste was literate – 'There's no one else in my house who knows how to read' – I thought he might have been useful to the dynastic André in running the family property, even as François le Champi was to the wealthy but uneducated miller who employed him in George Sand's story.

In addition, I knew that an Aussourd nephew and his wife had at one time made their home next door to great-aunt Jeanne and so near also to the Chaumette inn; that this Aussourd had in fact worked for Silvain-Germain in the inn at one point and that Silvain-Germain had been the witness to the birth declarations of his children. When I saw that a boy called Jean had been born in this household the month before Célestine, I thought that I had found the person I was looking for; that the young man who later styled himself 'Baptiste' or 'Jean-Baptiste', to distinguish himself from the numerous other Jeans both in his family and in others, had indeed shared part of his childhood with Célestine. I imagined them taking their first steps together across what is now a road but was then a safe space of chicken-pecked grass with a scattering of old grave mounds.

They may have done. But the problem with this satisfactory

solution, as I eventually discovered, is that this Jean Aussourd never reached manhood. He died in November 1848 at the age of four and must have been laid under the earth and the chickens not far from his home. The living and the dead then, and for another forty years, continued to share a common habitat.

Bu the 1860s the Aussourds were diminishing; whole households disappear. Old André himself finished his days well past eighty in the centre of the village near to his cousin Jeanne. Evidently the younger generation formed part of that drift to the towns that became so marked in the second half of the century. I decided that Baptiste's parents, whoever they exactly were, had probably joined this exodus by the time he came back to live temporarily on the family land. In the twentieth century there have been no Aussourds in Chassignolles, though there is one, with a variant spelling, on the Great War memorial in La Châtre, one of several hundred names beneath the figure of a weeping Berrichonne in a local cap.

The answer, however, was more simple, though I only came across it a year later, by chance. For another purpose, I was looking through stacks of early-twentieth-century newspapers in the hot attic of the Villaines' town mansion in La Châtre, now the municipal library. In the edition for mid-August 1923 my eye was caught by the death announcement of a Baptiste Aussourd of Le Magny, which is the small rural Commune between La Châtre and Chassignolles.

Back to the census, this time for Le Magny. And I realized at last that Le Magny too had a farm-hamlet called La Loge, and that I had passed by it many times walking from Chassignolles to La Châtre. Sure enough, there in 1861 was a Jean-Baptiste Aussourd, cultivating vineyards, living with his much older sister Marguerite and two elderly bachelor uncles. The family *were* related to the Chassignolles lot, but the connection went back to the generation of the original register keeper. By 1863, when the letter to Célestine was written, Jean-Baptiste was rising twenty-five, plenty old enough to be thinking of marriage when he took the path over the ford to court her.

Célestine did not write back '*de suitte*' to Baptiste, but several days later. His response reached her, again, by hand delivery. This time he started without any formal address:

I'm replying to your letter that you dated April 24. It affected me when I'd had a read of it and saw that youd spelt out plain to me that youd not decided to marry me for you must know that I can tell what that means.

I can see quite clearly from your letter that I neednt say any more. I havent put myself about to talk to your Parents because it wouldnt be any use. I wanted to know what you thought first of all, though I do think they wouldnt a been averse to it if I put it to them properly and to my knowledge . . . [Illegible sentence as the paper has been torn here by the sealing-wax.]

Listen, at the moment when it was in my mind to come and See you I really did think that we would be making a match of it. Now I think we should let some time go by. My idea is that I wont have anything to do with any other girl [*pas d'ennali voire d'autre*] till St Jean's Day is past, if that will suit you. At that time you can decide if you want me after all, for I know that you will seem as good to me then as you do now.

I can find myself a wife anytime I want. I dont say this to boast but just because these days I can hold up my Head wherever I go [*pour le momen je peut passé le tete Levée*]. I dont think youll meet anyone anywhere to say Ive behaved badly, I think Ive acted as right as any other tom-dick-or-harry who might be keeping company with you [*aussi onnaitement que lepremier garconvenu qui pourra te frequente*] but I wont say anything about that forthemoment.

All I can say is, I wish you from the bottom of my heart a husband who will always be faithful to you, for you dont deserve to be Cheated on.

This letter he ended with restraint and his surname only.

The two months' grace till midsummer did not change Célestine's mind, but Baptiste took years before finding another girl to his taste. He did marry in the end, when he was over thirty, a girl from the bell-ringers' village of St Chartier near George Sand's Domaine, and had a son. But by the end of the century, when he was about sixty, we find him on his own again at Le Magny with only his now-aged sister for company, though other Aussourds still lived near. Just to confuse matters, there was another Jean-Baptiste among them, a cousin or nephew, and a visit to the Le Magny cemetery established that *this* was the one whose death was announced in 1923. But my Baptiste (or rather, Célestine's) was in the family grave too. He'd died in 1909; he was not to know the trauma of the Great War that clouded the last years of others of his generation. No wife is mentioned; no son lies there. I hope, without entire conviction, that his life was by and large a happy one.

Those who knew Célestine in old age speak of her gentleness, goodness and 'refinement'. Evidently she had the gift of making others feel that whatever happened the fault could not be hers; her suitors never thought she was cheating *them* in spite of brooding remarks from more than one about others who might be courting her. It is true that, as the daughter of the inn, she was in a peculiarly fortunate position. On the one hand she enjoyed a status which ensured respect. The central character of Guillaumin's *La Vie d'un Simple*, a labouring peasant who marries an innkeeper's daughter, remarks that 'the daughter of the house seemed to me to belong to a station so superior to mine that I dared not lift my eyes to her'. But on the other hand a daughter serving in her father's establishment had social opportunities that were not available to other respectable girls, who would never have frequented an inn at that time as customers. Except at fairs (eagerly awaited) and church (also popular) most country girls at that time saw no one from one week's end to another but the people working on or near the same farm; in such circumstances they can hardly be said to have chosen their husbands at all. But Célestine's situation was more like that of a girl in La Châtre who might have her pick of apprentices, shopkeepers and perhaps even Something Better. She could afford to wait, either for a 'good match', or for the luxury of romantic love on her own part to which novelists such as George Sand and Henri Murger and their imitators had given currency.

The year before Baptiste Aussourd's attempt, she had already had one serious proposal of marriage. She may, of course, have had other, verbal ones, but the formal love-letter was then just beginning to take its place as a part of ordinary courtship: it was a sign of serious intent commensurate with the effort it cost most of the writers to put pen to paper. However, Célestine's first proposal came from someone well accustomed to written communication, and it arrived in one of the new 'envelopes' and by the post. In 1849 France had copied from England that system whereby all letters were paid for by their senders with a flat-rate stamp, and the price of postage fell to a level many more people could afford. Twice as many letters were sent in France in 1860 as in 1830, and the number increased each year. But village post offices had not yet come: this letter to Célestine was posted, in October 1862, in the small town of Ste Sévère, about ten miles away. With an impressive regard for middle-class correctness, it was addressed to *'Monsieur Chaumette, Secrétaire, Mairie à Chassignoles'*. On opening it, Silvain-Germain would read on the blank side of the sheet folded within: 'Would you be so obliging, Monsieur, [*Veuillez avoir l'obligeance*] to hand this letter to Mademoiselle your daughter, who will tell you the contents thereof.'

The correspondent's writing is as elaborate as his syntax, with huge curling capitals as in a school copybook. He was in fact the schoolmaster at nearby Sarzay. He puts this beneath his signature, either from pride or from anxiety that Célestine might not know. With a touching bogusness he has also put a PS in a less elegant hand, 'Forgive my ugly scrawl', as if hoping belatedly to create the impression of a spontaneity that is totally absent in this careful production. If Aussourd's letters read, paradoxically, like age-old peasant inarticulateness finding its own voice, Monsieur Allorent's composition seems redolent of the self-conscious world just being born: that of the *rentier* and the white-collar workers, of the ladylike wife and the *jeune fille bien élevée*, of trains and newspapers and morning coffee; a world in which eloquence was to be cultivated and yet where taboos and reticences unknown in simpler days were cultivated also. To Allorent, Célestine is 'Mademoiselle', of course, and *vous*.

'I did not want to write to you,' he begins. 'As I said, when we were together at the wedding, I wanted to come and visit you.' (One is not surprised to hear that their previous contact was the supremely respectable one of being guests at the same wedding. I cannot imagine Allorent being a regular customer at the Chassignolles tavern, or yet joining in the boisterous dancing at village festivals.) 'However, I must bring myself to tell you that I have remained inert in this respect without being able to explain why . . .' He continues in this vein for a number of lines before speculating tortuously, 'if, through your good-heartedness, I will find with difficulty an answer to my question?

'My hand trembles as I trace these few lines. I can hardly write to you at all when I remind myself that when I was with you I could barely speak – hardly stutter a few phrases, on account of the state of my heart. I felt you must have a bad impression of me [*J'ai cru que vous pouviez avoir bien mal jugé de moi*].' He goes on, however, to hope that in spite of his silences she may have realized his admiration for her. Since then his feelings for her have grown from day to day 'without my thoughts, crossing the distance which separates us, being able to question yours and form a chain of affection, one to the other . . .'

He is afraid of boring her, he says. He is, never fear, about to explain in one sentence his feelings for her – if she will allow him to. Since talking to her he had come to love her with *l'amour le plus tendre, le plus pure et le plus sincère* – 'the strongest desire and greatest happiness of which I could ever dream is to be alone with you in the gentlest of bonds. One word from you, Mademoiselle, will decide my fate –

'Will you have the goodness to pass on my deepest respects to Monsieur your Father and Madame your Mother. I am impatient to come and speak with them and with you.'

Against his signature he has written further, as if afraid he still had not made his point clear: 'I am most tenderly devoted to you.'

Impossible as it is not to be touched by such tender devotion, one can see why Célestine was not drawn towards marriage with him. She may also have suspected that, for all the underlying distress, some of his fine phrases were lifted from one of the letter-writers' manuals that were then in circulation.

'Allorent' is a local name; Ste-Sévère was probably his family home. It seems likely that in spite of his formality and his literary airs he was quite an ordinary young man whose new-found status had left him socially isolated. Cut off geographically and by lack of income from the town bourgeoisie, and by education and dress from their rustic neighbours, French country school teachers classically suffered in his way. Then and for most of the next hundred years, the Government policy was that there should be schools everywhere in the countryside, so that even children in remote farms might make their way there on foot. By the mid-1860s the Indre had 225 schools and there were over four hundred by 1870, most of them with one lone teacher (*instituteur*) in sole charge. It was the situation described, unchanged, at the turn of the century by Alain-Fournier in his novel *Le Grand Meaulnes*, which is set at the other end of the Berry: '. . . my appointment [is] as schoolmaster

in the hamlet of Saint-Benoist-des-Champs ... It comprises a few
scattered farms, and the schoolhouse stands alone on a hillside
near the road. I live a solitary life there, but if I take a short cut
through the fields I can be at Les Sablonnières in three quarters of
an hour.'

If Allorent in Sarzay was one such black-coated foot-soldier in
the Government's campaign to 'institute' France into one nation of
patriotic, French-speaking citizens, then Charbonnier, newly
appointed in Chassignolles, was another. He too was unmarried
in the early 1860s; perhaps the two young men were able to be of
some support to each other across the four miles of muddy paths
that separated the two villages.

There was no doubt that the Government's campaign was beginning to work. Teachers such as Allorent, or Charbonnier, whose
'zeal and devotion' were actually rewarded with extra pay by his
cautious fellow-villagers, were a far cry from the drunken old
soldiers and cobblers of a generation before. The Préfet of the
period in Châteauroux recorded his own satisfaction with the 'evolution' that was now occurring in the Berrichon peasant.

'His children, relegated to a solitary life, hardly clad, are now
properly dressed and go to be civilized at the local school.'

It would indeed be hard to overstate the solitary and uninspiring
effect on a child of long days passed alone minding cattle or
standing in a wintry ploughed field scaring away crows from a
planted crop.

The Préfet may have been a little optimistic. School was not, of
course, free, then or for another twenty years. And even when it
did become so (apart from the cost of books and paper) almost
one-third of country children did not attend regularly, particularly
in the summer, when there was much work to be done in the
fields. And 'children' at this point meant boys; girls did not attend
school officially till girls' schools were built or special classes
opened for them. Even so, according to the census taken in 1872
(which went into such detail for the first time) about one in seven
of Chassignolles' girls, including Mademoiselle Pagnard's grandmother, had learnt to read, and someone must have been teaching
them. Célestine, I assume, was taught by her father, the Secretary,
and he may have taught his wife too. At any rate, Anne Laurent
was to run the inn alone for years after his death.

What is certain is that by the time Célestine was a grown girl the *idea* of education, if not the reality, was established in the countryside. At the same time it was being discovered that 'evolution' might have its disadvantages. It was not only the peasants in need of their children's labour who regarded school as a waste of time; many of the bourgeoisie were equally disapproving, though in their case the disapproval was for the *other* people's children receiving education. In 1871 the Préfet of the Cher (the northern half of the Berry) complained that if he talked about increasing rates of school attendance people were apt to wag their heads and conjure up vistas of deserted farms and flocks of sheep roaming unattended.

Yet even then these forebodings were not new. Twenty years before, in the middle of the century, the *Écho de l'Indre* was writing in an editorial:

> ... There are complaints on all sides that the young are leaving the land and that the rural workforce is being depleted. It is shocking the contempt that the sons of country labouring men have for their fathers' occupations ... Everything they read [*sic*] and hear draws them towards the big cities. There, they only work at the less arduous trades which are more highly esteemed and they have more distractions and amusements – lively, noisy entertainments unknown in the countryside. Is it surprising that so many young heads are turned and join the rush to the great centres of population? There, luxury and pleasure awaits them, but also poverty and evil ...

And so on and so forth. This peroration was written a full generation before changing farming methods, spreading communications and general literacy began to have a substantial effect on the traditions of country life, and a hundred years before the major exodus began with the coming of mechanized farming. Yet it strikes exactly the same note as the later choruses of complaint in 1900, 1920 or 1950. It might almost be Georges Bernardet inveighing against the idle young *circa* 1980.

Evidently the young have *always* been disregarding the values of their parents, leaving the land and coming to grief among the bright lights of alien towns. They were no doubt doing so long before there was any question of education being to blame for it. In the poorer and more mountainous country immediately to the south of Berry there was already, by the early nineteenth century, a well-established tradition of men going forth to seek work else-where and only returning at long intervals to their own poor soil and their stoical families. The stonemasons from the Creuse formed itinerant labour gangs that were famous all over France: it was their work that transformed the major cities in the nineteenth century; much of Haussmann's Paris was constructed by them. Sawyers and carpenters also joined them from the forests of the Lower Berry. The Préfet of the Indre, the same humane functionary who had said in the winter of 1844–5 that the poor should be allowed to continue trapping birds to keep them from starvation, wrote a few years later: 'Each year in spring numerous workmen from the La Châtre area ... betake themselves to Paris to seek a means of livelihood. This traditional custom is all the more respect-able in that these labourers are for the most part decent men of tranquil habits.'

France needed this mobile workforce as much as the men needed the work. The Préfet wrote as he did because spasmodic official attempts were made, from the time of Napoleon to the end of the Second Empire in 1870, to limit the labourer's freedom to travel from one region to another; permits were required, sometimes total embargoes were imposed. Ostensibly the authorities feared the vagrancy and crime that might follow the failure to find work. The fact was they also feared, with some justification, that a large urban pool of uprooted labour would be seething with unacceptably radical ideas and potential rebellion. The life of one Creusois mason exemplifies just this and also the triumph of self-help and enter-prise. Martin Nadaud started his working life as an illiterate teen-age hod-carrier, travelling the whole way from the Creuse to Paris on foot in 1830. A natural leader, he set to work to educate himself and his companions. He became a banned trade-unionist under the Empire – ironically, since Louis-Napoleon initially favoured unions – but was welcomed back to France after 1870 as a cele-brated figure. He ended his career as Préfet of his native *pays*.

Although few economic migrants achieved quite such distinction as Nadaud, stories of people making good were plentiful through-out the century. A trawl through the *Journal de l'Indre* in the period when the railway was just linking Châteauroux to Paris produces the cheering moral example of another Creusois mason. He was said to have left his native land for Paris in the last years of the eighteenth century and there, through hard work, amassed a fortune, built a grand house of his own and died leaving his heirs one and a half million francs. However, other newspaper items of the same period convey the clear message that all that glittered in Paris was not gold. As a warning to the overconfident, one described the Morgue in lingering detail.

The ambivalence then surrounding the whole subject of education, getting on in life and leaving home is clear. On the one hand the French peasant was urged to make the most of himself, to wash, to speak French, to read, to use new farming methods, to adapt to a money-based economy, to look beyond his fixed horizons. On the other hand there were many complaints when this process led him away from the land, often to settle permanently elsewhere. Despised and patronized as he had often been, the very texture of France was his creation. Who will look after the *paysage* when the *paysan* has gone to the town? The question, with modern variations, inevitably haunts this account; it is a still more crucial question at the present day.

Even the local newspapers, in the middle years of the nineteenth century, carried inducements for fit men without encumbrances to seek their fortune at a distance – Paris, or California or the new colonies in north and west Africa. Some men were tempted; at least one member of Célestine's own family was. Most, however, stayed more or less where they were. It is the strikingly homogeneous and stable nature of life in villages such as Chassignolles that makes it possible to trace the fortunes of whole families, generation after generation lying in the same earth and in the pages of the same registers. And many of those names which eventually disappear from the village records – including Chaumette – did not journey far. A Chaumette breeds horses now near Neuvy St-Sépulchre, an easy ride west from Chassignolles. Another makes clogs in La Châtre to this day and sells them to a few faithful wearers, along with carpet slippers, sensible shoes *pour les dames d'un certain âge* and good-quality espadrilles for the more frivolous-minded. When I plucked up courage to enquire about his ancestors he was, like many people, reticent at first, uncertain of being able to provide the right answer – 'It's all so long ago' – and then progressively more interested. He produced his *brevet de famille*, part of the documentation with which all French citizens are armed against the fear of not existing, and offered the names of his grandparents. From these, to his surprise and pleasure, I could tell him his family-tree back six generations, through Silvain-Bazille and his father Pierre to the sacristan born in 1756, his and Célestine's common ancestor.

Through her choice of husband, Célestine might have gone on to make her life far from the confines of Chassignolles. She could have become part of that great migration from the countryside that transformed the main towns of every industrializing country as the century went by. The French historian Daniel Halévy wrote in 1910:

> The peasant population ... for so long mute ... had its own effect, without anyone realizing it, on the heart and soul of the nation. We owe perhaps to the countryman much of what is best in Paris ... The Parisian masses have come from the Upper Bourgogne via the valley of the Seine, or from the Auvergne, the Bourbonnais and the Berry via the Loire and the Beauce ... The tenements of Paris are in themselves villages come from the Centre.

Célestine might well have found herself in a Parisian tenement or in one of the newer blocks then going up as part of the Second Empire reconstruction. She had the opportunity. She did not take it; she went no farther than La Châtre and that only for a time. Perhaps this was her considered choice; perhaps it was another's decision, masquerading as fate. As Baptiste Aussourd remarked, 'your Parents ... have the right to decide your Destiny'. And yet it is hard to believe that a girl as sought-after as Célestine did not influence her own destiny, if not by what she undertook, then by what she refused.

Chapter 10

In the spring of 1864, when Célestine was almost twenty, she received two more formal proposals. It was a year since Baptiste Aussourd had been courting her and eighteen months since the school teacher had tried his chance. Another country winter had passed with its curtains of rain, its abrupt quilts of snow that cut the village off for days at a time. In the wide fireplaces, where the incongruous iron stoves of the late nineteenth century had not yet been installed, the great oak forests were being very slowly but surely consumed; for months, the fire was never allowed to die out entirely. The embers were carefully blown into life each dawn to reheat the soup that was still the standard country breakfast. But often in the dead of winter fires blazed the night away, for everyone still gathered at *veillées*, those night watches where some specific task was undertaken – carding wool, beating hemp, shelling walnuts, dipping rushes in melted tallow. Songs were sung and stories were told of ghosts and fairies and 'the old days' that, in the modernity of the 1860s, seemed to be retreating at an unprecedented rate. Later, towards the end of the century, when the traditional work parties had ceased to be central to the economy or the way of life, the *veillées* declined into simple card parties, pastimes for the old. But in Célestine's youth they were still going strong, encouraged if anything by the slight increase in prosperity – more people, more spacious kitchens, mulled wine. It was a last spurt and glow of a very old practice before the same prosperity brought its inevitable extinction.

But however much fun the winter *veillées* were, they were too public to further private relations. Indeed, the whole of life was public in these crowded homes where separate bedrooms, even for married couples, were almost unknown. To the young and desiring, winter was interminable and the stirring of spring a liberation that we can now, in our homogenized world, hardly imagine. Among the many blessings was that the transparent green haze on the trees would thicken into a screen, and woods would once again be fine and private places. The Chassignolles birth dates, taken over a long span of years in the mid-nineteenth century, tell their own tale. Fewer babies were born in the autumn than at other times of the year, with November, the low point, producing on average less than half the numbers born in the peak month of January. Obviously this does not relate to anything particularly propitious for birth in the dead of winter but to conditions nine months before: in February, the countryside was too inhospitable even for the most enthusiastic lovers, whereas by April the activity known ironically in the Berry as to *bergerer*, to 'go a-shepherding', was underway again.

But this was easiest for those with good reason to be out in the fields anyway. At Célestine's social level, the significance of spring was that once the roads and paths were drying out the fairs and *fêtes* began again. In the mid-century all social classes still participated: the retreat of the bourgeoisie into their new stucco villas had not yet got underway. But as the day's business drew to a close, 'The townspeople and others who'd come from a little way off climbed into their assorted wagons and were on their way before night came down on the rough tracks they had to follow. The small stall-holders packed up, and the local Curé went off to enjoy a supper with some friends of the cloth who had come over to watch the dancing.' (George Sand, *Le Meunier d'Angibault*)

Soon only the people of the immediate neighbourhood remained in possession of the dancing ring, all knowing each other, at their happiest now with no *étrangers* there. People of all ages and kinds took the floor 'including the old fat female servant from the inn and the hunchbacked tailor'. Music was made with pipes, drums and the Berrichon version of the bagpipes, and any adjacent inn stayed open far into the night. For these special occasions the innkeepers in the Black Valley were in the habit of building small green arbours outside their doors. The most respectable customers could sit there and frumenty was served to the ladies. When it was Chassignolles' turn to hold a fair I think it took place next door to the Chaumette inn on a convenient triangle of open land with a market cross in the middle, where today the modern primary school and playground stand. About the time Célestine turned twenty the crumbling cross was replaced by a new one, which is still inconspicuously there today, jammed up against the school wall.

A letter that Célestine received from a young man in Crozon in March 1864, and one from another boy elsewhere in early May, both refer to the big traditional festivals of the season which, under the guise of religion, marked the coming of spring: Palm Sunday and Easter were followed by the more obviously ancient May Day. Similarly the *fête* of St Jean at midsummer and of St Martin in November – quarter days when debts were paid, leases renewed or ended and hiring fairs were held in La Châtre – related to a pre-Christian calendar, only lightly disguised. A character in *Le Meunier d'Angibault* remarks that 'superstition is the only religion accessible to the peasant . . . God is nothing to him but an idol who bestows favours on the crops and flocks of anyone who lights a wax candle for him.' Certainly, decorated oxen and dances round purificatory fires, sometimes described by shocked observers as 'obscene', still figured larger in Célestine's childhood than the catechism classes administered by the local gentry that were later to become a feature of Catholic revivalism.

Yet organized Christian religion was becoming more present again in country villages than it had been all the first half of the century. In Chassignolles the unsolved question of repairs to the church, first raised by Geoffrenet de Champdavid, continued to haunt municipal meetings. It was still on the agenda in 1864, and by the following year the new mayor (another gentlemanly figure imposed by the authorities in Châteauroux) was declaring that the church was 'in a state of dilapidation and old-fashionedness [*vestusté*] which might not only have an evil influence [*une influence facheuse*] on the religious sentiments of the population but also endanger their security'. In brief, the old, squat belfry looked as if it was going to fall down. Steps were finally, expensively taken and the result was a tall spire pointing the way to heaven and a new, vaulted roof covered in brick-earth tiles rather than the old wooden ones. The spire itself was grandly covered in slate – only to be partly demolished by lightning twenty years later, when the whole saga of repairs and wrangles about cost was set off again.

The letter from the young man writing to Célestine from Crozon 'Mlle. Chaumette, habergiste à Chassignol ... Pour être remis qu'à elle-même' (personal delivery only) – is the only one in which a specifically Christian education seems to surface. Not that there is any overt religious sentiment, but the writer has a tendency to speak of 'confessing his fault' to his beloved (for not turning up to see her at Easter) and of receiving Grace by her kindness to him. The letter ends with a hope that he may love and cherish her for life, accompanied by a sketch of a flaming heart which appears to share the iconography of the Sacred Heart. Henry Lorant (for such was his name) seems to have conflated sacred and profane love into one.

Crozon-sur-Vauvre, some half dozen miles away, had been the site of iron forges for centuries. A Pissavy son from La Châtre had recently been paying court to the daughter of the ironmaster there; we shall revisit the place. Apart from the forges and the foundry, which employed many scores of men, Crozon was a tiny little village lost in the beautiful wooded valley of a tributary of the Indre, with its own miniature cliffs and deep pools left by past iron-smelters. In spite of the substantial trade, there was no proper road there even in the 1860s, though plans were at last being made to enlarge the path from Chassignolles at the time Lorant was visiting Célestine. He wrote a fairly correct French in a slightly careless hand, and at first I supposed him to be a clerk at the foundry. However, a reference in his letter to not being able to get away on festival-days because of the *Grande occupation* in his house at such times led me to wonder if he too was the child of an innkeeper, and so he turned out to be. The widow Lorant was running the inn in Crozon in the 1860s with the help or hindrance of several young sons. For an exact social equal, Henry's address to Célestine seems a little ceremonial:

'Mademoiselle,

Since I have had the pleasure of making your acquaintance I have not been able to rest for a single instant. For you have so much Grace and so many merits that I cannot Keep Silent any longer without making Known to you the desire I have to love you.'

This tone of high emotion (more borrowing from a manual?) is not entirely sustained. He tells her he has always desired 'to settle down [*placer*, the same word that was used by apprentices and maids securing positions] with a well-bred girl coming from a good and honest family'. He tells her he much appreciates 'your honourable father, who appears approving of my passion towards you [*mes délires*]'. Is it unfair to read a touch of patronage and self-absorption into this, or to think that he might have said something of what she might expect from him? On the following page, addressing Célestine as '*Ma Bonne*', more a jovial, husbandly term than a lover's one, he excuses himself for not appearing at Easter – 'You sent me a message by the Tissier lad that I had gone back on my word' – and suggests that instead he come to see her the following Sunday.

Well. She did not marry him. Even if he was right that Silvain-Germain regarded him favourably as a useful son-in-law for the business, Célestine was still at this point in control of her own destiny.

The boy who wrote to her in early May of the same year was never, I think, a serious prospect for her. He was the apprentice of the baker in La Berthenoux, a village on the far side of La Châtre. The village was famous in the Berry for a great cattle fair held there every year on 8–9 October before the autumn slaughter. By the 1860s this was beginning to change, as new fodder crops were being introduced that could keep cattle going throughout the year. Crop rotation had come in, even in the conservative Berry, along with commercially imported fertilizer, so land was used more efficiently than under the old fallow-field system. However, the October fair was still a place for serious trade, for the coming together of people driving their beasts on the hoof from all over the Berry and Poitou, and for jollity, dancing, thefts, fights and accusations of indecent behaviour or worse on the long walk home.

While it is clear from the young baker's letter that he had met Célestine at the previous October's fair and again at a recent spring one, he otherwise circles perpetually round the subject of his infatuation with her without conveying anything further. The helpless repetition of '*Oh Mlle Célestine*' cannot have furthered his cause.

Far more serious from her point of view seems to have been the suit of the young man who was writing to her six months later, exactly two years after the schoolmaster had proposed. His letter was headed Paris – crossed out – and then St Août, a village between La Châtre and Issoudun, but it is on the notepaper of a Paris liquor merchant in the Rue du Cherche-midi on the Left Bank – '*Manjouin et Cie, vins et spiritueux, Vinaigres d'Orléans, Absinthe et Vermouth*'. From this, and from his style – 'Mademoiselle Célestine, I have just received your letter of the 24th inst.' – I deduce that the young man was a commercial traveller, one of that new breed ironically described by Balzac in *L'Illustre Gaudissart* as having been unknown in the past but now 'social equalizers . . . representing the spirit of civilization and Parisian invention coming to grips with the good sense, the ignorance and conservatism of provincial France'.

Jean Dorian (such was his name) travelled for his firm in central France, where his family apparently lived. He may have spent some time in Paris to learn the trade and continued to make trips there as well as receiving his supplies. Such comings and goings were now, for the first time, made possible by the railways. The many plans for a cross-country line from Châteauroux down to La Châtre and beyond had not yet produced any results, but in the meantime two La Châtre families had begun running competing coach services geared to train connections: you could leave La Châtre at five-thirty in the morning for a guaranteed arrival in Châteauroux by four in the afternoon, this allowing you to take some refreshment and then catch a train which would miraculously get you to Paris very early the following morning, a mere twenty-four hours after you had left home! The same train could deposit you before midnight in Issoudun, Vierzon or Orléans. Another early-morning departure from La Châtre (4.15) would get you to a town on the Cher by 9.00 to connect with the 9.15, which arrived in Bourges at 11.05. Bourges was not only a substantial centre in its own right, but provided further connections to Paris and other cities.

Such a network, dependent on centralized, precise 'railway time' rather than local sun time, had been undreamt of twenty or even fifteen years before. It meant that travellers had only the shorter journeys to make by horse-drawn means: they no longer ran the same risks of ending in a bog or frozen by a snowstorm on a long, lonely road. Presumably the inn in Chassignolles was on Jean Dorian's itinerary. Although nearly three times as much wine was now being produced around La Châtre as had been earlier in the century, it was generally agreed to be mediocre stuff, an acidic rosé. Silvain-Germain would have needed better and more varied liquor to offer these days to a newly discerning public – or so Manjouin's rep would have tried to convince him.

Jean Dorian's writing is elegant and clear, his French almost as good as the schoolmaster's and more direct in style. Only one word defeated me for a while. It was *'fisiquement'*.

Mademoiselle Célestine,

I have just received your letter of the 24th inst. in which you tell me not to come back to your house. I will submit to your will if you really want it so, only allow me to ask you if it is truly of your own accord that you write me these words, or if it is your parents who have induced you to write in this way? Your mother tells me that she lets you make your own choices, but I wonder about this as I certainly can't believe it of your father. I am therefore led to suppose that neither you nor your mother have been frank with me about your feelings, something I find hard to bear – especially where you are concerned.

I do beg you, tell me what it is that puts you against our marriage, apart from the idea that you would have to come and live with my people and that you are afraid of not getting on with my mother, or that you don't want to leave home. Believe me, my dear and good Célestine, that if I were to marry you and you were to tell me that it didn't suit you to live in our house, my wishes would be yours [*je n'aurais pas d'autre volonté que la vôtre*] for, in marrying you, I would be hoping to make you happy and be happy myself with you. For I believe you to be so sweet-natured and good that the man who has the luck to marry you could have no other desire but to work and love you. Do not therefore imagine that if you asked me to set up our own home it wouldn't suit me. I would stop at nothing; we are both of us young and together we could go into a little business [*commerce* – shop or café] of any kind you like. I could arrange employment for myself in whatever would suit you best, but for my part I would prefer a business where we would be our own masters. Do not believe, Mademoiselle, that I am guided by self-interest for, no, I would not expect anything from your parents. It is entirely the love and feeling I have developed for you that has led me to believe we could spend our days happily together.

If, even so, I am so unlucky as not to appeal to you physically, then I must resign myself. However, I do entreat you to tell

123

me frankly if you are moved by the overriding wishes of your parents.

I will close now. According to what I hear, you are expecting someone else to visit you on All Saints Day. This does not worry me; I just want to know what your real wishes are and if you could look upon our union with pleasure. Being afraid that my letter might not be given to you, I shall send it care of Madame Merlin. You will therefore be able to think things through without your lady mother [*Madame votre mère*] concerning herself. I dare hope that you will do me the honour of replying directly from your own heart. In the hope and expectation that you won't leave me in uncertainty, allow me to embrace you a thousand times and to be, with the deepest respect, your devoted and humble servant –

A Marguerite Merlin had been the sacristan's wife and Célestine's great-grandmother. The Madame Merlin who was to hand on this letter must be of a later generation of Merlin cousins. She presumably did so successfully, or it would not have survived.

Of all Célestine's suitors, Jean Dorian strikes one as the most generally worthy on both emotional and practical grounds: 'the man who has the luck to marry you could have no other desire but to work and love you . . . we are both of us young and together we could go into a little business of any kind you like . . .' Had Célestine accepted the offer from this young *commerçant*, who was so representative of the future that was fast arriving, her later life might have been very different and, I am inclined to feel, happier.

But perhaps, indeed, she was not drawn to him *fisiquement*. Or perhaps – as seems equally plausible from what we can surmise of Silvain-Germain's strong character and what Jean Dorian hints about him – Célestine's father was simply set against his only and admired daughter leaving home and wanted a docile son-in-law for the business, such as Henry Lorant from Crozon. Perhaps Célestine really was 'so sweet-natured and good' that she inevitably deferred to her father's wishes. At all events, the commercial traveller did not win her.

Célestine was certainly an only daughter, and her presence must have helped attract custom to the inn. But was she an only child?

For a long time I was inclined to regard her as such. I had been categorically told by aged persons who remembered her that she and the man she married had inherited the entire business. This, given the Napoleonic law requiring parents to divide their estate equally among their children, was enough to indicate only-child status. Indeed this law itself was, by the mid-century, having an effect on family size. The desire to avoid splitting up the family land holding or business is traditionally advanced as the principal reason, if not the only, for the persistently low French birth rate at a period when the rates of other industrializing countries were rising. Historically the population of France had always been bigger than that of Great Britain. In 1800 there were twenty-seven million French people as against eighteen million Britons. The area that is now Germany had twenty-five million. But by the middle of the century the number of French had increased by only about three million; the British were overtaking them fast and so was Germany – a fact which became something of an obsession in French political life. It continued to be so into the next century and through three wars with Germany and is still capable of rousing governmental paranoia today.

In Chassignolles, the population increased in the first three decades of the nineteenth century by almost half as many again to close on a thousand, but this is mainly accounted for by more children surviving to grow up and by people in general living longer. During the 1850s and 1860s it stabilized. It began to increase again in the 1870s, but the rate was not dramatic. It passed the twelve hundred mark in the mid-1880s, and did not reach its peak of about fourteen hundred till the eve of the First World War. (It has been declining ever since.)

The more easy-going branch of the Chaumette family continued to have large numbers of children, as did other families with little or no land to divide, but it is clear from the censuses decade after decade that many of the villagers did not go in for unrestricted procreation. No matter that the Church disapproved of any deliberate limitation; no matter that the classic French folk story ends 'They lived a long time and had many children': the realities of life were otherwise. Silvain-Germain, with his role as Secretary, his inn and his one daughter, seemed to fit very well into this picture of ambition and prudence. As indeed did Célestine herself, who in turn was to become the mother of an only son.

I was, however, wrong about this. Célestine, I came to realize, had two brothers, though the fact that there is no casual mention of either of them in any letter written to her by a suitor may, in itself, be significant. I shall return to them later.

By the autumn of 1864 time was secretly beginning to run away fast for Célestine; that Destiny of which Baptiste Aussourd had spoken anxiously had almost caught up with her. Who was the boy whom Jean Dorian heard was planning to visit her on All Saints Day, about whom he bravely declared himself unworried? Perhaps it was the one who was writing to her in the first days of the new year. Although he addressed her as *vous*, this was probably a piece of letter-writing politeness, since he signs himself as her cousin and his surname was Laurent, that of Célestine's mother's family in Nohant. He wrote from La Châtre.

> My dear Célestine,
>
> The one who loves you is writing to you, but he does not know what you say in reply to what he said to you the evening before last in your house. And if what you say is the same as what he said, then Célestine I love you and will always do so. I would rather die than stop loving you. My dear Célestine, if your heart can answer mine these days will be the happiest of our lives [*le plus beaux jours de notre vie*]. If this matter should be accomplished, dear Célestine, I can promise you that you will find yourself in a position that could not be bettered. You won't have anyone to bother you; you will be on your own and happy with your husband Alphonse who will shower you with gentle kisses. Célestine, if you don't love me, tell me so, for no one yet knows about this but ourselves. I am waiting for your reply, dear Célestine, as you said you would write to me, but I can't wait longer, so I am sending you this letter. Please do try to come for the fair [probably a Twelfth Night fair] so that I can see you and we can have a talk. Or at least send me a reply at once, for, Célestine, as I told you, if the whole idea suits you then we must move quickly. If it wasn't for this, then we could take our time. Dear Célestine, I know you are going to say that I am young and that I haven't yet taken part in the draw [a reference to the lottery for military service] but you mustn't be bothered about that. As to age, I don't see there's much difference between us: I know I'm only nineteen and you, I think, twenty, but that doesn't seem to me an unequal match. Would you really rather have a husband eight or ten years older than you?

My dear Célestine, it's no use my writing any more now, even though there is more I could say than the paper could ever hold.

And so I finish my letter, my own dear Célestine [*ma bonne amie Célestine*] clasping you in my arms and kissing you with all my heart. Your cousin for life and your husband if it so pleases you. Laurent, A.

This letter was written on 3 January, and the remark about her surely not wanting a husband years older than herself is a loaded one. For just two weeks later, on 17 January at ten in the morning, Célestine was married in Chassignolles to Pierre Robin, the twenty-seven-year-old son of a family of oil-pressers of La Châtre. Her youthful days of competing suitors, of love-letters, of dancing at fairs and festivals, her *plus beaux jours*, were abruptly over.

> *Vous n'irez plus au bal,*
> *Madam' la mariée,*
> *Vous n'irez plus au bal*
> *Aux fêtes, aux assemblées;*
> *Vous gard'rez la maison*
> *Pendant que les autres iront.*

> (You won't go dancing any more,
> Married lady;
> You won't go dancing any more.
> No more fêtes or gatherings;
> You'll stop and keep house
> While the others go out.)

Traditionally, rural Berrichon wedding celebrations were lavish affairs that continued for three days on end, with a surfeit of food and drink, and a mixture of ancient pagan rituals and bawdy practical jokes. In the monotony and austerity that made up much of rural life, great store was set by these oases of excess and excitement. But I think that Célestine's marriage may have been a quieter occasion: certainly it was not long in the planning. In any case, the dead of winter in the Berry is not time for rollicking processions round muddy lanes tricked out in best clothes. After the church ceremony and another in front of the mayor, I expect they forgathered at the inn in the big room at the top of the outside stair and ate a lengthy meal. The women would have been in their best lace caps but the men by this date were mostly in the stiff, village-made suits they had worn for their own weddings, would wear for their children's and in which they would eventually be buried. Perhaps, as at Emma Rouault's rural winter wedding to Charles Bovary in Flaubert's novel of a few years earlier, the suits ranged according to the age and social position of the wearers from old, full-skirted riding coats, through frock-coats to various kinds of cutaways and modern jackets. The more humble relatives were clad in old-fashioned best smocks, pleated and belted. 'Everyone had had a recent haircut; ears stuck out sideways, chins were all freshly shaved, some so early in the dark morning that small cuts were left here and there . . .'

I see it as one of those very cold, absolutely still days in central France when hoar-frost outlines every leaf, stem, twig and spider's web beneath a grey sky from which the sun does not emerge all day to break the spell on this petrified landscape.

Why this abrupt transformation of Célestine from much-pursued girl into married woman? The obvious conclusion is that, in spite of being *une honnête fille*, she found herself pregnant, and the respectability of the family demanded that the situation should be instantly regularized by the young man apparently responsible.

At first I believed this to be the case. I did not find the evidence in the Chassignolles Birth Registers for the later part of 1865, but an excursion to the Hôtel de Ville in La Châtre produced the fact that Ursin Charles Robin, son of Pierre Robin, oil-presser, and Célestine Chaumette his wife, was born there in the Robin family house on 2 October. However, more precise female arithmetic indicated that if the baby was born more or less to term he would have been conceived in the early days of the year and that therefore, whoever his father was, in the brief time before the wedding took place Célestine could not have known that she was pregnant. If indeed the child came ten days early, then he was conceived in total respectability on her wedding night.

There still seemed the possibility that the baby was due in mid-September but came a fortnight late: in that case, Célestine would just have been becoming anxious in the first days of January. The idea of this foreboding, preoccupying her even as her young cousin came demanding her hand, was an interesting one: no wonder (I thought) she did not want to give his proposal an immediate answer.

However, when I re-examined the entry in the register for the wedding, I realized that the marriage could not have been as hastily arranged as that even if some behind-the-scenes uncertainty prevailed. The bans had already been read out correctly in La Châtre, which was the bridegroom's parish, six weeks before the appointed date and thus before any baby could have been on the way.

It is almost impossible that Alphonse Laurent, who was her cousin and who lived in La Châtre too, did not know of the proposed marriage when he came to visit her. His pleading letter 'from the one who loves you' takes on a more specific urgency – 'No one yet knows about this but ourselves . . . if the whole idea suits you, then we must move quickly . . . Would you really rather have a husband eight or ten years older than you? . . . there is more I could say than the paper could ever hold.'

He was hopeful; she had said she would write to him. Evidently a mere fortnight before she was due to marry someone else, she was not really decided. What was behind all this? It is possible that Célestine's father by then knew himself to be ill and was anxious to get his daughter settled without delay with the most suitable candidate. The trade of walnut-presser, always seasonal, would combine well with the running of the inn. Pierre is said, by the very few people in Chassignolles who still remember him, to have been a man with a pleasant manner. There is no letter preserved from him in Célestine's secret cache. Perhaps he never wrote her one.

All one can say with certainty is that she was not totally wholehearted about him, that she had sufficient doubts for another boy to urge his own suit on her till the eleventh hour – but that she nevertheless married him on the appointed day and they remained together for better or worse for nearly fifty years.

The young couple went to live in La Châtre, in a street leading out from one of the old town gates that were then still standing. As well as an oil-press, the Robin parents owned a vineyard outside the town; they were not themselves innkeepers, but Pierre's younger sister was soon to marry a man called Lamoureux and start a tavern in the adjoining house.

In the March Petty Sessions Célestine's father-in-law was fined one franc for allowing his chickens to run about in the roadway:

this practice, which would be common for another seventy years in the countryside and has not quite disappeared even today, was beginning to be frowned on in towns, along with free-roaming pigs and dogs. In La Châtre all the streets were now paved: the deep dirtiness of which George Sand had spoken with rueful affection twenty years before was a thing of the past. The remains of the town walls, and their bits of stagnant moat, were soon to be swept away. The stinking trades of tanning, wool-boiling and dyeing in the old quarter down by the river were beginning to decline with the introduction of more factory-made goods. These were sold in the shops with new glass windows on the currently named Rue Impériale, along with more exotic commodities that were imported via Paris from distant places and much advertised in the local paper: Chocolat Plantier for a fashionable morning refreshment, Kashmir shawls, Chinese fans.

The shops also held catalogues from the recently built Parisian department stores like the Bon Marché and the Samaritaine, the fantastic palaces of the new commerce as described by Zola in *Au Bonheur des Dames*. The time when even the gentry wore home-grown cloth, and ate from plates turned out by the potters in the next village beyond Nohant, was fast departing. Much was still made locally, but albums of fashion plates to inspire and instruct the village Jeanne Pagnards were ready to hand. For the small daughter of a prospering La Châtre tradesman there was a Parisian magazine to turn her, too, into a real lady: it was called *La Poupée Modèle* and featured little moral stories, advice, games and needle-work patterns.

Advertised alongside this in the newspapers was a patent medicine marketed in Paris but ostensibly of English manufacture, implausibly called Revalescière. This assured perfect health if taken regularly – 'repairs digestive organs, furnishes new blood, re-animates vital forces ... cures loss of memory, nerves, catarrh, hysteria ...' Genteel complaints for a newly genteel class. A far cry from the old Almanach recipes to cure warts, scabies and lumps, involving plants picked by moonlight, earth from mole hills and *la marde [sic] de chat*. It was even hinted that the fabled Queen Victoria took Revalescière. Since this cure-all features in news stories as well as obvious advertisements, I rather think the editor of the *Écho de l'Indre* had shares in the stuff.

Share ownership, under the Second Empire, was enlarging the

bourgeois *rentier* class. It never became as large in France as it did in Victorian England, but small provincial towns like La Châtre developed a significant number of people with some claim to education and refinement and nothing very much to do but run the place and cultivate social distinctions. The world described by George Sand, in which young La Châtre lawyers and local landowners shared the same entertainments as shop-workers, artisans and peasants, was beginning to slip into a past that already seemed the Good Old Days. The newspaper, while energetically fostering gentility, deplored 'our new, selfish habits'.

The editor almost certainly had shares too in the Anglo-French company that, in 1865, was trying to raise capital to build the much-demanded railway line through La Châtre. The notion of British involvement made everyone feel modern and smart. (England was then the world leader in railway building, having more miles of track than even the USA, a comprehensive network at a time when both France and her close rival Germany were still only planning and slowly extending their own.) The line that was to link the Indre valley with the outside world was the one that had been projected for the last dozen years between Tours on one side and Montluçon on the other: the editor harped on the crucial importance of such a line to the area's future and the need to allow the prospecting company to acquire the appropriate land. In the summer of 1865 an Open Letter to the Préfet of the Indre urged that a man of his 'renowned knowledge and devotion' would understand the necessity of compulsory purchase. This was, however, shortly followed by a wail that the company had proposed a site for the station in La Châtre that would not do at all – 'It is near Monsieur Vincent's limekilns, over a kilometre from the town.'

Since La Châtre is built on the side of a hill and its *beaux quartiers* by that time were near the top, it was inevitable that the station should be placed at a distance from them – and equally inevitable, had the newspaper only realized it, that new streets should soon afterwards cover the intervening kilometre. For the station was eventually opened on this despised site – but not for another seventeen years, in 1882. The debate about where the line should run, first in general outline and then in minutely argued detail, along with the financial and political vicissitudes of various fundraising schemes as central Government changed and changed again, lasted for most of that time.

The main problems were not, as it turned out, caused by people who resented the line coming across their land but by those who wanted it to. The days were past when the railway was accused of causing both droughts and storms and when surveyors from the unknown Elsewhere, with their spirit-levels and viewing glasses, were feared as necromancers who might be casting spells. Dissension now occurred because every Commune wanted the line to pass its way and loudly disparaged the claims of rival Communes a few miles off. The current Marquis de Villaines, whose family had exiled themselves at the Revolution, but who had inserted himself back into the local power structure as mayor of Ste Sévère, about ten miles from La Châtre, was particularly vociferous on the needs and rights of his own territory.

This long delay in linking the Lower Berry to the national network discouraged industry and confirmed the whole area in its deeply rural character, which persists to this day. The editor of the *Écho de l'Indre* had in fact been right.

It was a very hot summer in La Châtre the year of Célestine's pregnancy. In July the local paper wrote of 'Senegalese heat' and by September the numerous wells on which the town was dependent for its water were running low. The Sous-Préfet ordered that no water was to be drawn for other than strictly domestic reasons; to avoid people sneaking up extra pails under cover of dark, the pumps were to be chained from sundown to sunrise. This crisis gave further impetus to the plan to install a piped water supply – which was finally carried out, to the accompaniment of leaking pipes and litigation, some five years later.

In Chassignolles (where piped water was not to arrive for another ninety-seven years) the wells that stand in every other courtyard and most of the vegetable gardens were drying up that summer too. Life in a village that is running short of water is not pleasant or healthy. On 28 May, Silvain-Germain kept the Minutes as usual at a Council meeting that was called to fix the Communal budget for the following year – a year he was never to see. After that, his writing appears no more. He did not live to see the birth of his grandson either, but died at the end of August at home in the inn. His father, dead only four years earlier, had lived to sixty-six; his grandfather had lived to eighty-eight. Yet he himself was only forty-nine. The French method of recording deaths, while it

132

produces much incidental information on family relationships, does not offer a cause of death. A pity.

The death was reported to the Mairie at Chassignolles within hours by Pierre Robin, as a good son-in-law, and by a middle-aged Laurent cousin from a nearby farm (perhaps an uncle of the disappointed Alphonse?). Then, and at his son's birth in October, Pierre was still giving his occupation as *huilier*. Since Anne Laurent now found herself, within the space of a few months, without both daughter and husband and alone in the inn, you might have expected the young couple with their baby to have moved back to Chassignolles and joined her in the business. However, they did not – or not for some years. The census of 1872 finds the widow still running the place on her own, with only an eighteen-year-old Charbonnier girl to assist her. At that time Célestine and Pierre were still in La Châtre, but now they were running an inn in their own right. I know this because the last letter in Célestine's hoarded pack, written in 1873, is addressed to *'Mme. Robin (Chaumette), aubergiste, Grande Rue, La Châtre'*.

The Grande Rue was what everyone in La Châtre actually called the main street, whose official name was regularly altered through the decades according to the national political transform-ations. In the autumn of 1869 there was advertised for sale in the *Écho de l'Indre* 'an hotel in this town on the route of the new railway [*sic*] on the Rue Impériale opposite the entrance to the market-place . . . This is the only inn in the centre of town.' It was appar-ently a big place with fourteen rooms, including two dining-rooms, kitchens, attics, store houses and stabling, and it was advertised for weeks as if there was difficulty in finding a buyer. Presumably the fact that the La Châtre railway did not show many signs as yet of becoming a reality discouraged outside interest. By and by the advertisement was modified to 'For Sale or Rent'.

Today, the double-fronted Quincaillerie on the Rue Nationale opposite the entrance to the market displays a mass of desirable saucepans, heavily rustic bread boxes, wedding china in 'presen-tation caskets' and lamps whose bases seethe with globules of decorative oil. Behind the cramped street and the modern façade, the large old house stretches back into rambling spaciousness. It has long ceased to be an inn but its courtyard, reached through an archway, and its irregular, red-tiled outbuildings would, in wagon days, have made it very suitable for the purpose. Earlier, I have been told, these outbuildings housed pedlars and their wares. The house numbers have changed since 1870, but I think it was here that Pierre Robin, now in his thirties, embarked as a tenant on his career in the catering trade.

He must have realized that oil-pressing on its own did not offer much of a future. Walnut oil was still the basis for most home cooking and seasoning in the traditionalist Berry: indeed parties to crush walnuts have been described to me as still taking place in the twentieth century. But whereas it had once provided the fuel also for both street lamps and domestic ones, nut oil was being replaced by the cleaner, brighter kerosene (*pétrole*) that was now widely on sale. What was more, by the early 1870s the amazing modernity of gas lighting had come to La Châtre – although at first it was said that, as with the equally new water supply, the pipes leaked: 'Gas in the water and water in the gas . . .' A French joke about marital discord.

Did Pierre and Célestine make a success of the inn in the Grande Rue, I wonder? It was far larger than the Chassignolles inn, and though the La Châtre census confirms that they were by then innkeepers their one living-in servant does not sound sufficient staff for such a place. At all events, by 1876 they were back with Célestine's mother in Chassignolles, accompanied by Charles, who was now eleven years old.

Chapter 11

'I never heard tell of any brother or sister to Célestine.' Even Jeanne Pagnard said that when I first asked her. In fact I knew, when I thought about it, that this could not be right. Célestine had had at least one brother: his brief letter to her in the Grande Rue in La Châtre is the final one in the little cardboard case and dates from almost ten years later than the others.

It is addressed on one fold with copybook capital initials, but the letter itself is written in the careless hand of a young dragoon (trooper) who is in a hurry or slightly drunk or both. In the big northern towns, wine brought in by railway from the traditional wine-drinking areas was by then down to two sous – ten centimes – a litre: even on their miserable wages soldiers could afford a great deal of it. The letter is headed from Meaux in the Seine-et-Marne, a grandiose but unlovely city due east of Paris which was, and is, a major garrison town of France.

29 October 1873

Dear Sister,

The ten francs you sent me came as a great relief to me. I had some small debts that I couldn't get out of paying at once, seeing as we are leaving on Sunday. Now I find myself totally skint again. I did the whole journey back here on foot. The day before yesterday, I was appointed to a headquarters platoon.

I beg you, send me ten francs more in postage stamps, or, if you can't see your way to sending me such a sum, at least send me five francs. But I promise you that ten francs would be of the greatest use to me, and let's hope that one day I'll be able to let you have them back [*faut espérer qu'un jour je pourrai te les rendre*].

If you see Mother, will you tell her that I am very hurt by her letter, she has misunderstood what I said. And tell her that I will write to her when I get back from this tour on 17 November.

I end this letter by embracing you with all my heart,

Your loving brother, Chaumette, A.

PS. We are leaving Sunday morning, so I hope you will reply post-haste. Here's my address –

Chaumette, au 13ième peloton hors rang, 8ième dragons, Meaux.

I traced Auguste's birth record. He was born in Chassignolles to Silvain-Germain and Anne Laurent in November 1848. He was therefore four and a half years younger than Célestine and in 1873 was rising twenty-five. As you would expect, he appears on the village census for 1856 and 1861, but by 1866, when he was barely eighteen, he is gone, although his father had died the previous year and his mother was managing the inn on her own.

He figures no more in any Chassignolles register. This inelegant little letter cannot particularly have pleased his elder sister at the time she received it; it is not of the sort that would normally become a keepsake. I began to wonder if it was preserved because it turned out to be the last communication from a soldier who did not live to come home. The Franco-Prussian war was over, but skirmishes continued till late 1873 on the ceded territory of Alsace-Lorraine and round Metz, and a large number of men were still with the army.

The call-up for military service directly affected only a minority of Frenchmen for much of the nineteenth century, but it played a very important role in the collective imagination. Men were taken from all over France, speaking different *patois* and with varying customs, and were, in theory, summarily transformed into standard French citizens. It was due to military service, as well as to the great machine of French national education that was also getting into gear, that the concept of La Patrie was gradually being imposed on that of the *pays*.

But those actually conscripted were far from being a representative sample of the general population. Napoleon had introduced the system of drawing lots, and only those drawing a number low in proportion of the total (*les mauvais numéros*) were called to serve, usually about one quarter of the manpower available. In intention, this was a most egalitarian method. But in practice the intake was unbalanced by the substitution system, which flourished for two generations, till it was swept aside by the Franco-Prussian war and finally abolished by the new Republic. 'Substitution' meant that when a boy drew a losing number his family was allowed to pay, if they could, for another to take his place. Célestine's cousin probably had this in mind when he wrote to her: 'I know I haven't yet taken part in the draw, but you mustn't be bothered about that.' The result was that, for much of the century, about a third of the army consisted of bought men – 'the poor, the landless and the roofless', as a commentator on the quality of the troops sniffily remarked. 'Selling' a boy to a wealthy neighbour was often the only way a poor peasant family with many mouths to feed could get its hands on a sum of money for some badly needed purchase, such as a new cart or iron harrow. The going rate for decades was five hundred francs – a fortune to those who rarely dealt in money at all.

But most families, at every social level, did not want their boys to go. It was resented that the Government, who arbitrarily removed a much-needed worker from the family farm or business, paid no compensation. The standard length of service was five years for much of the time, seven between 1855 and 1868. The families feared, with good reason, that after being so long away, learning to play cards and drink wine and quarrel and go with strange women in cold, dirty towns, their son would be lost to them for ever. Indeed that was part of the Government's intention – to acquire an experienced force of men habituated to army life and untrained at anything else so that they would re-enlist as volunteers. Middle-class families and prosperous peasant ones began to take out private insurance against conscription, as against fire, flood or hail (the Mutuelle de l'Indre company organized one such scheme in 1863). Other fathers went deep into debt to buy a boy out; some close-knit Communes organized whip-rounds to help deserving cases.

And yet, for all it was dreaded, the *tirage* (the draw) was a time of celebration and masculine bonding. In the Berry, those whose numbers came up would march in formation to the local market town dressed in clean white smocks with ribbons in their hats, a home-made banner carried aloft. At the end of the day, the ones who had been passed fit for service were fêted in the local inns and joked loudly that they had been passed 'fit for marriage – fit for the girls', while those who were 'too small' or who had 'bad chests' or some other infirmity made themselves scarce, feeling humiliated. The classic song of the recruit on his way, '*Je n'en regrett' que ma Rosalie*', tells a different story from that of traditional peasant attachment to the family soil. When Rosalie suggests to her sweet-heart that her own father might help pay for a substitute, she is told by the departing boy: 'They won't find another fellow as big and strong to take my place.' Some twenty-year-olds, sick of a life where they never encountered a face that was not known to them, or that, more significantly, did not know *them*, must have been eager for a world elsewhere.

I felt that Auguste Chaumette might well have belonged in this category. It took some perseverance to establish the facts of his military career. Having traced the French military archives to the redoubt of Vincennes, I had difficulty in supplying the precise indications to have his record looked up: his writing was so bad that neither I nor several French citizens whom I consulted could decide at first to which company of dragoons he was attached, and there were twenty-six companies. It was suggested at Vincennes that I look up the local recruitment lists in the Châteauroux Archives for the year 1868, when Auguste reached the key age of twenty, to discover whether he had drawn a low number then and, if not, that I search the lists for 1870 when the war began and he was likely to have come under the general call-up. However, this apparently simple course of action proved not to be so: the rule, I was told by the staff in charge of the Salle des Archives, was that all military records were classified as secret for a hundred and fifty years after the birth of the soldiers concerned. Auguste had been born five years too late: to see if his name figured on a public list I should have to wait till 1998.

Since, in the same Archive, I had been free to consult census returns a mere thirty years old (in England and Scotland they have to be a hundred years old) the military authorities' concern for the privacy of long-dead individuals seemed to me excessive. The most sympathetic lady clearly thought so too, but endeavoured to make it seem reasonable.

'It's because matters to do with health sometimes appear on the military lists, you see.'

'You mean, someone might object to my finding out that their great-great-great-grandfather had flat feet?'

'Well, or tuberculosis. People might not want it known they had had that in the family . . .'

'After five generations?'

'I know. But you know how people are about their own family . . .'

I laid further siege to Vincennes who, fortunately for me, seemed to interpret the rules rather differently. Eventually a decision was taken on the regiment number and I got an answer. It turned out that in looking for a conscript and a possible death in battle I had not been quite on course. Chaumette, Auguste, it appeared, had escaped the draft in 1868. But in 1870, when the Germans invaded France, he joined up of his own accord.

The events in the north-east took their time to penetrate the *Écho de l'Indre*, but by 19 August they had ousted from the front page the pressing local issue of the summer drought. Stories about 'Prussian atrocities' appeared, a foretaste of the propaganda machine of the future, greater wars. The previous summer, and the one before, the big story had been the local celebration of the Emperor's birthday, a display of servile adoration and piety complete with fireworks, and special prizes to children who were dutiful to their parents ('They have the right to decide your Destiny'). This year, however, the birthday went unnoticed – in fact the Emperor was soon to be deposed.

The paper carried rumours of local lads being among the casualties: firm news was still slow to arrive then; army practices were in this and most other ways unchanged since the times of the earlier Napoleon. Young men previously excused from service, married men and those on the reserve list were warned that they might be 'called to the colours'. Substitution had at last been abolished under pressure of circumstances, and all were told to present themselves in La Châtre at seven one September morning along with the 'class of '70', the current twenty-year-olds. Those deemed not too short, tubercular or otherwise unfit were formed into rough ranks. They marched in a cheerful, undisciplined way to the sound of bagpipes the twenty-three miles to Châteauroux, where the realities of military life took over. George Sand, old now, saw them pass the gates of her manor as she had seen the troops of Napoleon's *levées* pass in her childhood.

However, by then many men had already enlisted voluntarily, swept along on a wave of new patriotism or perhaps reflecting that if they jumped before they were pushed they might do better for themselves. Auguste Chaumette had volunteered on 15 August, a traditional religious holiday and the day that the state of war became official. Five days later he was 'in Africa'.

This at first sight seemed so implausible that I wondered if the brief record I had been sent had been miscopied. Why, in the very fortnight when soldiers were being rushed from the colonial garrisons to *la métropole* to take part in what turned out to be the rout at Sedan, had this recruit been sent in the opposite direction? Expert advice, however, suggested to me that this was in fact a classic example of the ponderous workings of the French army at that date. (The Prussian one was far more efficient.) Auguste had apparently elected to join the Zouaves, an infantry regiment who did fight in France but whose headquarters were, as their name suggests, in north Africa. At that date this meant Algeria, since French hegemony over Tunisia and Morocco came later. So, willy-nilly, to Algiers or Mers el Kebir, any new Zouave was sent for basic training, regardless of other factors.

The Zouaves, who wore an ornate, Arab-inspired uniform, were a largely colonial company; just why Auguste joined them must also have a logical explanation, or at least a consistent one. It would have been an improbable destination for a young man enlisting in central France, but the very fact that he was in Africa already by 20 August shows, given the communications of the period, that he cannot have been coming from his own *pays*: the various stages of the journey would have taken far longer than five days. He must have enlisted much further south, most likely in some seaport such as Toulon or Marseilles. The Zouave regiments were regularly stationed there. and would have been a natural choice for someone who was in the area already.

Things begin to fall into place: his army service does not account for his being absent from home already by 1866, when his recently widowed mother might have been expected to need his help to run the inn. Indeed, being the son of a widow was often a good reason for getting excused from service altogether. So it seems that before he had even turned eighteen Auguste was elsewhere, and it would now appear that 'elsewhere' was the Mediterranean coast, a far more exciting place for a restless youngster than central France.

On 9 September 1870 he moved again, but simply to another

140

Algerian depot: he was transferred to the Chasseurs d'Afrique, a cavalry regiment. Presumably this more glamorous option was his own choice and he was familiar with horses: as an innkeeper's son, attending to the mounts of passing trade would have been one of his earliest duties. Perhaps, however, he was unconvincing as a rider, for he was returned to the Zouaves in January. At that time, far away in France, Paris was undergoing its winter of siege and the Prussian capture of Alsace-Lorraine was being bitterly contested. Auguste missed all that. He stayed in Africa till late September 1871 when, according to his record, he was *renvoyé dans ses foyers* – literally, 'sent back to his home hearths' or back to his people.

Maybe he did go home briefly, but we know that he did not stay. The records seem incomplete here, for he evidently remained in the army: two years later we find him writing to his sister from Meaux, having metamorphosed into a dragoon. He had apparently paid his family a recent, not entirely happy visit: 'I did the whole journey back here on foot . . . If you see Mother, will you tell her I am very hurt by her letter, she has misunderstood what I said . . .'

There are no other notes on his movements. His record ends '*libérable du service actif le 10 août 1875*' – almost exactly five years from the day when he first joined up.

'*Libérable*' – entitled to be released. He did not necessarily avail himself of this right. 'The historical archives have no further information on the individual concerned. There is no file on him, a usual situation in the case of Other Ranks.'

It seems highly probable that he never again returned home.

We know that his sister kept, all her life, the scrawled demand for money signed with a hasty endearment. We know that thirty years later, in the 1900s (the earliest period that anyone now alive in Chassignolles can recall), his very existence had been forgotten. Of course his sister and a few childhood friends could not have forgotten, but no doubt they had long ceased to mention him. It would seem that, regardless of the provisions of French law, he had effectively disinherited himself from any claim on the inn. His mother had been gone since 1884, dead of that cancer of the breast she tried to treat with lumps of raw steak in what is now Jeanne Pagnard's kitchen.

Maybe, when Auguste did leave the army, he drifted with his 'small debts' from Meaux to Paris or to another of the expanding northern cities, where he became caught up in money-making schemes, successful or otherwise. Or maybe he was drawn south again, back to the Mediterranean, and any original intention to contact his family again and repair 'misunderstandings' faded and faded until it was extinguished by guilt and time. But I think it most likely that he returned to Africa and settled there, and that this accounts for his total disappearance. *'Tout ça, c'est la faute de l'Afrique,'* as another old adventurer declares at the end of Pagnol's *L'Eau des Collines.*

There were opportunities there for active men without families: even in La Châtre you could discover that, in the 1860s and '70s. What more natural than that he should simply remain in a place where it was never cold and where even the most humble-born Frenchman could have a servant to wait on him? His obscure life history encapsulates a whole era in France's development and her participation in the glories and follies of nineteenth-century expansionism. From the Auguste Chaumettes of France derived the bitter Franco-Algerian conflicts of the mid-twentieth century.

This is not, however, the whole of the story. Célestine, it turns out, had not one vanished brother but two.

In the seventeen years between 1833 and 1850, twelve Chaumettes were born in Chassignolles but nearly all belonged to the branch descended from Célestine's great-uncle Pierre. Submerged in this tide, whose various combinations of Silvain, François, Louis and Félix recur like some natural cycle, I almost overlooked the fact that one other Chaumette of Célestine and Auguste's generation was born to Silvain-Germain and Anne Laurent. His name was Ursin and he was their first-born, coming into the world in 1843.

I was for a while inclined to think that this hitherto unsuspected brother so close in age, who seemed to have been lost to village memory as completely as Auguste and who had not even left a trace in a letter, had perhaps died in childhood as did his neighbour, little Jean Aussourd. Otherwise, why had he not taken on the inn, at that time when a son almost automatically followed the father into a business if the family were fortunate enough to have one? French law gave him an automatic share in the place; older Berrichon tradition would have favoured him in any case, as the eldest. So his absence in adulthood was still stranger than Auguste's.

But there was no sign in the Chassignolles register of an early death, and when I got to the census records I found Ursin in place. He was there in 1856 'without profession' (the sign of a family comfortable enough not to need the earnings of a thirteen-year-old) by which time Anne Laurent's widowed father from Nohant had also joined the household. By 1861, aged eighteen, he was still at home but had become *'leur fils taillandier'* – 'their son, a tool maker'. This was a skilled trade, slightly more prestigious than that of a general smith but learnt in a smithy. Antoine Pirot, whose father was a blacksmith, had followed a similar calling. It was just the kind of occupation to be recommended to a young man who, once married, would also take on the inn: such was the classic pattern then and well into the twentieth century. On the evidence of this, Ursin was all set to succeed his father as a prominent member of village society, and should have gone on appearing in the records throughout the decades.

But he does not. By 1866 he had gone, never to reappear. In fact he was most probably gone well before: the tone of Henry Lorant's letter to Célestine of 1864 suggests that he (Henry) saw himself installed in the inn. Certainly Ursin does not seem to have been present during the eventful year of 1865. He was not an official witness at his sister's wedding in January; more significantly, he was not there in August either, when his father died. It was the new son-in-law, Pierre Robin, who was not even living in Chassignolles, who represented the family.

Come to that, Ursin was not there either at his mother's death, nearly twenty years later. It is this very lack of further evidence, and of any apparent trace in village memory, that tells its own tale. But what tale, exactly?

The most obvious and comprehensive explanation for Ursin's desertion was the one that I had originally assigned in my mind to Auguste – that he had drawn a 'bad number' in the military lottery. This would have removed him for seven years and quite likely for ever. Back again to the Archives in Châteauroux and this time, as the sympathetic lady remarked, I was in luck. This was 1993, and Ursin had been born in 1843, exactly one hundred and fifty years earlier.

A hundred and sixty-seven twenty-year-olds appeared in La Châtre from villages round about on the appointed morning in the spring of 1864, minus a few who had failed to return from jobs elsewhere and would now be sought by the police, or who were away with a good excuse and were represented by their fathers. They drew lots, each man plunging his hand in turn into a basket of numbers. Only those with numbers up to eighty-five were then called for interview and examination by a committee of local mayors.

I did not have to seek long for Ursin: he was number twenty-nine. It was noted that he was born and living in Chassignolles, son of Silvain-Germain, that he was able both to read and write and that he was a tool maker. His height was 1.74 metres – about five foot nine inches, tall for that place and time, even taller than the *beau farinier* of George Sand's story. But, unlike Sand's rustic hero, he was also marked as *faible* – 'weak'.

The final decision was taken by an army surgeon; it is scribbled against Ursin's name in his different, impatient hand: '*Faible de constitution. Improp.*' 'Unsuitable.' The army had turned Ursin Chaumette down, and since a century and a half had gone by I was allowed to know it.

But did 'weak constitution' simply imply that he was a skinny, gangling creature without the apparent strength for route marches? Or did it refer to something more specific, such as recognized poor health – a history of asthma, perhaps, or the dreaded *phtisie* (consumption). There is also, of course, the possibility that *faible de constitution* was used as a general euphemism for boys whose weakness appeared to be in the head, but the fact that Ursin was a tool maker and literate would suggest that he was not stupid.

I played for a while with the idea that he might have been just rather odd: the sort of young man who then, today and in any era, causes his family pain by his apparent inability to be or think quite like other people – the sort who may drift away and be lost to view. It was unusual to disappear from home in rural France at that time, but, in spite of the travel permits a working man was supposed to carry, it was not really difficult and probably most disappearances never got signalled to the authorities: the new highways were busy with wanderers. From the mid-nineteenth century a trickle of search notices put out by local Mairies hint impotently at family feuds, mental illness, tragedies that will never now be fully elucidated. 'Louis Got, aged twenty-one, born at Vatan [in the Berry], left that town several weeks ago to work as a tailor in Paris. He was seen on 6 July in Vierzon . . . and said that he was going to look for work in Romorantin. At that time he still had with him his trade papers and a silver watch . . .' That young man, of similar age and social status to Ursin Chaumette, disappeared without trace in 1866.

There was, of course, the simpler possibility that the weakness discerned in Ursin by the army surgeon was a straightforward one which, before long, killed him off. Or he could have died in some accident – an injury at work that turned septic, a fall from a roof, a bolting horse and cart . . . But nothing appears in the Chassignolles Death Register for Ursin for the rest of the century.

Today, and for the past two generations, marriages and deaths anywhere in France are automatically reported back to the Commune where the birth was registered and noted in the margin of the original entry. So a completed twentieth-century entry encapsulates at a glance the life journey, both actual and metaphorical, of that particular individual. But during the possible life span of Ursin, or indeed of Auguste, this coherent system was not yet in force. Just once or twice I found pasted into the register a declaration from a distant Commune concerning the death of someone ordinarily resident in Chassignolles. For instance, a Charbonnier son died in Versailles in 1843 at the age of nineteen while working there as a builder's labourer, and even at this early date the Versailles Hôtel de Ville efficiently sent notification of this to his native village. But there is no such document at any date relating to Ursin, any more than there is for his younger brother. Nor, needless to say, is Ursin mentioned on the family grave.

But surely, one might say, the most likely explanation is that Ursin, like so many countrymen in the latter half of the nineteenth century, took himself and his particular skill off to a nearby town where he could hope for a more comfortable and modern existence? That is entirely plausible as far as it goes, but as an explanation for his complete disappearance it does not go far enough. Metal-working was an expanding trade; developments in agriculture were requiring more elaborate tools. By the 1860s the first of the horse-drawn reaping machines were beginning to clack in the fields that, for a thousand or more years, had been harvested with sickles and scythes. The earliest (hand-operated) mechanical thresher was actually invented locally, in Vierzon, during Ursin's childhood, a small but distinct advance on the exhausting flail. If Ursin had opened a Quincaillerie Agricole in La Châtre, Ste Sévère,

145

Neuvy, Issoudun or any other of the small towns around, he could have done nicely. But in that case he would have remained locally known, returning to Chassignolles at times of death and marriage, a continuing if off-stage presence in the family history.

Even if he had gone much farther away, to the growing industrial town of Nantes or to the Atlantic seaboard or to Paris, he should not have been totally lost to his own *pays*. Most nineteenth-century migrants to the big cities joined kin or friends there, a network that linked certain jobs or trades with specific country areas of origin, so a sense of regionalism was retained. ('The tenements of Paris are in themselves villages come from the Centre.') Often such migrants returned in old age to their childhood home, having inherited and kept their part of the family goods. Even today, the habit is not lost: people in the Berry cling tenaciously to small pieces of land or redundant farm buildings deriving from share-outs several generations back. The way in which property is neces- sarily allocated helps to perpetuate ties that might otherwise have been relinquished. Proprietary reference is made to 'cousins' even when these are several times removed, and they are always addressed in the intimate *tu* form in spite of the fact they may be virtual strangers.

In this way, Ursin's existence and that of his descendants, if any, should have remained a matter of oral record. I should have been told: 'He let his sister have the inn, as she was there, and he kept an orchard they had as his share.' Or yet: 'Célestine and her hus- band must have bought the brother out', or even: 'She had a brother, I seem to remember, but he was never interested in the inn.' Instead, where Ursin should have been, in however shadowy a form, I encountered only empty space. Many years later, when Célestine became a widow without resources, it was as if this brother, like the younger one, had never been.

I began to form the theory that that able and respected man Silvain-Germain, who seems to have had a strong personality ('Your mother tells me she let's you make your own choices but . . . I certainly can't believe it of your father') somehow alienated both his sons as soon as they reached manhood, and that each left home with sufficient drama and decision that even his death could not bring them back. Or was it their mother Anne who was the real cause of tension: might she have remained on reasonable terms with her 'sweet-natured and good' daughter but driven the boys away? ('If you see Mother will you tell her I am very hurt by her letter . . .') Either way, it cannot have been a happy story. It also looks, on reflection, as if the period of nearly ten years following Silvain-Germain's death, when Anne ran the inn on her own before Célestine and Pierre joined her, may represent a continuing uncertainty as to whether either of the absent sons might not after all reappear and reclaim the succession. And, perhaps, a reluctance on the part of Célestine and Pierre to go and live with her themselves.

Célestine's own son, born after Ursin had gone, was initially registered as Ursin Charles. Perhaps the intention was that brother Ursin should be godfather, as was the custom of the countryside. But later the boy was always referred to as 'Charles', as if the very name of Ursin was forgotten.

Many months after I had consigned Ursin, like Auguste, to the file of unprovable supposition, I received some confirmation from an unexpected quarter. I was visiting Suzanne Calvet in the neat turn-of-the-century house by the main road into Châteauroux, where she and her husband have finally retired from the hotel trade. (This move is explained by the fact that Châteauroux was Monsieur Calvet's *pays*, for which he developed a yearning in old age.) Madame Calvet received me with warmth and huge slices of a local delicacy called *clafoutis*, a confection of cherries in a paste of flour, eggs and sugar. The daughter of generations of Chassignolles innkeepers, she brought out for me rolls of old legal documents which she described as mortgages taken out by her grandfather, Ursin Yvernault, 'Because he spent all his money treating conscripts going off to the war to white wine and oysters in Tours! . . . He was a very generous man, but had no head for business.'

Madame Calvet has always had an excellent head for business, allied to a capacity for work undiminished by her substantial size, but she was not in the habit of looking closely at obsolete legal documents. While a couple of them did indeed indicate forced sales of property to meet loans taken out 1915–20, the rest were much older papers; they related to the original acquisition of these lands or houses by Ursin's father, Jean, some fifty years earlier. I pointed this out. 'Oh yes, him. Well, he wasn't nearly such a good-tempered man as my grandfather. When he was in a sulk about something he wouldn't speak at all – he used to write instructions to his servant boys in code on the door of the barn instead . . . Or so I've been told.'

'His poor wife.'

'He had two. The first one died. She was my grandfather's mother. He had a whole lot more children with the second. Sulks or no sulks, he was *un chaud lapin*.'

But, while I was interested in Jean Yvernault, my attention had been caught by another name that stared up at me out of a document – Ursin Chaumette.

The date was 1868, four years later than any other trace I had found of this Ursin and three years after the death of his father. In that year, it appeared, he was selling up the Chassignolles property he had inherited as his share of Silvain-Germain's estate, consisting of a house somewhere in the village and two pieces of land elsewhere in the Commune. Silvain-Germain had acquired part of these from his own father François and had added to them by further purchases: the inn, even in those early days, must have been profitable.

The fact that Ursin was in sole possession of these properties would suggest that the inn itself had not been left to him. The sale – to Jean Yvernault, carpenter and cabinet-maker – was registered by the La Châtre lawyer whose name appears on most conveyancing documents at this period, but Ursin did not return to the area to sign the agreement of sale in person in the way that was, and is, customary. Instead, he nominated his mother to act for him – at some stage in her adult life she had acquired some degree of literacy, or at any rate she could now sign her name. It rather looks as if he wished to liquidate his Chassignolles interests without further involvement.

So he had indeed gone off elsewhere, but the mere fact of his doing so does not in itself explain his complete severance from his *pays*. He was by then living at an address in Bourges about forty-five miles away. Such a distance was much less significant than it would have been twenty years before, but it was still some seven hours away by the once-daily coach and train connection. In other words, it was far enough to allow him to cut his links with home if he was so minded, but quite near enough for him to have kept in touch had he so wished. All in all, it seems that he did not.

He was still a tool maker and had taken a wife, a girl born in Bourges.

The temptation to pursue his wraith further through the late-nineteenth-century census records of Bourges, a town larger than Châteauroux, is one which, in the interests of my own sanity, I shall resist.

Around the time I picked up Ursin Chaumette's scent again in Suzanne Calvet's sitting-room, Jeanne Pagnard said to me: 'About Célestine Chaumette being an only child . . . I told you that, but it does come to me now there was some story . . . About a brother who disappeared.'

'Where?'

'That's the point. He disappeared. No one ever knew what became of him.' But she could not tell me any more. The period was just that much too remote, too far over the rim of memory, even that of her grandmother who had been such a mine of information on the last quarter of the century. Ursin Chaumette's defection dated from the mid-1860s and Grandmother Chartier herself was not born till 1857. And if the story of disappearance into the blue related rather to Auguste, he apparently disappeared from Chassignolles at the same time, only revisiting briefly on leave from the army in 1871 and 1873.

Even folk memory, so durable, eventually blurs and fades, conflates two people into one, telescopes generations and at last extinguishes. The most colourful, long-mythologized figures pass in the end into the great, quiet dark, becoming as if they had never been born: even family ties, so tenacious in rural France, are eventually relinquished. I have said that Chassignolles people will happily claim cousinage with remote connections, but it is evident that, by unspoken consensus, a halt has to be called somewhere. All those whose roots in the Commune go back far enough are probably related to one another in some measure, but once the link goes back beyond great-grandparent level oblivion begins to descend.

As a footnote to the family-tree of the Chaumettes, I happened to notice from Madame Calvet's documents that the Jean Yvernault who bought Ursin Chaumette's village property was in fact the young man's uncle by marriage. The dead first wife of this sulky but persistent progenitor turned out to be the young sister of Silvain-Germain, she who as a child was called 'Felissé'. So Madame Calvet, whose café-hotel led us to Chassignolles in the first place, is herself a direct descendant of the Silvain Chaumette, the sacristan, who was born long before the Revolution, who lived to be eighty-eight and died in the year Célestine was born.

Chapter 12

In departing for Bourges, Ursin Chaumette was very much a figure of his time, though not necessarily a laudable one. In France as in England, the idea of the village as good and the town as intrinsically evil was appealing to a growing nineteenth-century romanticism.

Once changes were working away elsewhere, a static rural existence without the possibility of improvement or social mobility came to be seen as desirable, healthy and 'natural'. In contrast, urban life was allegedly 'sick' – this vague sickness comprising everything from alcoholism, gambling and loss of religious faith to snobbery, adulterated milk and bad drains. From the Second Empire onwards, life on the land was less apt to be described as a matter of harsh conditions and brutalized feelings: a softer and more positive image took over. It was given wide currency in Millet's two phenomenally successful pictures, 'The Gleaners' (exhibited 1857) and 'The Angelus' (1859), which between them conveyed an impression of the thrift, piety and generally unchanging values of an adequately fed and decently clad peasantry. These portrayals, apparently of timelessness, actually of a particular moment in France's evolution, were distributed in the form of cheap prints (thanks to new processes) to homes all over France. It is significant that they caught the popular imagination so strongly just when the age-old practice of gleaning for grains was declining because of the new and more efficient reaping machinery. In both pictures, and most obviously in 'The Angelus', the light is that of the day's ending which carries its own subliminal message: the paintings, apparently naturalistic, are elegiac in mood. The fictionalizing effect of nostalgia is already evident.

The reality was that both town and country were, in their own ways, part of the same evolving pattern, and the opposition between them was more complex than popular art or laments about the young deserting the land could suggest. Indeed, had rural life continued at the same deprived level, dominated by the need to eat, with all other considerations secondary, arguably *more* peasants would have been leaving the land, from simple necessity. At the time Célestine was born, Balzac wrote, referring to the Berry: 'country people have a profound aversion to change, even to changes which they acknowledge might be useful to them'. But this very remark indicates that change in the countryside was stealthily on its way. A generation later the industrial and commercial development that was transforming urban France was introducing new skills, trades and amenities not just in country market towns but in the villages as well.

Land, too, was being regarded as more valuable now that it was being more productively used, and those in possession even of a smallholding found themselves in slightly easier circumstances. Most of the unused heathlands in the Berry disappeared between 1860 and 1880, apparently without the traumas and class conflicts of the British Enclosures of a hundred years earlier. In Chassignolles, grazing held by the Commune was auctioned off in lots in 1870, on the grounds that 'most of the inhabitants get no benefit from it'. The money was put towards that perennial community expense, the improving of roads and paths; that same year the road between Chassignolles and La Châtre was at last being widened and made up with hard core. Needless to say, there were complaints that the process was taking too long and that meanwhile the right-of-way was 'so full of pits and piles of stones' that its state was much worse than it had been before and 'dangerous to both horses and carts'.

In another ten years the right of *vaine patoure*, the grazing of flocks on tracts of ownerless land, was formally abolished. At the same period the more intense land use seems to have put an end to rural squatting and begging, driving the remaining paupers into the towns. From then, too, attempts were made to chase gypsies into the towns. The continuing fear *des nomades et des forains* probably reflected, and reflects, the ancient fear of strangers in one's 'own' countryside, but the more specific sense of the ownership of land that came in after 1870 gave the old, superstitious dread a new rationale. Gypsies were widely accused of stealing animals and crops and lighting fires: they still are today. They seem to raise an atavistic loathing, even in normally tolerant people.

The woods, also, had been gradually cut back, partly to claim more land for agriculture and partly to supply building materials and other needs for the growing towns. In the Berry, wood fired the new local industries such as cloth-, glass- and china-making. The forges and foundries that had traditionally absorbed much wood in their furnaces, keeping whole tribes of woodcutters in full-time occupation, continued to use even more between 1840 and 1860, though this turned out to be their final spurt: the collapse of the ironworks of the Berry, when it came, was swift and complete.

The erosion of the deep forests and deserted moorland had its effect on the wolf population. There had, as well, been an indiscriminate campaign against them since the 1840s, with a bounty paid for wolf or cub carcasses in any season – the same myopic obsession that is currently eradicating the last wild predator, the fox, from France's countryside. Wolves became rare in the Indre after the 1870s, and by the 1900s the Department could no longer realistically be regarded as a wolf zone. Yet wolf stories, scares and sightings continued up to the First World War and even beyond: the wolf lived long in the imagination of rural populations and is not quite extinct even today. I have talked to old people in Chassignolles who, while they know that 'the last wolf in the region' was killed in the Bois de Villemort in the year of their birth or whatever, believe that the archetypal enemy is still to be found somewhere in France – in the next Department or 'in the mountains'.

Daniel Bernard, an historian of the Berry who interviewed a number of old people who were still alive in the 1970s, the last generation who had heard wolf stories directly from their own parents and grandparents, found that in the collective memory the disappearance of the wolves was put down to the coming of the railways. In particular, the line from Tours to Montluçon that arrived at long last in the Lower Berry at the beginning of the 1880s was perceived as having been the literal engine of change: 'When the trains came, that frightened the beasts and they took themselves off.'

When Balzac wrote of the Berrichon's inherent aversion to change, almost as a matter of course he equated material change with improvement. This view was, in one form or another, almost universal among educated people for the whole of the nineteenth century. Even those who bewailed the passing of the Good Old Days in certain defined ways, did so without any formulated idea that the march of progress could be impeded or that progress in general was anything but a Good Thing, a journey out of darkness into light. This assumption has, in turn, informed our own historical perspective. The nineteenth century saw a physical transformation of every country in western Europe on a scale unknown before and unrivalled since, even after another hundred years of continuing change. Traditionally, therefore, the history of the nineteenth century tends to be recounted as a series of staging posts on the long route to present-day technology, expectations and values.

Even if we now question some of these values and feel that much of the technology has brought ills as well as benefits, we still see the story in the same basic shape. Indeed, our perception of it as a story derives from our sense that the drama of nineteenth-century change and development was all leading to a climax that we in the twentieth century have witnessed, as the unfolding themes of a novel lead to its grand scene. The characters from the earlier chapters of this saga have all disappeared by the closing ones, but we, benefiting from an authorial overview, have been able to trace the links, the plot.

Almost inevitably I have found myself adopting this approach, Yet, as the quintessential French historian Braudel himself has pointed out, it is possible to look at chronology from the opposite end and therefore to interpret both past and present differently – to see, not the past as prologue and preparation for the present, but the present as evidence for the persistent survival of the past.

It has been the unbroken threads between the Chassignolles of the past and that of the present that have drawn me into the web of its history in the first place, and it is on these threads that the story is strung. The drama of change was not in the end as decisive as it seemed, nor was the movement all in one direction: rather, like the cycle of the seasons, the life of Chassignolles reached its equinox and then began to decline once more.

But for the moment let us pick up the evolutionary story again in the heyday of Célestine's life as a young married woman, and the beginning of its own Belle Époque for the village and for thousands of others like it.

The village to which Célestine, her husband Pierre and their young son returned in the mid-1870s was being documented more completely than ever before, thanks to the burgeoning Third Republic that followed the upheaval of the war and the Paris Commune. The 1872 census, the first of the new, centralized regime which was finally to weld France into one nation, was particularly detailed.

For the first time the census-taker (Auguste Charbonnier, the energetic school teacher) was required to note literacy, or its absence. The great majority of the 590 people over the age of twenty could neither read nor write. Of those who supposedly could, fifty-nine were male and only fourteen female, but the figures have been altered to make disparate totals agree and there is a note that some could only read. Among those under twenty – nearly half the population – the literacy rate is somewhat higher, thanks no doubt to Charbonnier himself. The difference between the sexes is, however, less marked. This could hardly have been due yet to the influence of the girls' school, since this had only started the year before. It was the project of a well-born personage, Mademoiselle Guyot, a relative by marriage of the Pissavy family, who were by then a presence in Chassignolles. It was run in her house, with the help of nuns from a teaching order; it continued even after the secular girls' school was opened in 1904 and is still fondly remembered by old ladies who attended it. For decades during the present century it went on existing in the vestigial form of catechism classes for village children.

The 1870s, long a watershed in folk memory between the old world that harked back before the Revolution and the twentieth-century one that was on its way, forms a watershed in the records also. The Pissavys, busy turning themselves into new-style landed gentry, given to good works and improvements, coexisted then with Jeanne Aussourd, *belle amie* of the Sieur Vallet, who had been a Seigneur of a far older type. Jeanne's aged cousin André was also still alive, and so were other survivors of a time beginning to seem quaintly antique. Besides André, the census records two other 'widowers of over eighty, and four widows' plus 'one widow of over ninety'. This person, a Marie Villebasse, was born in Sarzay in 1781 and was evidently an object of pride: her name in the lists is written in a special flamboyant hand with thickened strokes.

(Today's incumbent in the role of oldest inhabitant, a sprightly and formidable person born in 1897, is similarly revered and is known, in ceremonial French style, as *la doyenne de la commune*. 'I am told that I am,' she said dismissively to me in 1992. Of course she knew she was. Years of birth, even months, are a matter of public record in France, in a way that leaves no room for the polite discretion that clouds the topic in less-documented Anglo-Saxon societies.)

Occupations in 1872 were still overwhelmingly agricultural. But a second inn had been added, the one run by the Yvernaults that was handed down in the family, passing to the granddaughter who became Madame Calvet: it survives as the café-hotel of today. Thirty-seven men were employed up at the quarries that were owned by the family who spirited Mademoiselle Pagnard's grandmother off to Paris to sew rosebud dresses. Mademoiselle Pagnard's great-grandfather had opened his grocery shop some seven or eight years before; his was still the only shop in the village, but by 1876 there was a second one, run by the then-sacristan's wife, and also two tailoring shops. No bakery as yet, though by the 1880s one was installed, worked by a man who hailed from another village and whose Chassignolles-born wife had opened a third inn. The wine trade was clearly flourishing.

In 1872 neither the Chaumette inn nor the other one as yet had any accommodation worth describing on the census form as 'hotel rooms'. This had to be noted because, unlike the earlier censuses, this one was an extensive, even exhaustive document that, in asking its questions, took an urban habitat as the norm – rather inappropriately, perhaps, for France was still a predominantly rural country, with half its national income derived directly from agriculture. Land was not yet accepted as security for loans: it comes as no surprise to see that there were no banks or insurance companies in Chassignolles. The population did not number any heads of railway companies (though there were two men and three women living 'entirely from income derived from land holdings or invest-ments': a miniscule *rentier* class). No one was down as a beggar, there were no 'acrobats, charlatans, exhibitors of wild animals or other curiosities'. And no *fille publique* (the dispiriting term for an officially registered prostitute). Nor, even though a certain amount of inbreeding must have occurred in all those households where both marriage partners were born in Chassignolles, was anyone listed as an idiot, mad, blind or deaf and dumb. Perhaps there were genuinely none, or perhaps it was a matter of village pride not to recognize the fact, at least in public.

In Chassignolles in 1872 there were 42 workhorses (only the richer farmers as yet used horses), 83 donkeys, 684 *bovines* (which includes both milk-cows and the oxen that were still the usual plough animals), 3,498 sheep, 371 pigs, 514 goats, and '2,760 assorted poultry'. An 'approximate number' of 160 dogs was noted, roughly one dog for two out of every three households. The no doubt equally numerous cat population is not recorded, but their hundredth-generation direct descendants are there to this day. Tiny, from centuries of strenuous hunting and minimal feeding, they are still begging at the same doorsteps, insinuating themselves through the same slots in barn doors, stalking the same field paths. Their brindled coats are a race memory of the infinitely more distant wild ancestors of the forests, from which they are descended.

It was in these years after the establishment of the Third Republic that many of the village houses were either rebuilt or substantially improved. Floor tiles were laid over the bare soil of France, glass appeared in the window-spaces, the ox and the ass were moved to a separate stable. The first roofs of slate, imported by rail from other parts of France, began to appear, a source of pride to the occupants and a sign of their social aspirations. (In the late twenti-eth century slates are frowned upon, and officially banned as inap-propriate to the area.) Here and there proper bedrooms with dormer windows replaced the old lofts, just as carved wooden beds with mattresses replaced straw palliasses infested with minute animal life. The chamber-pot appeared, and also the earth closet as a standard arrangement. (This remained the norm in Chassignolles for the next hundred years.) In earlier days, many houses in the village and even in La Châtre had no *commodités* whatsoever. Women used a bucket and made a daily trip to a discreet hedgerow or thicket; the men of the house, less concerned with privacy, sociably availed themselves of the backyard manure heap.

Among the new or rebuilt houses of the 1870s were ours, Mademoiselle Guyot's, and the substantial farm on the outskirts of the village that the Pissavy connection turned into a country seat. Happily, all three houses escaped the vogue for slate and are roofed to this day with the red-brown tiles that are made in the region. In the case of our dwelling (long known as the Pope's House, because the original owner looked like the Holy Father of the period) the availability of old materials probably played a part. But Mademoiselle Guyot's house was raised on a field site that had previously contained only a cow-byre and a flax store belonging to the indigenous Charbonnier family. Given the status of the Guyots (the father was a lawyer in La Châtre) it must have been a conscious decision to build something that would look like a nicely converted Berrichon farm rather than the kind of alien villa that was by then beginning to spot the face of rural France. The result is a house that, externally, reminds one almost more of the country-cottage dream that was developing then across the Channel: it has dormer windows, Virginia creeper and rose-beds on the lawn. The interior, however, is resolutely French, with four undifferentiated rooms and a spacious kitchen all opening in a democratic way out of a tiled hall. It is still lived in by a member of the family, and is a repository of the bourgeois comforts and elegances of former days: crucifixes above high wooden beds, brass-bottomed pans, miniature colanders for making *tisanes* in china bowls, a coded royalist silhouette of Louis XVI and his queen disguised as an urn and a willow . . .

The Domaine had an even more fortunate escape. With its landscaped park (more English influence) and its agricultural functions removed to a home farm with a tenant farmer, it might well have been rebuilt as one of those nineteenth-century mock-*châteaux* whose vertiginous pitched roofs and turrets suggest indefinable nightmares, Victorian dreams for sale that almost no one in the late twentieth century wishes to buy. However, the two principal buildings of the old farm were merely enlarged into something grander but still local in style. This transformation was underway after the harvest in the late summer of 1870: it is recounted by present-day members of the family that the men raising the roof-tree to accommodate a new upper floor said: 'Don't ask us to go too high, M'sieur Victor – the Prussians might see us!' The Prussians were then on the Loire, a long way to see even with the clearest of eyes, but uncomfortably near for Berrichons who had known no invader since the British were seen off in the fourteenth century.

How had Victor Pissavy, the son of the Auvergnat cloth merchant and one-time master of pedlars, transformed himself into a country squire? To explain this requires a brief backward excursion through the generations.

In 1864, the year before Célestine Chaumette had her own son, a first and only son was born to another local girl. Marie-Rachel Yvernault was the daughter of the ironmaster at Crozon, Louis Yvernault, born the same year as Silvain-Germain though into a different social class. (He was no relation to the Yvernaults of Chassignolles who were to open the second inn. The name is common in the Black Valley: it is said to be derived from Roman legionaries wintering round La Châtre.) Louis and his twin brother ran between them the water-powered foundry at Cluis, where the local iron ore was extracted and smelted, and Louis owned the forges nearby at Crozon, where the smelt was heated again to incandescence and hammered into iron for industrial use. There was another family foundry and forge in the north of the Indre.

At Crozon a great embanked reservoir, a system of conduits and a lower pool had long been installed both to power the bellows for the forges and to cool the metal down again. Louis Yvernault put modern steam-driven hammers in place of the ones that had been wielded by muscle power on the site since the seventeenth century and probably much longer. Opposite the engine sheds of the forge he constructed a row of model workmen's cottages. He built for himself and his bride a four-square gentleman's residence a hundred yards off, with box hedges and a monkey-puzzle in the garden and (of course) a wrought-iron gate. This modern Master's house superseded the seventeenth-century one right on the forge yard which, in its turn, had superseded an adjoining fifteenth-century one with finely carved stone doorways and window arches. A weather-worn coat of arms and a lookout tower on an earthworks behind hints at an earlier, feudal occupation, perhaps of very ancient date. The iron trade must always have been closely associated with power and conflicts, since weapons were forged for many centuries before the ordinary ploughshare was made of metal.

Like the many other forges in the area, the Crozon ones became busier than ever before as France's industries developed and the demand for iron grew. In 1840 thirty thousand tons of iron were produced in the Berry alone. According to a respectful history written in the twentieth century for circulation among Louis Yvernault's descendants, the foundry and forges between them employed three hundred men, including the woodcutters and charcoal-burners who supplied the furnaces round the clock. At night the sky was lit with a pink glow for miles around, and the woods echoed with the clang and thump of metal and the hiss of steam.

The authorized history is careful, however, to mitigate this picture of crude, entrepreneurial force with instances of Louis' modern enlightenment and piety (the latter being equally modern *circa* 1840). He provided work for the unemployed and urged those employed on the land in the direction of crop rotation and chemical fertilizers. He built a school for the Commune staffed by nuns and also endowed a new church and cemetery. He was, of course, nominated mayor.

Although Marie-Rachel spent her childhood in the new house within the sight and sound of her father's modern machinery, Crozon was essentially as it had always been: a self-contained world with its own wagon routes and charcoal-burners' paths, its own dynasties of workmen, remote from civilization amid its pools and the Spanish-chestnut forests on which it fed. There was not even a proper road there from La Châtre, and at night wolves could be heard howling close at hand. Family lore, less reverential than the official account, has it that Marie-Rachel's mother, Louis Yvernault's bride, whom he married in 1836, did not want to live in this savage place, and that she was only induced to marry by family pressure. They were both very young and they were first cousins; in addition, their own parents had been first cousins, but since Louis was an orphan by then and in charge of his inheritance one must suppose that this claustrophobic arrangement fitted in with his own ideas of what was appropriate and desirable. Unions of this kind were common at the time, such was the bourgeois preoccupation with keeping accumulated family wealth from being dissipated.

Taking a further step back in time, where several different strands in the web of history unexpectedly meet, it is worth recording that the formidable Yvernault brothers had inherited not only all their father's extensive property, much of it in land in various adjacent Communes, including Chassignolles, but their Uncle Charles's share also. This black-sheep uncle had got deeply into debt in Paris as a young man, where he had lived dangerously in the world of Revolutionary intellectual ferment and its aftermath of outrageous, febrile fashions for red neck cords, see-through muslin and assumed speech defects. As the price of rescue from his financial predicament, and perhaps as a punishment for harbouring Advanced Ideas, he had had to surrender his patrimony to his white-sheep brother (Louis' father). 'But what am I to live on now?' he asked as he signed away his income.

The story runs that the brother replied: 'Bah, I'm allowing you to keep our little mill over at Angibault. You can go and be the miller there.'

'Me – a miller? But – '

'What alternative have you?' asked his brother rudely. There was no alternative. Black-sheep Charles betook himself to isolated Angibault, where, dressed 'like a half-bourgeois', he resignedly directed the operation of the mill's great water-wheel and sluices: a far cry from the Café Procope and the Seine. The young George Sand, who met him when he had been there a good many years, wrote of him in her preface as 'a gentleman of a certain age who, since he had associated in Paris with *Monsieur de Robespierre* (thus he always referred to him) decided to let nature have its way round his mill locks and streams: the alder, the briar, the oak and the guelder rose grew there in profusion.'

In her novel, George Sand transformed this melancholy, dispossessed nature lover (who sounds more like a disciple of Rousseau than of Robespierre) into one of nature's socialists, a young and high-minded working miller, the *beau farinier* of Angibault who defeats low cunning and triumphs in a pure love. Purity was not particularly evident in Charles Yvernault's life, but perhaps the generally democratic image was further enhanced by the presence in the mill of a young unmarried peasant housekeeper who, over the course of years, became the mother of five children.

So, at any rate, runs the alternative or word-of-mouth family history. The memory of hushed-up scandal still carried enough of a charge in the 1920s, a hundred years later, for it to be omitted by the pious chronicler of the received version; he is silent, in any case, on the whole George Sand connection, since the family traditionally disapproved of everything the writer represented, politically and socially. The chronicler's widow, one of Marie-Rachel's granddaughters and the teacher of catechism to the village children, was particularly firm in this view. In old age she burnt packages of George Sand's letters to another member of the family which had come to rest in her Chassignolles attic. Their potential value, both literary and financial, was considerable even then and would today have been enormous.

According to one of the letter-burner's descendants, the peasant family who tenanted and worked the mill at Angibault for several generations were well known in the area to be related to the grand family of Chassignolles, though neither side ever mentioned the fact. He himself inherited the mill when young as his part of the family goods, and once said genially to the miller in the course of a conversation about funds for repairs: 'After all, Monsieur, we are cousins, aren't we?' The elderly man gave him an anxious sideways look. 'Well, yes, M'sieur Jacques . . . but low be it spoken.' And moved on at once to other matters.

When I plucked up courage to visit old Madame L, Marie-Rachel's last surviving granddaughter, in the Domaine at Chassignolles, she received me kindly in a décor of tapestry-seated chairs and family portraits. She said nothing of the black-sheep Charles or of certain other things. But she discoursed on Marie-Rachel and showed me a cabinet photograph of this girl, who seemed to have become something of a family icon: a pretty but strained little face between the lank, centre-parted hair and the bunchy dress of the period.

Marie-Rachel, who was born to the ironmaster and his wife in 1841, was the fourth daughter to arrive since their marriage five years before and the only one to survive infancy. The unfortunate mother was consoled by her husband with the thought that 'When we lose them all we should really rejoice, since they go to swell the heavenly choirs with more voices to praise the Lord.' This, however, was no longer a time when babies in the French countryside died off wholesale; the received version of the history goes into no details, but one may surmise that the marriages between cousins over two generations had resulted in an accumulation of recessive genes, leading to weak or malformed babies. Another pair of Yvernault cousins, though more distant ones, also married at that period, had a daughter who, while she lived a long life, was described in the census of 1861 as *boiteuse*, 'lame' – an admission that, in a genteel family, may indicate rather more than just a club-foot.

Marie-Rachel, however, was 'a beautiful, healthy child' who grew up in isolated Crozon as the sole focus of her parents' tender care. It seems they had decided to have no more. Everything was to be for this daughter. Long afterwards her mother, by then the sole survivor of the trio, wrote of her 'life so pure, so hard-working, so pious, so charitable, so gentle, so gracious . . . She was gifted, from her earliest years, with a tenderness which I never found wanting, she loved to give, it was one of her joys. She also possessed, from earliest youth, a sense of orderliness . . . She never left anything half done . . .'

To this holy picture of a girl too good for this world, the bereaved mother did, however, add one transforming detail: Marie-Rachel was once, as a small child, found praying in her room at an unexpected time of day, and said when questioned that she was asking the Mother of God to lower the price of wheat. Since the grain riots (see page 90) occurred when Marie-Rachel was six, this anecdote has an authentic feel.

It was customary for girls of good family, whom their parents hoped to marry well, to be sent away in their teens to board at convent schools. There, it was hoped, they would accumulate enough docility and expectation to co-operate in a suitable marriage, and also shed the country accents they might have picked up from peasant nursemaids or little local playmates. Louis Yvernault and his wife accompanied Marie-Rachel to distant Paris by the convenient new railway line from Châteauroux and established her with the well-born Sisters of Sainte Clothilde in the Faubourg St Antoine. According to the brochure of this establishment: 'Nothing is neglected that may embellish their personalities. While following current developments in the education of the female sex, the school aims above all to conserve their simplicity of heart. In brief, the wish of the Ladies is to see their pupils combine firm principles with amiability and gentleness, and learning with a modest reserve.'

One cannot help thinking that life held more promise for the daughter of a local innkeeper.

The Yvernaults made regular trips to Paris to visit their daughter, and brought her home once a year for a summer holiday. In 1857, when she was rising sixteen, dysentery was widespread in the Berry. According to the chronicler:

> Louis Yvernault, with his usual kindness, visited the sick to bring them moral comfort and material assistance as necessary. In the midst of this, he had to leave for Paris with his wife to fetch their daughter ... carrying the disease unbeknown with him. He became ill, and on arrival at their hotel in Paris had to take to his bed. He died on 27 August, after several days of acute suffering.

Madame L of today, partisan for her own countryside, claimed that it wasn't a local germ that killed great-grandfather but cholera picked up in Paris itself, that known centre of sickness physical and spiritual. Whatever the truth, one feels a pang for this usually masterful and energetic man of barely forty, dying of terrible diarrhoea in a hot rented room full of Second Empire draperies, with only hotel servants to wait on him and his distraught and genteel womenfolk. Marie-Rachel herself subsequently wrote an account of the whole event: 'not a complaint nor a regret ever passed his lips ... "Have confidence in God," he exhorted us, "He is so Good!"' When it became apparent that God was going to let His faithful servant down on this occasion, Louis changed his reflection to 'Don't be so distressed. What is this life compared with Eternity?' All three of them seem to have had the absolute and concrete conviction that they would be reunited in a better world, together with the first three baby girls who had preceded them and would be waiting there – possibly transformed like their sister into perfect *jeunes filles*. No wonder the Catholic Church in France at this period rather discouraged second marriages: the practical problems posed in Eternity by such temporal readjustments would hardly have been manageable.

Louis Yvernault returned to Châteauroux as he had come, but in his coffin. The train arrived at four in the morning and it took a horse-drawn cortège another six hours to negotiate the valley of the Indre and reach Crozon. There, the entire workforce of the forges was lining the route to see the Master laid away in his own new cemetery.

Marie-Rachel settled once again into being her mother's constant companion: 'My darling girl kept away from all dangers. She never read a novel, preferring serious works; she would take my advice and have me read aloud to her while she sewed . . .' In fact *so* serious was this paragon (as one can believe from her photograph) that the family doctor had to suggest little excursions, a change of air from time to time for her health's sake.

The received story is that, in spite of all this, Marie-Rachel fell in love, making her own choice rather than leaving it to her mother but exercising that choice 'keeping in view Faith, wisdom and reason'. Her intended was Victor Pissavy, one of the four sons of the energetic Guillaume Pissavy who had left the Auvergne to establish his cloth-peddling business in the Berry. All four boys had been educated as gentlemen at various religious boarding establishments, but when Victor met Marie-Rachel he was back in La Châtre working in his father's warehouse. By one of those coincidences which are of no particular significance but please by their neatness, this warehouse was the same rambling old building that the young Robins were to take on as an inn eight or nine years later.

According to the chronicler, Victor Pissavy was 'an attractive young man, slim, physically supple, dressed in the style of the time in either a jacket or a cutaway which particularly suited his height. He wore a high, stiff collar, a waistcoat and cravat of the same shade, spats, and always had an elegant gold-knobbed cane in his hand.' The perfect dandy. The embodiment of the new middle-class commercial *chic*. One wonders if Marie-Rachel's dead father the ironmaster would have entirely approved?

There is a hint that his widow did not. The official version, from her own pen, is that she and Marie-Rachel went to Paris to ask the advice of the girl's erstwhile confessor at Sainte Clothilde and that the hopeful Victor accompanied them on this expedition. There seems to be something wrong with this story: suppose the confessor had been disapproving, would it not then have become quite improper for Victor to be in Marie-Rachel's company at all, even with her mother present?

Madame L, speaking some hundred and thirty years later in the pretty drawing-room of the property in Chassignolles which Marie-

Rachel brought to Victor as part of her dowry, assured me that the marriage had indeed been 'a love match' but said that the young man had at first asked for her hand 'incorrectly' (a term that would suggest he simply failed to ask Madame Yvernault's permission before proposing) and that the Paris confessor had been called in to arbitrate and soothe everyone.

Their great-grandson, my main source for the alternative family history, had a different version again. According to him, the Yvernault family did not consider a son of the *nouveaux riches* Pissavys a good enough match for the daughter and sole inheritor of Louis. The Master of pedlars had transformed himself into a wholesale draper, but sheets, even wholesale, were much less socially acceptable than iron, selling was inferior to manufacturing – and then there was the matter of the family's relations with That Woman at Nohant. Victor's doctor brother, Édouard, was known to be on cordial dining terms with George Sand. Whether or not the whisper had reached Madame Yvernault at that time that Édouard Pissavy was also the lover of George Sand's daughter Solange, I do not know, but certainly this was a contributory factor to the indignant burning of George Sand's letters in Chassignolles two generations later.

As if to confirm the family's worst suspicions about the Pissavys, Victor (I am told) schemed with Marie-Rachel to stage an elopement. Perhaps there was indeed more courage, passion and guile than appears in the repressed little face in the photograph or in her mother's account, for however seductive Victor was he could hardly have brought off his plan without Marie-Rachel's active participation. Maybe she had managed to read a romantic novel or two on the quiet without her mother's knowledge. She had probably met Victor through her La Châtre cousins, the Guyots, for it was with the connivance of one of their servants that she managed a meeting with him in the town one night. The young couple went off together, not to reappear in their respective homes till the next day. 'And after that, of course,' said their great-grandson gleefully, 'they had to let the boy marry her. There was nothing else for it.'

Perhaps this was what was really covered by Madame L under the heading 'incorrect behaviour'?

Nothing of this surfaces in the official version, where there is no hint that Victor Pissavy was ever on anything but excellent terms with his wife's mother – as indeed he had to be. In 1864, after two and a half years of marriage, Marie-Rachel gave birth to their son, another Louis. She died shortly afterwards of what the chronicler calls 'a crisis of albumen', and which we would recognize today as the consequences of untreated toxaemia of pregnancy. For reasons both human and financial, the bereaved young husband and the doubly bereaved mother-in-law could only make common cause over the upbringing of another cherished only child.

At the time of Victor's marriage the family firm in La Châtre was tactfully wound up, having served its commercial purpose in launching Guillaume Pissavy's sons into professions such as medicine, banking and the law. Victor too, once married, embarked on law studies, which in his case were intended rather to embellish his future life as a gentleman of leisure: the young couple made their plans to remodel the big farm in Chassignolles as their country residence. When Marie-Rachel died, Madame Yvernault moved there to take charge of little Louis. He was thus brought up an Yvernault as much as a Pissavy, and eventually added his grandmother's name to his own.

The received version is that Marie-Rachel's death so affected Victor that he never remarried. The fact was that this handsome widower of barely thirty could hardly take a new wife without compromising his inheritance from Marie-Rachel, including the property in Chassignolles, to all of which he was entitled solely as trustee for his son. He was an intelligent and forceful man, and the role of local squire in a time of evolving rural prosperity was far too attractive to abandon: had he not in any case sacrificed a continuing lucrative career in trade to take on this role? He made sure, however, that he retained certain business interests in La Châtre which required his presence there, sometimes overnight. Later, when young Louis was sent to school with the Jesuits in Poitiers, and Grandmother Yvernault accompanied him there to ensure that his delicate health was properly monitored, Victor was able to revert to a more bachelor life and spent most of each winter in La Châtre.

In a wood of oak, ash and larch that forms part of the Chassignolles Domaine's extensive property, a small iron Virgin with a Child in her arms stands on a stone plinth in the recess formed by three tall trees. She is a typical statuette of the second half of the nineteenth century; her pretty, impassive face is commonplace, but her lonely situation invests her with a certain austere power. I have visited her in all seasons: in summer when the woods are green and gold and alive with woodpeckers; on a day in deep winter when the hoar-frost on a spider's web made a breathtaking lace veil against her iron cheek; and again in very early spring when the whole bare wood above the carpet of dead leaves was suffused with a blue, expectant light. For a long time I assumed that her presence was due to some half-pagan cult in this wood that a late-nineteenth-century Curé had Christianized with a new, respectable figure. Madame L, however, believed that the Virgin and Child had been placed there in the 1860s as a memorial to Marie-Rachel.

But, if so, why does the plinth bear no inscription?

Georges Bernardet – who will re-enter this chronicle as it nears his own birth date and the family from which he sprang begins to appear in the Minute books – told a different story and one whose specificity carries a ring of truth. The statue had, he believed, been put there in memory of a boy who was in some way connected with the Domaine. This child had been climbing a tree in the wood after a magpie's nest, had fallen and broken his neck. 'Not a child of the family, no. I think the Monsieur Pissavy of the time was his guardian, or somesuch.'

'Which Monsieur Pissavy? Monsieur Victor or Monsieur Louis?'

'Ah, I couldn't say that. My grandfather, he could have told you.'

Another entire, intricate story, irrecoverable now as last year's dog roses.

But meanwhile what of the forges of Crozon?

After Louis Yvernault's abrupt death in Paris, they were directed for several years by his twin brother with the help of a resident manager. But at that time the local iron trade, which had flourished so in the new industrial area, suddenly began to fail, victim of the very same forces of evolution and change. Just as the new roads that had been a boon to pedlars ended up making them unnecessary, so the proliferating railway lines, which demanded iron for their own construction and carried it to all parts of France, began to bring in iron from elsewhere in competition. Cheap imports from neighbouring countries undercut the product of central France, even though overproduction had already driven down the domestic price. In addition, veins of ore were being worked out and the forests themselves were being cut for charcoal at an uneconomic rate. In any case charcoal-firing was out of date and had elsewhere been abandoned. On the Loire, Henri Martin's coke- and coal-fired forges were turning out a new, superior material – tempered steel. All over the Berry by the 1860s small, undercapi- talized forges, which had been working for hundreds of years but could not afford to convert their machinery to use coke, were going bankrupt. As a contemporary wrote: 'The workshops are shut, the paths are abandoned, the buildings crumble, the teams of workmen are disbanded and the woods grow thick once more . . . Silence is re-establishing itself in the forests and the villages of the Berry.'

The Yvernault family, or at any rate the Crozon branch of it, saw what was coming and got out just in time. In the same year, 1861, that Victor Pissavy abandoned the cloth business to marry Marie- Rachel, her family were liquidating their own interests and placing the money in land. The forges of Crozon were sold (I was rather surprised to discover) to the Parisian engineer with the Creole wife, who already owned the quarries. Perhaps it was an asset- stripping exercise; at any rate even he could not make them profit- able, and in 1868 the furnaces were at last allowed to go out. The night skies were dark now above Crozon. Weeds and water birds colonized the great pools.

The forge still bears that name today and the various buildings stand, not so much ruined as fossilized by time, by more than a century of summers and winters and the endless altered people that have come and gone. The house with the monkey-puzzle is tidy but shuttered; nettles grow in the kitchens of the workmen's model cottages under the broken slate roofs. Straw, sacks, barrels, discarded harrows, a rusty Deux Chevaux and an antique tractor occupy the echoing works. In the yards where the conduits ran and heavy trucks were pushed around on Louis Yvernault's modern rails, chickens and geese wander. The fine seventeenth- century house is smothered in flowering creeper, its hand-wrought roof shingles perilously sagging. It is occupied, more or less, by an elderly couple engaged – more or less – in subsistence farming. The fifteenth-century house next door gapes roofless to the sky, a shelter for rabbit hutches; while the medieval lookout tower on the mound, from which the forge foreman used at one time to observe his workforce in the yard below, has become a territory for goats.

Thanks to the mining engineer, Marie-Rachel's inheritance was secure, but another branch of the family was not so lucky. The foundry in Châtillon, on the far side of the Department, was not sold in good time: in 1866 it was advertised fruitlessly for weeks in the *Écho de l'Indre*. The business went down with many debts, a burden that was to haunt the younger generation for the rest of their lives. A retreat into formal bankruptcy would have been a relief but this they refused, either to avoid the shame or from a highly developed sense of honour toward their creditors. One daughter escaped into marriage, one son emigrated to Minnesota, where he apparently prospered. The official chronicler remarks regretfully: 'He was on the point of coming back to France in 1890 when he died, leaving no children, and his family in France who should [*sic*] have inherited were unable to recover a penny.'

The other son became a railway clerk with the Paris–Orléans–Châteauroux line, till his mother died and he retired early to live in La Châtre with his sister – she who was 'lame'. Needless to say, neither of these incidental casualties of nineteenth-century progress ever married. They lived in a cramped little house in a row built on the site of the one-time town moat, valiantly practising what have been described to me as 'sordid economies'. The phrase implies worn, shiny jackets, mended grey cotton stockings, casseroles of horse-meat, heart and lights, bread always a day old so that they were not tempted to eat too heartily of it . . . One lamp, never lit till dark had fully come, winter nights made interminable by early bedtimes that saved on wood for the stove . . . All the entrenched tradition of old-style French penny-pinching frugality that still today, like a necessary shadow, accompanies that other French tradition of abundance, quality and *douceur de vivre*.

It was not simply that they were poor relations, though they were. Their aim was to pay back in the end all the money owed since the 1860s failure. They saved and saved, doggedly converting their accumulated *sous* into gold. For the whole of the nineteenth century and even after, the value of gold was unaltered in monetary terms: 290.32 milligrams equalled one French franc, as if the franc was a fixed measure like the metre or the litre. It did not occur to most people that it could be otherwise, certainly not to this pair. The years went by, life changed around them, the Great War came and the right to exchange money for gold was suspended as a 'temporary', emergency measure. Four years later when the war ended the emergency did not. The cost of living inflated; the brother and sister's resolution remained fixed. At last, one day in 1923, they achieved their goal: every debt was honourably repaid.

A few weeks later France finally abandoned the gold standard, with a substantial devaluation. This meant that the gold with which they had paid their creditors would, if they had only delayed, have been worth far more. It also meant that the annuity they had bought to live on, by selling their one remaining piece of land, was reduced to paper francs, each worth only about a quarter of the precious gold francs that had been used to purchase it.

Two years later they both died, within a few days of each other.

By chance, Célestine Chaumette (who was born the same year as the crippled Mlle Yvernault) was also living then in La Châtre, in two rooms in an old house not far off. She was alone.

There are lives that descend into silent tragedies that, piecemeal and partially hidden, never warrant statuettes or memorial histories, which have no place of honour in family lore, but whose inaccessible pain tugs wordlessly at the heart.

Chapter 13

In 1871, following the establishment of the new Republic, Victor
Pissavy became the mayor of Chassignolles and remained so for
thirty years. He was no Republican; as the family chronicler cir-
cumspectly put it, 'his preferences were conservative and imperial-
ist', but evidently both he and the village felt that for him to be
mayor was befitting. No doubt his dead wife would have thought
so too, for from then on he modelled himself on her father, of
blessed memory, who had ruled his own Commune some twenty
years earlier with a degree of benevolent despotism: *bourgeoisie
oblige*.

Like Louis Yvernault in Crozon, one of Victor's first acts as
mayor was to offer the Commune a religiously-run school – this
time a girls' school, the one that was to be organized in her own
new house by Mademoiselle Guyot. It was a common pattern in
the countryside at this stage: the boys' schooling was coming to
be seen as the financial and social responsibility of the Commune,
while the girls could attend only an establishment run by private
charity. It may seem enlightened of Monsieur Pissavy and Mademoiselle Guyot to want the girls to be educated too, but such
initiatives began to run into trouble in the next decade when, under
Jules Ferry, the principle was established of secular State education
for all – *'gratuite, obligatoire et laïque'*, in the ringing phrase of the

time: dedicated anti-traditionalism creating its own tradition, its own glory.

Indeed, by the 1890s, the conflict in France between Church and State was reaching its final spasm before the Church finally retreated to its own separate high ground, taking refuge in the moral and social clout it wielded. In Chassignolles, this national contest found local expression in fervent proposals for the building of a new, non-religious girls' school on the same lines as the boys'. It therefore seems no coincidence that at this time Victor Pissavy was replaced as mayor. A letter of the period to the Préfet from the new mayor, a villager called Appé, spoke of *'la population républicaine et clairvoyante de Chassignolles'* ('the Republican and far-sighted members of the community') being at loggerheads with 'the reactionary population' who, he alleged, were campaigning in a way that showed bad faith and disloyalty towards their erstwhile fellow-councillors. It is not hard to see where the nexus of this reactionary feeling was supposed to lie.

The chronicler of the Pissavy family remains silent on this row.

The neighbouring Commune of St Denis de Jouhet, where Victor Pissavy possessed a farm, suggested that he might like to come and be their mayor instead, but he had the grace to decline their offer. He was then in any case in his mid-sixties, though he was to live on at the Domaine, a powerful figure, into his eighties. He is still remembered as having 'done a lot' for Chassignolles, though the oldest inhabitants did remark to me that he was very careful with his own money – the family characteristic, no doubt, which had made the Pissavys astute tradesmen. After the school affair the mantle of benevolence was assumed by his son Louis. He was gentler in manner than his father and less physically robust; I have been told by one person that he was 'a bit of a soft touch' and by another that he 'really loved country people, understood them and knew how to talk to them spontaneously without hurrying them'. He had, of course, been reared by his grandmother, whom he is said to have 'adored' and whose own memories went back to simpler, less class-conscious days.

Let us return, for the moment, to the 1860s. Once the Guyot girls' school project had been agreed, the cause of enlightenment plus piety found its next object in the cemetery question. The time-honoured practice of inserting the dead into the open land around the church, which was not even a defined churchyard in the English style, was causing unease. Old bones surfaced every time a new grave was dug. 'It has become impossible,' Victor Pissavy pointed out, 'to continue burials there without complete prejudice both to respect for the dead and to public hygiene.'

As in other villages all over France, proposals for a separate cemetery had already been made from time to time, but had foundered on expense and on the vague feeling that the land round the church was the proper place. It was customary to stop for a brief communication with the dead on one's way to or from Mass; with them lying hygienically in a separate plot behind a wall it wouldn't be the same. As early as 1810 there had been discussion about extending the burying ground by the church over some vegetable gardens and a ditch – the remains, I think, of the monks' moat and fish pool. This plan was never carried out, though the approximate site today has come into the possession of the dead by a different route: it is where the war memorial has stood since 1921 in its own railed garden.

In the 1830s there was further discussion: a piece of land several hundred yards off was acquired by the Commune and appears hopefully marked as 'cemetery' on the 1843 map. However, no burials took place there – no one wanted to be the first – and eventually the site was swallowed up by a road division to avoid a steep slope on the way out of the village towards Crozon.

In 1871 the Council reluctantly agreed with Monsieur Victor that the churchyard would no longer do and voted one thousand francs for a new ground. (At the same meeting they neatly decided that, in this case, they could not afford to contribute any more money to the long-delayed completion of the Crozon road.) Eighteen months later land was finally purchased on the western edge of the village, on a small escarpment with a pleasant view. This already, however, took up over half the thousand francs allocated. Thereafter the progress or lack of it in the laying out of the cemetery, the need for new ditches to drain it and the raising of the wall, is an intermittent item in the Minutes for years. By 1876 the Commune had to borrow to meet a projected cost nearly three times the original one, and 'extra expenses' continued to surface.

The cemetery belonged to the Commune rather than to the Church, which was another sign of the developing separation between Church and State; however, perhaps the drain it represented on resources created a general feeling that the more secular needs of the living should come first. As ever, tensions that were really about deep-seated priorities and attitudes to life expressed themselves as arguments about relatively small sums of money. The same year the Council refused a request from the village Curé for further funds to repair the presbytery. He had already had some in 1871; now he wrote to the Council pointing out that more had been promised him – that the Bishop in Bourges was 'astonished' that it had not been paid, that he had continued to show *délicatesse* and patience, but . . .

Even Victor Pissavy evidently thought this letter out of order, for it was judged to be 'in an improper tone, unworthy of priestly dignity' and it was unanimously decided that the request would not even be discussed. The Curé of that time was a stripling of twenty-eight, born in La Châtre, replacing Jeanne Aussourd's crony the old mass-server. He did not last long, but other Curés of the last quarter of the century were more successful at leaving their mark on the village in the form of crosses here and there, much encouraged by old Madame Yvernault.

Not till 1884 was the new cemetery finally completed, just in time for Anne Laurent, *veuve* Chaumette, to move into one of the first grave-plots. It is conveniently situated near the main gate, where the rings for tethering horses are still set into the wall.

Individually owned graves were in themselves a novelty to the ordinary people of rural France. This is clear from the discussion when the Council fixed the price of concessions – something that, as the Minutes cheerfully remark, would 'allow families to satisfy their feelings of pious respect while at the same time procuring an advantage to the Communal coffers'. In the past, when one generation succeeded another in the same space of earth, and the wooden crosses above ground decayed with the passing seasons as did what lay beneath, a true levelling in death had taken place. For a few years, a grave-mound might be known and recognized, but as time passed a democratic oblivion took over. As a Berrichon novelist (Raymonde Vincent) has recorded: 'Among the very old, an occasional person would still know who was buried where from way back, but most of these dead were effaced from the memory of men.' Only with the new cemetery, in Chassignolles as all over France, was the family tomb to become another piece of property, to be marked, fenced, tended and decorated accordingly.

Yet ironically, though the new Chassignolles cemetery inaugurated the era of permanent personal memorials, it hastened eradication of older markers in a way that caused suppressed resentment and grief. I know this from Denise Bonnin, who was born Denise Apère or Apaire (even in the twentieth century the family had not quite decided how to spell its name) in a very old, one-storey farmhouse where she is still living ninety-odd years later. I have, cumulatively, spent many hours with Madame Bonnin, while waiting with my milk can for the cows to come home. Deaf, heavy, lame and a little resentful of age but perfectly sensible, she has always been ready to talk about her family. One summer evening, when light streaked the sky long past ten by the double-summertime clock that 'the cows don't understand' and the milk had still not been brought in by her harvesting son and grandson, she told me: 'My father would never drive his cart through that narrow place by the church – there, where the café on the corner of the square used to be.' (She meant the Café Chauvet, the one-time Chaumette inn.)

'. . . Why? Why, because he knew his mother was buried somewhere down there. That's what he said anyway. And he didn't want to drive over her bones.'

Denise Bonnin did not locate this fact in any chronological framework. The time before the cemetery existed was just the mythical Olden Days, static as a tapestry, as in Georges Bernadet's view of the monks, the hawks and the hounds. But she vouchsafed the fact that she had been the youngest child, with both her parents turned forty when she was born.

What she did not know was that her father, Jean Apaire, carpenter, usually known as Jean Beaumont, had also been a late child. From the records in the Mairie, I established that he had been born in 1859 when *his* father, another Jean, was forty-nine and his mother was forty-two – elderly parents for that or any other era. His mother was a Geneviève Pirot – a sister, it turned out, of the luckless convict Antoine – and she died, aged fifty-three, in September 1870. Her youngest son was then two months short of his eleventh birthday, so he would indeed have seen his mother put into the old ground beside the church. Later, when still a young man, he saw this same ground levelled and then, as the village changed and prospered and carts and gigs multiplied, surfaced with gravel and subsumed into the roadway.

The formal confirmation of Grandma's story was received with wondering pleasure by the assembled Bonnin family: it might almost have been a tangible object. It was as if they had, till then, believed that the past was a private and fragile place of which they were helplessly inadequate custodians, and that, like them, it would pass away utterly. The further information that, according to the record, the mythical mother under the road by the church had died here in the farmhouse, and therefore no doubt in the large, dim, several-bedded chamber which is still a shared bedroom today, produced a thoughtful hush, a faint shiver. The Bonnins are probably the only family left in the Commune whose occupancy of the same house runs back in a straight line from child to parent into the era before the Revolution, and they are given to dynastic axioms ('In our family, we have never liked going upstairs'). None of them, even teenage Francis, can be unfamiliar with the face of death. A few years ago Grandpa, a survivor of the Great War and a renowned singer at the Third Age Club in the Mairie, went to join his fathers: he lay in state in the farmhouse while all the neighbourhood trooped in to visit him. Yet evidently the thought of all the earlier births and deaths that must have taken place within the walls of their home, crowding it with the noiseless ghosts of people with hair and gestures and voices akin to their own, struck them now with unaccustomed force.

To pin down the past before it escaped again into myth, Georgette Bonnin (in her sixties, and the current family linchpin) fetched a pencil and took a piece of paper off the back of the kitchen calendar. With some discussion about spelling (one 's' in *naissance* or two?), the facts I had garnered were recorded. The paper was then put back in the table drawer where there also turned out to be Jean Apaire's military papers, lying there as peacefully as when they were stowed away on his death sixty years ago, along with a few of his ironmongery bills for nails and screws. 'He was called up for military service, see, like everyone.' (This was true after 1873: one of the democratic reforms of the Third Republic was to abolish the lottery system.) 'But he never did more than a few weeks' reserve training, because both his parents were dead by the time he was twenty and he had to support his sisters. Also, he'd had an elder brother killed in the army.' Presumably in the Franco-Prussian war.

Over the course of time, I was to hear a good deal of this Jean Apaire. Poor in land, he sowed his first crop of wheat with a bushel gleaned – goodness knows with what labour – by his wife and sister from the stubble in other men's fields. But he was rich in skills. He specialized as a *scieur de long* – a long-sawyer, a trade for which the Berry was known. In the days before sawmills, it was the long-sawyers who reduced tree trunks to planks in the first place, and who were called in halfway through the construction of a house to cut the roof timbers to size once they had been installed. I heard how he used to walk all over the district to different jobs, sometimes many miles away, carrying his saw and its trestles on his back, at a time when the labourer's day lasted from sun-up to sun-down however long the hours. How he could 'turn his hand to anything and was always ready to do a favour for a neighbour'. How once Monsieur Victor himself, seeing him at work on the new girls' school, jovially gave him a hand with an awkward beam (considering what had passed concerning this school, this seems extra good-natured of Victor Pissavy) . . . How another time Monsieur Louis took a picture of him up repairing the church tower, small as a sparrow . . . How once he broke his leg, falling from a roof in La Châtre, and was laid up for a long time, his leg weighted with sandbags, and the doctor said he should go away to hospital in Paris, but instead he saw a local bone-setter and after that the leg healed although he was left lame.

'The bone-setter said that if he'd gone to Paris like the doctor wanted he'd have come back with a wooden leg,' concluded Madame Bonnin triumphantly. She has never been to Paris herself, though she did once go to Lourdes in the 1950s, when the Curé organized a trip there that included a whole, epoch-making night on the train each way. She has only once, in her entire life, been to Châteauroux, less than twenty-five miles away, and that was on a school trip when she was twelve, organized courtesy of the Domaine.

Jean Apaire is another of those vanished personalities, like Bernadet's grandfather, of whom it is recalled that he could neither read nor write 'but could calculate anything inside his head'. He must have been a man of determination and natural aptitude, for he taught himself what numbers meant by observing the kilometre posts on his long forced walks. It is remembered in the village that he once figured out, with the assistance of diagrams he drew in the white dust by the roadway, how to build a spiral staircase to fit into a corner in an old house that was being renovated. Since he was unable to consult any handbook, he must have had to work out the necessary geometry from first principles. 'And the foreman on the job, who was a stranger, was amazed that this little fellow in clogs knew so much!'

Jean Apaire's was the last generation in which it was possible to be untouched by the French national education system. After the early 1880s elementary schooling was free and, at least in theory, compulsory. There were also sporadic attempts to run classes in basic literacy for adults, and by the late 1890s the declining number of councillors 'declaring themselves unable to sign' was down to one.

Today, Jean Apaire seems to represent for his sixty-year-old grandson, and even for his great-grandson, who never knew him, an archetype of which they feel themselves to be inferior reproductions. Yet it seems to me that they and Georgette have tenaciously continued in their own lives the same strengths and multiple skills, the same unobtrusive complexities. Unlike Jeanne Pagnard, Suzanne Calvet or *la doyenne de la commune*, all of whom have, in relative terms, been elsewhere and seen the world, the Bonnins have no notion of presenting a story for its own sake, much less of being entertaining at someone else's expense. Their piecemeal account of days gone by falls limpid from their lips; they are at once interested in everything and surprised at nothing, but they have their own reticences. What more, I sometimes wonder, do they know about their close-knit family that they do not choose to tell me? I think of Jean's name, 'Beaumont', apparently from a hamlet in another Commune where he inherited some land. I think of Catherine, Jean's sister: twenty-two years older than him, never married, the mainstay of the family once the mother had gone into the earth beside the church, lived for the rest of her life in Jean's household. Something of a family pattern seems traceable here, that is still apparent today, as in a fabric, down the generations.

In the 1880s Chassignolles, along with many other villages, began to assume the physical aspect it retains today. An important element in this was the construction of that monument to homogeneous Republican ideals, the Mairie and School combined under one roof. The schoolhouse that had been built with such opposition from Vallet forty years before was sold and became a café. The councillors abandoned the upper room of the inn and acquired, for a population of around twelve hundred, a municipal building grand enough to service a considerably larger community, rearing up higher than the roofs of the barns, complete with a public clock. On the upper floor Auguste Charbonnier, still teacher, had a spacious apartment: indeed the Commune were so pleased with themselves that they at once petitioned the Préfet of the Indre for a grant for a junior teacher to assist him, on the pragmatic grounds that one could easily be accommodated now without getting in the Charbonnier family's way.

No building in Chassignolles, except perhaps the renovated Domaine, had ever been planned except by a group of men standing talking and measuring things with strides, but even in prospect the purpose-built Mairie-School was impressive to all. A loan was to be raised, and designs were drawn by an architect from La Châtre. However, the planning, like that of the first school, did not go entirely smoothly. With a bizarre symmetry, the spirit of Vallet manifested itself, this time in the person of his daughter, the improbably named Frauzine, she who married 'a gentleman called Choppy' considerably older than herself. By 1880 she was a rich widow who happened to own a sheepcote and pens in the village on a large site that was considered the only suitable one for the new construction.

But Madame Choppy did not want to sell. It was decided by the following year that if she was really so opposed to progress she deserved to be expropriated. By the summer of 1882 she was still refusing to 'bargain amiably' (*traiter à l'aimable*) about the price to be paid for her land, so the Council fixed it at 3,600 francs. Needless to say, in spite of huffing and puffing, they settled a few months later for 5,000. Needless to say also, after another year the building under construction turned out to cost more than the original budget. Nevertheless, level-pegging with the cemetery, it was opened on schedule in 1884. The future, long heralded, was at last beginning to arrive.

The whistle of the train was much nearer now. The station in La Châtre had been opened two years before, with a grand banquet, the local bagpipe band and a last-minute confrontation between the Mayor of La Châtre and his opposite number in the adjoining Commune, on whose territory the station had had to be built and who demanded recognition of the fact. Later the same year the first-ever chance came to see the sea, an unknown mystery to most of the landlocked inhabitants of central France. A special train was advertised, leaving La Châtre for Tours one Saturday in late August at 7.15 in the evening. It acquired other coaches further up the new line at Châtillon and at Loches, and joined up with a train at Tours that had come from elsewhere in the Loire valley. Then the whole procession steamed off towards the Atlantic coast, arriving at Les Sables d'Olonne (a name redolent of the new age of the excursion ticket) at 5.45 the next morning. There, after what one can only hope was an unforgettably golden day on the beach, and was certainly a long one, they returned to the railway coaches shortly before ten in the evening, and spent a second night sitting up crammed together on slatted wooden seats under swinging oil lamps, before at last reaching La Châtre just in time for work on Monday morning. If you wanted a seat with some padding in the second-class coach, that was five francs extra, but there was no first class – and no restaurant coach or *commodités*, in those days before corridor trains. The whole enterprise was designed as a popular one and billed as the experience of a lifetime. Participants were warned to bring only such baggage as they could keep beside them 'without annoying others'. Fashionable bathing wear would hardly have been in the wardrobes of La Châtre and its neighbourhood at that time, and I imagine the baggage consisted of capacious baskets of reassuring home food and drink to keep everyone going: *rillettes du Berry*, *pâtés de pommes de terre* and local *vin gris* that you could trust. Who knew if anything suitable would be obtainable in that strange land called the seaside?

Mass summer holidays were not to become general in France for another fifty years, and then hardly affected country dwellers. All the same, this post-harvest excursion seems a far cry already from the days when the Atlantic coast meant the intimidating port of La Rochelle, place of imprisonment in the hulks or near-definitive departure for the New World.

The following year, the Mairie of Chassignolles expended 22 francs – nine more than the cost of the excursion ticket – on acquiring for the first time a map of the Indre. No longer would the geography inside a man's head, the knowledge of how far he could walk in a morning or a day, suffice as a perception of distance.

Almost as soon as the Tours–Montluçon line was in place, more railway schemes were being suggested. This time, these were 'local interest' lines, branches designed to connect one market town with another and with their satellite villages, and they were proposed in bewildering quantity. It can be difficult now, when almost all these small lines have disappeared again from the maps, to determine which were built as fully-fledged lines with cuttings, embankments and country stations, which were more like suburban tramlines (*tortillards*), and which were never more than a hopeful pencil line across the map and a fervent endorsement from local councillors, who thought that a station was just what their village needed.

After 1890 every Commune hoped for its own railway, and Chassignolles was no exception. The two lines which seemed to offer the most likely prospect were the one running west from La Châtre to the old Roman town of Argenton, and a more problematic one that eventually made its way south from La Châtre to Guéret in the heart of the Creuse, where the foothills of the Massif Central begin. This line, which did not actually open till 1906, was proposed first in 1890: the intervening sixteen years were occupied by lengthy argued decisions as to which remote old villages – Crozon? Cluis? – should be transformed by its passage, since there was no single obvious route for it. At first it looked as if it might cross straight through Chassignolles. Even in 1900, by which time it had become clear that adjacent St Denis de Jouhet was going to be the favoured village, the Chassignolles council was still urging the logic of a station near at hand, between St Denis and La Châtre. The Croix Pendue crossroads was surely the natural place? Indeed Les Béjauds farm might make an excellent site for a station . . .

One can see the desired station, out of a standard railway pattern-book, rising effortlessly in village imagination above the trees, even as the new Mairie had in reality. If it had come, the prospects for Chassignolles might indeed have been greatly changed, but it was not fully appreciated in the village that railway lines, unlike roads, always take the flattest feasible route. La Châtre itself had had to settle for a station on level ground outside the original town. Many villages, such as Sarzay and Crozon, found themselves with an isolated station bearing their name but in practice too remote to be of much use. One such country halt in the Indre was *so* remote that it was derisively known as the Gare aux Loups –

Wolf Halt. Chassignolles, a little higher than any neighbouring village and always rather proud of the fact, never really stood a chance of a station on its doorstep.

In any case, the other proposed local line, from La Châtre to Argenton and then on to Poitiers, was by the 1890s assessed as 'nationally desirable', which meant it received finance from the appropriate ministry in Paris. It was already being built to cross the edge of the Commune, where Chassignolles' land ended at the old main highway, two and a half miles from the village itself. In 1901 Louis Pissavy-Yvernault was at some pains to explain to his fellow-councillors, who were still talking hopefully about a station at Les Béjauds, that the Guéret line must fit in with this Argenton one. With the two lines running parallel for several hundred yards near the main road, they could ask for a station there. No, it wouldn't actually be a Chassignolles station – but there were good paths in that direction; the inhabitants of the Commune would find it useful for deliveries of fertilizer (that abiding preoccupation) and for sending off their goods; they could also use the trains to go to markets and fairs north, south, east and west . . .

The numbers of these distractions had increased enormously in the last thirty years of the century, replacing the older, semi-pagan religious expeditions made on foot. Cheered by the thought of fairs, the Council reluctantly agreed to a station on the main road, but stipulated that it must be a proper station, with a platform and someone to accept parcels. Three years later, when the line was open, there were loud complaints because the earliest morning train coming from Argenton did not get into La Châtre till after ten in the morning – and whoever heard of arriving that late on market day?

In the end the Guéret line, when it did swing away from the Argenton one, still only cut across a far corner of Chassignolles' land – the Bois de Villemort. The Council, however, made sure that the railway company built them a special halt there too at a level crossing. The last wolf was driven out and civilization, in the form of a full-time crossing-keeper in his own house, had officially come. In practice, the miniature *château* of Villemort was the only other property near enough to the halt to derive much benefit from it. It was by then occupied by a family of tenant farmers called Gonnin, of whom we shall hear again.

The line was opened by the Minister of Public Works, travelling on the inaugural train, to be greeted at each new halt with flags, bunting and Sunday hats. On the territory of Chassignolles there assembled Mayor Appé, the Council, the two village teachers who had finally replaced old Charbonnier, a teacher's little daughter with a bouquet of roses, and almost the entire population of the Commune come to watch. A young pupil at the brand-new Chassignolles girls' school drew a careful picture in her exercise book called 'The Arrival of the Train at the Station'. The station – gable, clock, name-plaque and all – is easily recognizable; so is the curve of the line – but the engine itself has been much drawn and then rubbed out, as if its impressive size and sheer complexity were too much for the conscientious artist.

The branch lines also brought, for the first time, a trickle of urban visitors to see such historical, literary and artistic sights as the Berry could offer. Cultural tourism was, like seaside tripping, taking its first hesitant steps. The guide book was born, centred on railway timetables and on the station hotels with water-closets and gaslight that were superseding the old high-street inns as respectable places to stay. One informal guide, published in the first year of the new century, complained that neither of the two book shops in La Châtre had anything by George Sand. One of the assistants explained: 'You see, it's because everyone hereabout has read her books already' – which may, improbable as it sounds, have had some truth in it. The scandalous Republican, alias Bonne Dame de Nohant, dead these twenty-five years, had been sanitized into a Great Writer and therefore a text for generations of schoolchildren to copy in their best calligraphy.

The writer of the guide seemed surprised and put out to find La Châtre a quiet little town with a river still dirty from the remaining tanneries, but modern improvements pleased him no better. He took himself off to Nohant, which he similarly regarded as 'very small and ordinary' (perhaps he expected a Second Empire mock-*château*?) but added: 'However, Nohant today possesses a railway station, situated on the banks of the Indre near one of those mossy water-mills that George Sand so loved.' Warming to his then-and-now theme, he complained that quaint old beliefs were dying out, extinguished by the daily newspapers from Paris that the trains delivered. Another nearby market town (Neuvy St-Sépulchre, whose basilica church cultivates a drop of the Precious Blood) was actually lit by electric light! Cluis, where George Sand had gone to eat the vast, oozing, goat-cheese cakes for which the woodland forge-villages were famous, had coaches leaving in different directions for two main-line stations, and its own line was to open shortly. On another local train 'the people around me only stopped talking about farming to have a brief go at the Paris Exhibition and the war in China. No use here trying to turn the conversation to Great Beasts or werewolves!'

In fact la Grand' Bête, once such a reputed creature round La Châtre, was not quite extinct. Twelve years later, just before the First World War, it took to leaping out of bushes at dusk on country roads when young girls were passing, and making *des propos inconvenants*, as the French primly called indecent suggestions. It disappeared for good, however, when a well-equipped girl threw pepper in its masked face.

During the 1980s the line through the Bois de Villemort past Crozon in the direction of Guéret ceased to be used even for freight. Mare's tail and bracken fronds are growing between the sleepers, the rails are lifting. Soon saplings and scrub, gorse and briars, will reclaim the embankments and the cuttings, as they have been reclaiming the Argenton branch line since the end of the Second World War. The secret lanes to nowhere, losing themselves in bogs, that are the setting for George Sand's pre-railway country romances, have by the accident of time and chance been re-created. The keepers' cottages at the many obscure level crossings are shuttered or have been turned over to other uses. The station on the main road two and a half miles from the centre of Chassignolles still has its blue enamelled name-plaque and unmistakable railway clock, but it has been lived in for many years by an elderly carpenter and his family. In the 1970s he built us a fixed ladder inside our house, using local oak and rule-of-thumb methods that Jean Apaire would have recognized.

It is easy, now, to underestimate the important role the little lines played in opening up remote parts of the country. Their era was unnaturally brief. Arriving a generation later than the typical British branch line, they were overtaken, even in their first heyday, by the coming of the petrol engine. From the 1920s, the lorry, the country bus, the charabanc and finally the private car gradually began to replace the trains. Their life did not even span one human existence. Madame Caillaud, Chassignolles' oldest inhabitant, saw the first train arrive with the Minister of Public Works on board when she was a small girl at her parents' side: her hair had been curled specially for the occasion. Later, she and a boy would meet on June evenings in 1914 beside the track where it ran through the dark woods. Before she was an old woman, she saw the line fall silent again.

Chapter 14

In Chassignolles in the last decades of the nineteenth century and the first years of the twentieth, the Inn prospered. After Anne Laurent's death in the mid-1880s we find Célestine and Pierre in sole possession, along with their son Charles, now a young man. Pierre became a municipal councillor for a while. The name 'Hôtel Chaumette-Robin' was now displayed in large letters on the side wall of the whitewashed building. A big room with a wooden floor was built out towards the stables. It could accommodate a larger party than the old upper room reached from the outside stairway, but it was principally a place where dances were held, an improvement on the dusty old square.

There were two other well-established inns, one kept by the wife of Chausée, a smith, on the opposite side of the church, and the other by Ursin Yvernault, son of Jean. With the increased refinement of village life, at any rate among the craftsmen and shopkeepers, the inn was seen less as a drink shop for rural labourers and more as a respectable venue for business transactions. But while both Chausée and Yvernault were essentially vintners ('*vins en gros*') storing large quantities of wine and selling it by the barrel as well as by the glass, the Chaumette-Robin establishment was something more. It offered coffee, lemonade and 'kept a good table' in the back room that now served as a restaurant. It was genteel enough to attract visitors out on a Sunday drive in the pony cart or carriage on the now-gravelled roads. It had stabling at the rear, and was regarded as *the* inn to the south of La Châtre for miles around.

It is remembered that Célestine, now in middle life, set the tone of the establishment. If a customer showed signs of putting away a great deal of liquor, rather than encouraging him she would say softly to him so that his friends could not hear: 'Now, *mon fils*, haven't you had enough? . . . Why not think of going home? . . .'

'. . . Even though,' Madame Caillaud added meaningfully, 'this affected the inn's takings.'

Commerce was expanding. The census for the mid-1890s lists in the village in addition to the three inns, two grocers (one still the venerable ex-pedlar's), three blacksmiths, a baker, several clog-makers, a cobbler, two tailors, two dressmakers (one Mademoiselle Pagnard's grandmother employing two apprentices), one remaining weaver (the inevitable hard-up Chaumette cousin), two carpenter-cabinet makers, a wheelwright (Mademoiselle Pagnard's father) and sundry other specialized occupations such as plasterer, post-master and 'owner of the *alambic*'. This was a travelling still, which converted the skins and pips of each grape harvest into a fiery liquid known as *la goutte*. An elaborate blackened contraption of pipes and boiler, it is still to be seen today in November parked steaming ghostly on a grass verge in a quiet part of the village; though the band of people left with the right to make use of it is shrinking every year and no more are being given licences. A hundred years ago it was busy for six months of the year, for every self-respecting local family by then had their patch of vines for their own delectation. The phylloxera plague of the late 1870s was a blow, but it was not the financial disaster in the Berry that it was in areas where finer wine was grown to sell. In any case, in Chassignolles the energetic Victor Pissavy presently organized the Communal buying of a hardier, American strain of plant.

Meanwhile his mother-in-law Madame Yvernault, supported by Mademoiselle Guyot and the nuns of her school, were organizing a liberal distribution of wayside crosses. There was a Virgin now too by the cemetery, to keep an eye on a disused loop of old path that had become a favourite stroll for couples on summer evenings. The doctrine of the Immaculate Conception, and hence the cult of the Virgin, had received a boost since Her timely apparition at Lourdes and the development of that small Pyrenean town by the promoters of railway tourism. A shift had taken place since the days when a central character in *Le Meunier d'Angibault* had complained of the peasants' superstitious attachment to wayside shrines. Now, it was the well-to-do who went in for cults and symbols, and for the refurbishment of old chapels that were then opened with pomp by Monsignor from Bourges. Religion in France might be under secularist attack but, as in England, it was socially correct. The more prominent Chassignolles households such as the Graizons (Madame Caillaud's family), the Pagnards and the Robins, gravitated towards the Church as part of a lifestyle that included schooling at Mademoiselle Guyot's establishment and good relations with the Domaine. Yet, overall, unquestioning religious faith no longer held the place in life it once had.

Fear was in retreat. Many people were still poor – the applications to the Communal benevolent funds show this – but the very fact that the funds existed, encouraged since the 1880s by legislation, was an advance on the past. Prosperity is a relative concept, and the historian who takes a longer view of this period has to note that in the last part of the century France, compared with her European neighbours, was economically depressed – that the prices obtainable both for farm products and for manufactured goods suffered from outside competition. Nevertheless, the perception of the ordinary Frenchman, rich or poor, was that from about the middle of the century the standard of living had begun gently to rise. It continued to do so, with pauses but without major setbacks, far into the following century and indeed almost into the present day.

By the Third Republic, the world in which you could easily die of cold and hunger, in which starving vagrants roamed the countryside and any stranger or even neighbour might cast the evil eye on you, had passed into history. The brutalized peasantry, direct descendants of the feudal serfs, was largely replaced in popular tradition by the peasantry as the spiritual guardians of France, and now called *nos braves gens de la campagne*. The Wicked Lord had been replaced by the Pissavy-Yvernaults; the schoolmaster was mightier than the Curé, and the newspaper told you more than the Almanach had. Paraffin and acetylene lamps were chasing away the hobgoblins that had thrived in the dark beyond the rushlight's tiny spark. Drained swamps, covered wells, disinfectants and respectable earth closets down the garden were proving more effective against sickness than prayer had ever been. Fertilizers, imported seeds, mechanical reapers and steam-powered threshing machines were delivering the earth's bounty more reliably than religious processions for sun and rain. Even though such processions still continued sporadically in the Berry into the 1920s, there was no longer, by the 1890s, the same need to place desperate trust in the old saints of field and spring. And if magic spells were no longer expected to work in a literal and demonstrable way, then nor was prayer. It is a natural sequence to which no religious leader has ever found an entirely satisfactory solution. More than wolves were driven out by the trains.

There were other modern inventions that must have seemed more remarkable yet to Célestine's generation, who, in their own youth, had pioneered the written communication sent by post. Telegrams, at first brought on horseback from the office in La Châtre, had been known for some time. But in 1898 the telephone suddenly makes its futuristic appearance in the Minutes of municipal meetings. This was the work of Louis Pissavy-Yvernault, then in his thirties, and his friend and relation by marriage Paul Dutheil, a regular army officer, later to become a General. Dutheil's father was a lawyer and landowner and the family occupied the only other 'big house' in the neighbourhood. These young men were making Chassignolles an offer that, though generous, must surely come under the heading of enlightened self-interest. The telephone line had arrived in Châteauroux five years before and was shortly due to be installed in La Châtre. To extend it to Chassignolles would cost 100 francs a kilometre – 700 francs in all, which was reimbursable by the State. But the cost of an actual instrument and its installation would be 300 francs, and this sum was what Pissavy and Dutheil were offering. It was not a vast amount to them, for differentials were large, but it is instructive to see what it represented to the ordinary villager. At this period, the annual income of a smallholder or a farm-worker in central France often amounted to less than 600 francs a year – much of this sum notional in the case of the smallholder who consumed his own produce or bartered with his neighbour. Even such a respectable and sought-after job as rural postman paid only 800–1000 francs a year, depending on length of service. Wages were higher in the towns, but so was the cost of living.

In fact the telephone did not operate in La Châtre for several years more, and I do not know if the offer of a subsidy was promptly taken up in Chassignolles. But certainly ten years later a phone was in place in the Mairie and in the post office premises – also then owned, as it happened, by the Pissavy-Yvernaults. Night telephone calls from one Mairie to another, with urgent instructions to millers to open sluices, helped in 1911 to avert the worst consequences of a flood which rivalled that of 1845, the year after Célestine was born.

In 1904, Célestine turned sixty. Her generation might well have been excused for thinking that the half century just ended, their century, had seen such changes that little more need be anticipated. Modernity, the official goal of progress, had surely more or less arrived and the future could not now hold many more new inventions?

With the disadvantage of hindsight, one feels daunted on their behalf that the vast further technical developments of the twentieth century, with their attendant capacity for destruction and social dislocation, were only just beginning. But to the ordinary citizen in the early 1900s all technological development had so far seemed more or less benevolent; such dissident views as were expressed tended to be on the lines of 'what you gain on the roundabouts you lose on the swings'.

One theme continually surfaces and, after 1900, intensifies: the complaint about the drift to the towns and the threat of rural depopulation. It is true that, from about this time, the practice of the men going off only seasonally to labour in the cities was replaced by a more permanent exodus. Wives tended now to accompany their husbands and find work themselves as maids, shop assistants or concierges. The Guide to Central France quoted in the previous chapter spoke of the boys and girls of the Berry all going off to work in the factories of Vierzon and Montluçon – an anxiety that seems rather overwrought considering that scores of Berrichon villages like Chassignolles were then reaching their peak of population. Another, more subtle version of this unfocused angst expressed itself in complaints that those who *did* stay on the land were the least able and ambitious of their generation, though this may have been the view from the city and based upon urban values. The alternative view was that even in the country the modern young were too sharp for their own good, and over-interested in *fêtes*, cafés, billiards and the latest styles in clothes. As the aged central character of *La Vie d'un Simple* expresses it to a companion, watching young girls coming out of Mass: 'If they could come back, the women of the old days, those who've been dead fifty years, wouldn't they be astonished to see these dresses?'

To which the other old man answers that 'it' (time and progress) might 'all go back again': a countryman's cyclic image of time.

In general, at the turn of the century as in 1850, 1870 and indeed in 1920, 1950 and 1990, it was felt that old ways were passing, that folk customs were in decline and that the rising generation no longer respected the traditions of their parents and grandparents. Certainly it was true by then that the young no longer had to sit around in the long evenings participating in these traditions. The old social cohesiveness, born of necessity, had inevitably weakened a little. The young peasant whose father had had to do his courting in the fields and trudged through mud and fords to the weekly market, now had not only the branch-line railway but often a pony and trap and a decent road to use it on. Or, increasingly after 1900, he had a bicycle, that great new aid to freedom. It was during this rural heyday that regular Saturday-night dances (*bals*) were established, rotating week by week from one village or small town to another. These remained the principal entertainment and meeting ground for the rural young till after the Second World War, and still play an important part in country life. Later reminiscences of them therefore cast a valid light on earlier times.

Georges Bernardet, born in 1913, recalled the dances of his own youth as some of the happiest memories of a life otherwise spent in incessant toil on others' farms. When, in 1938, he had inherited a little land of his own and saved up enough to rent some more, he felt able to marry and that was a matter of pride to him. But there was a flaw in his pleasure.

'Saturday came,' he told me once. 'The Saturday after our wedding. And I thought, Ah, good, the dance is at St Denis this week. We'll take the cart down there with a few friends. And then I thought, Ah, *merde*, I can't. I'm married now. My dancing days are over. Not the done thing to dance once you were fixed up. But I hadn't thought about that beforehand, and I'd always enjoyed dancing so much. I felt really put out.'

> *Vous n'irez plus au bal*
> *Madam' la mariée . . .*

He and Madame Bernardet, who'd also enjoyed her youth, sol-aced themselves with late-night card parties – that vestige of the old *veillées*, where the conversation still tended to turn to the possibility of there being the odd wolf about in the region or of the wisdom of singing in the dark on the way home to keep evil spirits at bay. 'And then when they turned out into the night,' Bernardet remarked, 'they'd be so frightened they'd take to their heels at the sound of each other on the far side of a meadow! . . . But even if it had been a spirit or a ghost, what then? What harm could be done to us by people who were once just creatures here like ourselves?' It took more than dead ancestors to perturb him. Dislike of any group was more apt to be expressed by him as a mild, measured contempt, the same for Germans, Communists, gypsies, the rats in the barn and young people who didn't know what work was. Late in life, however, some of his ideas expanded or mellowed, under the influence of the television documentaries about distant places that he enjoyed. It is true that television has been a largely negative influence in rural life, isolating people of all ages, especially the old and the young, behind their own front doors, but to Bernardet and some others of his generation it has been a belated chance to see and learn things on which their brief schooling never touched.

Today the old card parties, like the Saturday-night open-air hops on the village squares where the shuffle of feet was as loud as the live music, are themselves seen through a veil of nostalgia. The rural dances that take place today happen in specially hired han-gars complete with revolving lights. From hired equipment hugely amplified music fills the night air with vibrations, for one night turning a sleepy village into a vision of the wicked city. And yet . . . disco dancing has replaced the once-shocking foxtrot and tango just as these once overtook the polka with its scandalous Second Empire reputation. A generation before, in the youth of George Sand, it was the waltz, and the very idea of dancing in couples, that shocked those to whom dancing had always meant folk dances in circles and squares. How great is the real change? When, in the mid-1980s, our son attended a rural *bal* in the Indre valley, he reported that, in spite of the volume of noise, it was extremely decorous by urban standards. Most of the assembled youth of the area knew each other, many were as ever related, and a large amount of very proper cousinly kissing on both cheeks took place. There was little heavy drinking, since these boys and girls had been accustomed to alcohol at home from childhood and getting drunk has no social cachet in France at any level. Even the presence of a group of young soldiers on leave did not lead to any disturbance. Bernardet would have recognized the atmosphere from his own youth. Célestine would have done so, from the dancing under the stars that rounded off the festivals of her youth once the townspeople and the stall-holders had gone home. What the historian Daniel Halévy wrote in 1907, in the first edition of his ongoing work *Visites aux Paysans du Centre*, still seems to be true today:

> Progress has taken place, yes – but so what? Past times were hard; does it really make so much difference if they are no longer? To compare the present with the past is to calculate – so much more of this, so much less of that – and happiness cannot in fact be quantified in this way. Comparisons have to call up memories in review. But happiness is a state of mind without memory ...

Many people undoubtedly were happy in Chassignolles by the 1900s, benefiting from just those changes that others deplored. But the era has now, in its turn, assumed the pristine glow of a golden age, the time of irretrievable safety on the far side of a momentous historical divide: in this case, the First World War. 'Village life was never the same after that war,' I have been told by the very old. The same perception as their ancestors, perennially discovered in a new form.

Marcel Jouhandeau, who was born nearby in the Creuse in 1888, did not subscribe to the idea that any essential changes had taken place by the 1900s. He wrote in his memoirs:

> There are eras that are destined to be blessed ... The first forty years of the Third Republic seem to me to have been such an era. From 1890 to 1914, how fair was my native place ... This happiness was no doubt due to the fact that everyone had received much the same upbringing ... From this derived something miraculous: a moral unity, a confidence, a relaxed trust and mutual helpfulness. We all spoke the same language and hardly needed to speak because we understood one another anyway. Everyone shared more or less the same ideas about what mattered ... What a delight and a source of strength to have to do only with people you have known since

childhood and whose family have done nothing that you don't know about for the last hundred years!

How happy such a narrow world really makes everyone is debatable. Lifelong enmities and griefs can flourish in it just as much as peace and security. But nevertheless I do feel that many of the growing population of Chassignolles at that period enjoyed their lives more, for simple, practical reasons, than previous generations did, and more innocently and optimistically than the post-war generation could.

This lost era will be the first one in Chassignolles not to vanish entirely into myth on the disappearance of its last witnesses. By 1900 photographers no longer had to confine themselves to carefully posed, breath-held portraits such as the one taken of Marie-Rachel in the 1860s, but could take exterior shots of daily life. These were made into picture-postcards, much used in those days for ordinary communications, since telephones were for the rich or for emergencies only. Half a dozen different postcard views of Chassignolles survive, including one of the new girls' school looking prim and rather forbidding, one of the Yvernault café with the extended family and retainers drawn up in front of it in their Sunday clothes, and one of the Chausée establishment similarly arranged. There are also two of the roadway at this point crowded with decorated carts, men in bowlers and some with musical instruments, women with cottage-loaf hair and figures to match, a boy posing proudly with his bicycle, others in Pierrot costumes, some blurred little girls who hadn't stood still when they were told to – and several raised umbrellas. People grin self-consciously, others stare dutifully into the lens. The sky lours.

'C'est la Cavalcade!' Denise Bonnin's sight, at ninety-two, is no longer what it was, but she instantly recognized the scene as a grand festival organised by Messieurs Chausée and Yvernault in mid-Lent 1912 as an encouragement to business in the village. It was one of her happiest memories. 'We girls from the school [the religious school, not the new State one] put on a special show, like we used to each Christmas. I was dressed up as a boy with a moustache!' In more prosaic terms, the two-day *fête* was only half successful, since torrential rains descended as they do so unpredictably in this region near the mountains, and a planned procession, complete with comic turns, all the way to La Châtre, had to be abandoned.

Madame Bonnin identified a tall girl in white in a decorated cart as the Queen of the Fête, who she knew to have been Blanche Yvernault from the café, but though she pored over the picture for some time her old eyes would not let her recognize anyone else. I felt frustrated in the same way, though my own inability had a different root. 'Once . . . on this familiar spot of ground, walked other men and women as actual as we are today, thinking their own thoughts, swayed by their own passions, but now all gone . . .' Here, among this cheerful stolid crowd on the postcard, must have been a number of people whose names I have seen so often in the records that I feel I know them – and yet I had no means of connecting these names with the faces before me. Appé, no longer mayor but the senior municipal councillor, must surely have been there, and Ageorges, the current mayor, whose relatives ran a café in the old schoolhouse, and the assorted teachers male and female, and the teacher's daughter who had presented the Minister with flowers on the inauguration of the station half a dozen years earlier? In the interests of promoting trade, the commercial bour-geoisie of the village was seemingly out in force: surely there was a Chaumette or a Robin in an odd corner, unrecognized? And what of the less respectable element? The *Écho de l'Indre* did not have much occasion, apart from the Cavalcade, to mention Chassignolles that year, but the village did appear several times in relation to one of its inhabitants, call her Stéphanie, aged twenty-six. With two men younger than herself, she was arrested for drunkenness in La Châtre during the summer, and by September the citizens of Chassignolles were sending a petition to the police to complain of her 'immoral acts'. It is hard to imagine what these can have been that so aroused the wrath of the normally rather tolerant country people. Her father was a builder: she had grown up in the village in the ordinary way among people who 'all . . . shared more or less the same ideas about what mattered'. What happened there? I should like to have been able to spot her among the crowd.

Another postcard eventually proved less frustrating. It showed a wrinkled peasant woman in apron, clogs and white cap, a basket on one arm and an umbrella on the other. It seemed to be posed, and when I first glanced at it I took it as a sign that the traditional peasant world was then just beginning to slip from reality into folklore. But Denise Bonnin took it for granted that this was a photograph of a particular individual whom she ought to remember too, and spent some time shaking her head over it in irritation. Sure enough, when I came to look at the very small print on it, it read, facetiously but with precision: *'Une demoiselle chassignollaise de 1828'*. The figure also turned up, tiny but with the same recognizable stoop and accoutrements, in a general view of the church.

So, a real person with a place and date of birth. Back to the registers. These revealed eighteen girls born in 1828, of which four were still recognizable in the census for 1901. Of these four, one was Jeanne Pagnard's great-grandmother (she who was taught to cook by the teacher's mother). Wondering if I had achieved an identification, I took the book to her, but before I could embark on an explanation she said: 'Oh, that's Marie Chièbe.'

'Marie who?' (*Chièbe* is a dialect word for 'goat'.)

'Chièbe, Chièbe – I don't know what her real name was, but people always called her that. A little old woman, quite alone in the world, who ran errands for people to earn a few *sous*. See, she trotted round with that covered basket, she came from over at Les Girauds, I think . . . No, I don't remember her that well myself, but my grandmother told me that picture of her was taken by the Curé they had then. He was the only person in the village with a camera. People teased her about it afterwards, but she was that proud of having her picture taken. He gave her a copy, of course.'

'I've seen that card in an exhibition in La Châtre, with a note saying she hasn't been identified.'

'Huh, well you'd better remember then, so *you'll* know when I'm gone. Daugeron, the Curé's name was. Very nice man, quite progressive for that time.'

I also showed Jeanne Pagnard and the Bonnins the careful drawings of Chassignolles in the 1905 school exercise book that had come my way. It had belonged to a ten-year-old girl, Adolphine, the daughter of yet another blacksmith. It had been given on to me, long after her death ('I know you like these old things'), by the woman who replaced her at the side of her bereaved husband – an outsider, with whom the village never really came to terms. These drawings are more informative and remarkable in their way than the postcards, since they show scenes such as apple-harvesting and the interiors of houses with a child's eye for specific physical details. Evidently no one explained to Adolphine that, in a picture, you do not draw lines with a ruler; farmhouses stand to rigid attention in her world, rain falls in regularly slanted curtain rods across a landscape of elms, sheep, ducks and Chassignolles' unmistakable church, rising correctly from its huddle of roofs. She was evidently a perfectionist, which is why the challenge of a moving railway engine, seen in perspective, defeated her, but she was also talented and almost abnormally observant. In spite of some rather odd perspective and proportion (the houses are unrealistically high, as they would be to a child) there is an absolute authenticity about the faded crayon drawings.

Denise Bonnin and her son and daughter all remembered Adolphine ('*La Duchesse*') well, but they were less interested that day in telling me about her than they were in discussing with nostalgic appreciation her exact depiction of a reaping hook or a donkey harness or a particular make of oil lamp. They were also keen to establish where each drawing had been 'taken' from, arguing about changed rooflines and evoking the checker-board hedges of now-vanished vegetable gardens. Only later did Georgette remark to me that Adolphine, who married her father's assistant, was *phtisique* (tubercular) and died childless in her thirties. Her mother subsequently drowned herself (said Georgette) in a water cistern in the garden behind the smithy, while everyone else was at Sunday lunch.

Denise Bonnin's own older sister died 'taking a cold on her chest' during the Great War, after her husband had been killed.

I look at those busy, happy drawings and at the fresh faces of the young men and boys in the postcards of the Cavalcade, and I feel glad that the future is always hidden.

It is true that in the early years of the new century Célestine herself does not seem to have been happy. But this was for personal and particular reasons.

In 1894 her son Charles had married. He was then twenty-nine and his bride was a girl of not quite twenty, Blanche D, born near Tours. I have been told she had relations nearer at hand, in St Denis de Jouhet, or perhaps in Crevant towards Crozon. The wedding was not held in Chassignolles and I have been able to discover little else about her antecedents. She is said to have been a good-looking, dark-eyed girl, bigger than her slim husband. The name 'Blanche', then fashionable, suggests social aspirations, and apparently she was well educated and articulate. Her mother was dead and her father, who may have come from Paris, was said to be 'a man of means'. In other words, a suitable match for Charles, as an only son.

What I do know specifically is that Blanche, although joining her husband in the family business, brought with her an extensive trousseau in a way that had not been customary when Célestine was a bride but had become so by the 1890s. The days when a new young couple simply took their places round the wide hearth with the existing household, sharing the few hand-made pots and pans, the home-stuffed goose-down quilts, were past except in the poorest families. I think it was probably to accommodate Charles and Blanche and their personal chattels in suitable style that adjacent buildings at the back of the inn were made over at this time into extra living space. With Blanche came sets of 'best' and ordinary sheets and frilled pillow-cases – some lace-edged, like the lace-edged petticoats, camisoles and drawers that had also now become an indispensable part of a young wife's outfit. There were also heavily embroidered linen tablecloths and a stack of very large damask table-napkins: each of these had 'R-D' (the couple's joint initials) in the centre in red thread, each woven with minor differences, as one would expect from bespoke work. They were extremely good quality and wore very well. I know this for a fact, since we are using some of them in Chassignolles today, a hundred years later.

The carved and polished oak presses in which all the linen was kept, and which I saw in another house in the village in the 1970s, were, I think, part of the furnishings of the inn and the work of a local carpenter – perhaps of Jean Yvernault, around the middle of the century. But, along with Blanche, the family acquired a couple of spoon-backed padded chairs. There was also a padded *prie-dieu*, the prayer-stool that had by then become an approved article of furniture in a genteel bedroom, and a small padded footstool. Both these were worked in *gros point* woollen tapestry, another refinement which had by then belatedly reached the village. The footstool depicted a small, neat cat, its eyes worked in silk for greater brightness. I have been told that the embroidery of both the *prie-dieu* and the stool were done by Célestine as a gift to her daughter-in-law, and that the stool was intended for her to rest her feet upon both before and after her baby was born.

Zénaïde Robin duly appeared in 1895. The next thing that happened was that Blanche went mad.

That, at any rate, is how the disaster is described in village lore. Today, one might refer to post-puerperal psychosis, which responds readily to medication. Or one might speculate about its having been simply a nervous collapse, with manic features. No one still alive today remembers the baby's christening, even Madame Caillaud was not born till two years later. But a number of people remember having heard about it in childhood: 'There was dancing; people did then, after a christening. And although it wasn't long since her laying-in, Blanche would join in. And she danced, and she danced and she danced all night – she wouldn't stop . . .'

'People kept saying to her, "But you must sit down, *ma chère*. Take a little rest. You'll wear yourself out. Think of the baby . . ." But it was as if she really couldn't stop. She just danced and danced . . .'

I am reminded of the bewitched girl in Hans Andersen's *The Red Shoes*, whose feet were condemned to dance for ever, attached to her or not. But this story is simply a latter-day version of ones that had been current for centuries in Europe, of dancing epidemics that broke out, either in the wake of plague or as a result of individuals being cursed. Some sufferers were said to be in a state of sexual arousal; some, in the tradition of classic schizophrenia, heard voices urging them on; while others apparently believed continual dancing to be a protection against sickness. As late as the seventeenth century, in Basle, a servant girl is reported to have made herself ill by dancing for a whole month. 'She ate and drank but little, but danced continuously till she had wasted all her strength and had to be taken to hospital, where she was cured.'

The fact that Blanche's first disquieting episode took this form may be fortuitous, but it is also true that individuals 'go mad' according to the traditions and preoccupations of their particular society. Dancing, as I have said, occupied an important role at that time in the life of the village young, and the Chaumette-Robin inn possessed the village dance floor. The fact that a married woman, newly delivered of a child, should choose to assert herself by frenetic dancing hardly augured well for the future happiness and stability of the marriage.

Blanche recovered – but relapsed. Over the next few years this became a pattern. Presumably the Robin family tried to keep her away from dances, but I am told she would sometimes become 'quite wild', would talk incessantly and have 'strange ideas' – unspecified, perhaps for reasons of delicacy.

She does not appear to have received any treatment for her condition, not even the soothing bath-cures that were all that medicine could offer then besides opiates. Indeed, where would she have gone? Twenty years before, in an unprecedented move, the Préfet of the Department had asked the Commune of Chassignolles to contribute to the support of one of their fellow-inhabitants who had had to be confined in the madhouse in Limoges, but he was there because he was said to be *aliéné* – 'beside himself' – and beyond the control of his family. The ordinary hospital in La Châtre, the ancient religious establishment that put babies out to nurse, was small and rudimentary, a combination of orphanage, infirmary for simple physical injuries, and refuge for the destitute old. By the 1890s large, purpose-built asylums were rising in the French countryside as they had a little earlier in Britain, but there was none in the Lower Berry and in any case such places were merely for care and shelter. For anything resembling treatment Blanche would probably have had to go to Paris. There, at the Salpêtrière Hospital, Charcot, the high-profile pathologist and mentor of Freud, had pioneered the idea of hysterical ailments; 'neurasthenia' was now a fashionable concept. However, the whole subject of insanity had become caught up in *fin de siècle* debates about 'decadence', the evil influence of cities and the erosion of moral certainties among uprooted people: such causes could hardly have seemed relevant to Blanche Robin in Chassignolles.

At any rate, she stayed at home. Balzac's remark, made earlier in the century, was no doubt still appropriate: 'Who has not encountered the admirable devotion that people in rural areas show towards the sick, the sense of shame lying in wait for a housewife if she should abandon her child or her husband to the care of an institution? And then again, who is not aware of the reluctance of rural families to pay for the keep of one of their number in a hospital or asylum . . .' (*L'Illustre Gaudissart*)

When Blanche was in a particularly wild phase she had to be locked in her bedroom. Later, when it became apparent that the situation was not going to improve, part of the stabling at the back of the inn was made into a small garden room for her, separate both from the family quarters and from the inn. Zénaïde, an intelligent and sweet-natured child, was brought up largely by her grandmother. By the time she was in her teens she was sent to board, first in Châteauroux, and then in a convent school in Bourges to become a *demoiselle*, away from her mother's influence.

The choice of Bourges seems to have been merely the obvious one: the town, the old religious centre of France, was full of convents. If Ursin Chaumette was still there, the family in Chassignolles did not know it, but I think it far more likely that he and his weak constitution had been inconspicuously extinguished some time in the 1880s or '90s and that his widow had maintained no contact.

The long-term effects of Blanche's condition on the Chaumette-Robin establishment can be only too well imagined. Pierre and Célestine were in their sixties by now: logic and tradition would have suggested that the day-to-day running of the inn should be progressively handed over to Charles and Blanche. But – to use Jeanne Pagnard's turn of phrase – 'For the innkeeper's wife to be mad is most inconvenient' ('*Ça n'arrange rien*'). Although Blanche was indisputably intelligent, and not malevolent, her nervous, intense manner, even in her more peaceful times, put people off. Customers drifted away to the other inns. The Chausée establishment, on the other side of the church, near the Pagnards' various workshops and the corner where the male clientele liked to relieve themselves, had been rebuilt as a four-square, slate-roofed house with proper bedrooms: it now called itself 'L'Hôtel de France'. Jean Chausée had become the prime organizer of village festivities and was generally considered very go-ahead. He even drove – for a while, till an unfortunate accident – the first petrol vehicle the village had seen.

Business declined at the Chaumette-Robin inn. Its stables were little used now: that is how the space could be spared for Blanche's bower. It wasn't, however, all Blanche's fault, says Jeanne Pagnard. Charles was a good cook: he had been sent away in his teens to do a course as a chef and he had, like his father before him, a pleasant manner 'at any rate with outsiders'. But, as the only son and sole inheritor, he had been spoilt. And he was lazy as a dormouse. Mademoiselle Pagnard used the word that, in correct French, is spelt *fainéant* – 'do nothing', but which in the country accent is transformed into *feignant*, which has overtones of pretending to be busy while achieving little.

Madame Caillaud, of the same generation as Zénaïde, also remembers the family well. Her own family, the Graizons, had been on genteel visiting terms with the Chaumette-Robins for half a century.

'I don't think that Célestine – well, I knew her as Madame Robin of course – ever *said* anything about her daughter-in-law and the way things had turned out. She put a good face on it. Quite right too. But all the same . . .' Charles, according to Madame Caillaud, was undoubtedly amiable but unrealistic, a dreamer – 'a little cracked [*fêlé*] himself, actually, as if madness was catching!'

She added a terrible detail. When she was a child, accompanying her mother to church on Sundays, they would usually encounter Célestine. More than once, outside the church, Madame Caillaud saw her mother slip money from her own gloved hand to Célestine's shrinking one with a sympathetic murmur: 'Take it, *ma chère*, please take it.' It was not the country custom to make such a gesture. The danger of absolute want was still perceived as being too close at hand for general peace of mind. Literally anyone might be at risk, and so most people, in atavistic fear and self-protection, preferred to look away. Perhaps, in fact, Célestine herself would have preferred it so.

To her, the sought-after girl from the prosperous family she had once been must have seemed very far away by then. As far as the two brothers who should have been there to buttress her: gone their ways these thirty or more years. She had, as the implacable French saying puts its, *mangé son pain blanc en premier* – eaten the white bread of life first, so that only the bitter rye remained for her in her later years. She could not possibly have foreseen this.

In the end bankruptcy, the spectre of ultimate disgrace that haunted the French commercial classes of that period, did not quite overwhelm the Robin family, though failure did. In May 1909 the decision was taken to sell up, and not just the inn but all the family property. For several weeks the advertisement appeared in the *Écho de l'Indre*:

'To sell or rent as one Lot: L'Hôtel Robin and all its adjoining buildings situate at Chassignolles, as from St Martin's Day: meadow, vineyard, other parcels of land, garden, stable yard, store house, barn and the hotel business. Apply to Monsieur Robin, at Chassignolles.'

But there were apparently no takers at the asking price. At any rate, the family were still there running the inn two and a half years later, though they may by then have disposed of most of their other assets.

Finally, in 1912, the inn was sold for a knockdown price to a family from Le Magny with the name of Péru. Péru was a blacksmith specializing in farm machinery and his wife had been keeping one of the several grocery stores in the village. It would appear from the table of land holdings that this purchase passed through the intermediary of the Pagnard family, who also bought a building or two by the church to add to what they already owned there. The Péru inn – or rather, café, since the Pérus did not have the ambitions for it that Célestine and Pierre had once pursued – was one of five such establishments now in Chassignolles.

Not quite all the property was sold. Charles and Blanche moved into a small house that had been built in happier times on a site originally acquired by Françoise Chaumette near the gates of the Domaine. It was the house that Zénaïde was to occupy with her Australian painter several decades later. Like most houses in the Commune, it had its own patch of land on which minimal subsistence farming could be carried on. By the census of 1921, Charles Robin was listed at that address as *cultivateur*. They kept no servant, not even a little farm boy.

Célestine and Pierre did not move in with their son and daughter-in-law. In old age, for the first time in their lives, they went to live quite on their own. They returned to La Châtre, where Pierre had grown up and still had relatives, and where they had once run the inn on the main street.

Now they settled in the old town, in a narrow lane sloping steeply down behind the church in the direction of the river. Rue des Chevilles ('the street-where-pegs-are-made') is one of the oldest in La Châtre. It was there in the twelfth century, and though none of its houses is probably that old several certainly date from the later Middle Ages. Today it has a dilapidated and semi-abandoned air, and it would not have been much better on the eve of the Great War. A retired Chassignolles schoolmaster (another Pirot), who was a child in La Châtre at that time, evoked for me the poverty of what was then known as the *basse ville* – the dirt, the barefoot children, the men who worked in others' vineyards for a pittance, the women who grew lettuces and leeks in their tiny gardens by the river and trundled them around the more prosperous quarters begging housewives and maids to buy. At that time, and indeed till the 1970s, there was no main-drainage in the old town: the dirty water ran from waste pipes under windows into an open drain. Today, this has been remedied and the streets smell clean for the first time in hundreds of years. In the more picturesque corners some cautious gentrification is taking place, but so far the Rue des Chevilles is untouched by new paint, geraniums, *style rustique* shutters or freshly exposed stone lintels.

The reason I know of the move to the Rue des Chevilles is that I found Pierre Robin's death recorded in the town hall in La Châtre. He did not long survive the departure from Chassignolles. His occupation was given as *vigneron* – vineyard worker. He was seventy-seven years old.

He died at nine o'clock one November morning in 1914, and his death was formally declared an hour later by that nephew who had been a new-born child in the house next door when Pierre and Célestine were young marrieds. One must hope that the nephew, now a railway employee, and other Robin relatives, were in a position to help pay for the funeral.

In Chassignolles, the report of his death made hardly a ripple. The Commune had other deaths on its mind. The young men and even the not-so-young were going off to war. The chief miller had been called up – how would the corn be ground? So had one of the bakers, brother to Ursin Yvernault of the café. The Chaumette-Robin inn was already part of a world that had gone.

III

A Time for Reaping

Chapter 15

It was just before nine at night. The frogs were making their usual racket in the still water of the pool, and in the depths of the sky the stars had already appeared. Soon everyone would be going to bed, but it was a beautiful evening and each person wanted to make it last. Most of them were stretched out on the dry grass of the verges that separated the houses on each side from the dusty white road. Bats flew low in front of open doors before disappearing into the gardens, slipping between the branches, glancing by the edges of haystacks and the walls of barns, leaving a faint trail in the air behind them, a sign of fine weather to come.

I too have often seen bats disporting themselves on fine evenings as I go down for the milk at Les Buts. So runs the opening paragraph of *Campagne*, an autobiographical novel published in 1937 by Raymonde Vincent, evoking a peasant childhood in the Berry in the early years of the century. The book opens on 3 August 1914: what the morrow was to bring, as well as fine weather, was the declaration of war, announced in the isolated countryside by a drummer on foot just as for the Napoleonic wars a century earlier. The noise temporarily silenced the frogs and it could be heard coming from a distance over the hot landscape. The tap and rattle of the drum was alternated with the sound of a voice: at each farm gate the Garde-Champêtre stopped and read out aloud the list of men from the Commune who were to report at once to the nearby town.

Of course this description relies, for its effect, on the reader understanding all that the coming war was to mean. At the time, however, in the remote countryside, the war came as a complete surprise to most people, who much resented being pushed around by Them in Paris, particularly with the harvest only half in. There was wild talk in some places of the young men taking to the forests to avoid the *levée* – another echo from Napoleonic times. By a strange revolution of time and chance this did come to pass in the Indre, not in 1914 but in the next war, when France was occupied and Frenchmen were threatened with forced labour in Germany.

Raymonde Vincent's testimony is particularly valuable because at that time she herself was living on an isolated farm, away from even that modicum of progress which by then was established within the villages. She was one of those who, as Daniel Halévy wrote: ' . . . lived far from towns and main roads and remained for a long time mute and unrepresented. Yet they were there, they did things, loved, and had their effect without anyone realizing it on the heart and soul of the nation.'

But Raymonde was not mute; she was one of the first generation to benefit fully from universal free education. In her book, the aunt who helps to bring her up cannot read, her hard-pressed father ('The Master') can read only 'with difficulty', but she and her elder brothers go to school, at least enough to become literate. In her real-life teens, after the war, she worked as a *petite main* for several textile businesses in Châteauroux. At eighteen she took the road to Paris, where, after various adventures and a period posing as an artist's model (the classic route into a different existence) she married a university lecturer. But she retained an affection for the rural world from which she had escaped, and it became the stuff of her books.

She evokes the Berry with a sure touch – the black lace of the forest at the end of winter against a pink sunset sky that presages spring; a wavering string of lamps going home on a wet night; a winter's day of mist and the voices of hidden crows. But beyond the simple physical scene she conveys the loneliness of the landscape, even in a time when the fields were more populated by labourers than they are today; and the way the children, whose job it was out of school to mind the flocks, spent countless hours with no distraction but their own thoughts.

'How immense the world is on a day of strong wind, when you can see only the slate roofs of the big house through the bare trees of its winter-naked grounds. A herd of cows stand with bent heads beneath the unceasing rain. It seems that nothing will ever change, that time has no weight.'

If the child cowherd was lucky, he might have his head stocked with stories, such as were still told on winter nights round the fire while the *veillées* survived, or gleaned from sparse school history lessons or from a more chance source:

> Robert had been living for a long time already in the constant company of the highly coloured, solemn and passionate characters of legend ... They spontaneously left their own world to enter his. There was, for instance, a great medieval lord, discovered one day in a page from an illustrated paper which had been used to wrap up something Aunt Victoire had brought back from market. This lord had a most noble nature. Robert was struck with enthusiasm for him, and the two of them undertook a long, mystical journey that lasted more than a year. During this time Robert was to be seen galloping back and forth across the meadow astride a stick, raising his arms in the heat of the chase ... stopping at last by a hedge and launching into a speech in a noble language of his own creation before the invisible crowd that now surrounded him.

A little while later, when constrained by the Curé to attend catechism classes, the child finds in the Gospel stories new food for his imagination, and tries to walk on the duck pond. He feels sad when he learns that Christ finally ascended to Heaven, but comforts himself with the thought that He might appear one day in the home field along with the cows.

Once past twelve, all schooling was at an end. A child from a poor family would be likely to be sent off to work on another farm in the traditional way, a life that might be still more lonely and monotonous:

'[The two boys] had found Elizabeth, who was minding her goats in a small pasture in the middle of the woods. She was sitting in a sheltered place wrapped in her large cloak, and she was occupying herself by striking the frozen ground with a hazel branch.'

Once they were separated on different farms, brothers and sisters rarely had the time or the opportunity to visit one another. 'Sometimes the others would be forgotten for a while, but when contact was suddenly renewed the earlier indifference seemed dreadful and one's whole being swelled with remorse.'

We might as well be in 1814 as 1914; in some respects so little had changed. Nor did it even after the First World War. Georges Bernardet, born in 1913 to parents with little land and many children, spent his first years in a hamlet on the far side of the Domaine which was the last one in the Commune to have its mud track surfaced with gravel. 'There was no road there – nothing,' he told me. 'We had nothing. We never went anywhere, not even into the village.' Georges himself escaped into rather more fortunate circumstances in his sixth year. But he still had to undergo a period of hard labour on another's farm in his teens. He considered himself lucky simply in that he got a 'good master' who 'trained him up properly' to rise at four a.m. to feed and water the horse so that it would be ready to be put in the harness between six and seven.

Other boys of his generation fared harder. I have been told of one – still alive today – who was treated 'worse than a beast. Made to sleep in the stable, he was, and sometimes nothing to eat but what was given to the pigs.' This had shocked even at the time, for traditionally on a French farm there were few of the social distinctions that obtained in England, and all, from master to little swineherd, ate democratically round the same table.

And yet by Georges Bernardet's childhood times *had* changed. Hand-outs had gradually become available to relieve the worst of poverty: minimal and inadequate as such assistance was by the standards of the later twentieth century, it would have seemed a blessed luxury to earlier generations. For much of the nineteenth century, the destitute, as such, are absent from the Minutes of municipal meetings. Among the necessarily parsimonious discussions of paths, fairs and money to pay a teacher, their particular plight does not even figure. But from the eve of the Third Republic onwards payment of medical expenses begins to be mentioned. At first these were just individual grants for exceptional cases. In June 1870 the Council had a special meeting about one of their number, a poor relation of the innkeeping Yvernaults, and agreed ('*ayant mûrement délibéré*') to pay for him to stay in the La Châtre hospital to get a damaged hand treated 'since he is genuinely indigent'. Some years later, when La République was beginning to make central funds available, a grant of ten francs per month was actually obtained from the Préfet for one 'very poor and sick old man', and a similar sum for another in the early 1880s. It does not seem at this date as if illness in itself was regarded as suitable for charitable relief, but rather that money was given on the ground that illness or age or both combined were preventing the individual from labouring to earn his own or his family's bread; thus all the early recipients are men.

By 1883 we find the mayor (Victor Pissavy, of course) drawing up a whole list of people who, in his view, should receive free medical treatment. In another ten years a national law was passed codifying such rights and – at least in theory – obliging the Communes to pay for their own. In many places the new law was not enforced, but I have the impression that even before the 1890s Chassignolles, led by the Domaine, had a fairly clear concept of its responsibilities. The descriptions of illnesses also became more specific: for instance, in 1888, a sixty-seven-year-old tenant farmer was reported as having 'pulmonary catarrh, and a hernia which has already once dangerously strangulated, also varicose veins in his legs. His children, who are servants in others' households, are having to support him out of their own small earnings.' The same year a member of another long-term village family was said to have 'pulmonary emphysema and asthma' while his wife had 'gastric problems'.

In 1905 came more legislation, this time in relation to the aged poor, and after this small sums are quite often voted in council meetings for women as well as men. Concepts of medical treatment were also beginning to progress beyond emergency action on hernias or broken bones. In 1909 and again in 1911 two separate sick women were actually sent to 'take the waters' at Évreux-les-Bains, a thing inconceivable in the days when the Communal population had been smaller and less prosperous. But it was decided that, even when a sick person had been in receipt of relief, no money could be paid out for burials.

Of course none of this limited largesse touched the needs of failing innkeepers and their families, struggling to keep up appearances and avoid commercial ruin. As ever, social distinctions within the Commune were real, even if on a small scale compared with the vast differences within urban society.

By 1913 there had been more legislation, this time concerning the payment of old-age pensions to peasants and factory workers even when they were not quite incapacitated; assistance was also to be given to pregnant women and to large families. Of these provisions, the pensions seemed by far the most miraculous advance, and many of the old could hardly believe their good fortune. They remembered the days when as a matter of course you went on working for your bread till sickness or death claimed you – the one often following soon on the other, since it was not the custom to attempt any treatment for a useless old person's ailments. Now here was the nice postman turning up every week on their doorstep with money for them. It has been recounted to me that one old lady, 'La Mère Philomène', could not understand why he did it. Her name makes her sound faintly exotic, and the census reveals that for most of her long life she was the one person in Chassignolles to be born in a far-off place. She had been a foundling child in Paris in 1837 and was put out to nurse in the Berry, where she stayed. By the end of the First World War she was eighty, a widow, living alone in a little separate dwelling at the back of a farmhouse a stone's throw from our own house; she went out cleaning for others. She decided that she ought to give the postman a present, both in genuine gratitude and to ensure his continuing support. She obtained a rabbit, killed and gutted it, and set off happily with it to the new post office. But the postman's reaction was disappointing. As a French civil servant he stood on his dignity:

'It's my job to bring you money. I don't want your rabbit. You take it home and make yourself a decent meal with it.'

Perhaps he was afraid that if he accepted the rabbit word would be all round the village that he solicited gifts from the poor and needy. She insisted, he refused more brusquely. Finally she cried: 'I won't eat it! It would choke me now . . .' flung the furry corpse down on the postal floor tiles and banged out of the office.

If only poor Mère Philomène had waited till the end of the year her rabbit would probably have been accepted. Either in consequence of a collective gratitude to the distributor of pensions, or as a result of a much older and more equivocal desire to placate the bringer of news from afar, it is still today the custom in rural

France to make presents to the postman on New Year's Day, either in money or in kind. In a Commune with hundreds of households, the cumulative effect of all this giving adds up to a substantial subsidy to the postman's basic salary, and is recognized as such when the appointment is made.

In its gradual evolution of a primitive welfare net, France was merely keeping pace with other developed countries – old-age pensions were introduced in England in 1909. But the French legislation of 1913 concerning help for large families had a more specific intent. The tendency, apparent ever since the Napoleonic wars, for the population of France to grow more slowly than that of neighbouring countries, had persisted. In 1871 France had 36 million people and only three and a half million more in 1911. In the same period the British population had grown from just under 32 million to forty-five and a half million, but the most spectacular contrast was with the German Empire: there, 41 million had grown to nearly 65 million.

What was worse, from the point of view of the French government, was that this difference could only increase, for the French birth rate was the lowest in western Europe. Long before August 1914 the Government knew, even if the people of central France did not, that a confrontation with the German Empire was looming, a further round in the hostilities begun in 1870. It is from this period that one can date the governmental obsession with numbers, with 'missing' young men who should have been born to be cannon-fodder, and the conviction that national strength depends on a steadily increasing population – an idea not extinct in France even today.

It is in this context that the Government decided to give financial help to large families. Needless to say, this had little effect on most of the citizens of villages such as Chassignolles, who saw husbanding the family property as a much greater virtue than procreation. It is clear from the birth rates that most couples did want to limit the number of children born to them and more often than not succeeded. The few large families tended to be born to those with little or nothing to husband, for whom children might be optimistically regarded as a source of pride and an eventual security. To this minority the new law, with its allocation for bread to each new child, must have come as a salvation, and among them was Paul Bernardet, *cultivateur*, father of Georges and eight other children. All of them survived to grow up, which seems some sort of proof of the law's positive effect.

'Poor man,' said Paul Bernardet's daughter-in-law to me. 'He did what he could, but that was so little to go round. He'd nothing, and he wasn't even particularly strong. And she was lame. Had been from birth. That didn't help.'

'Her foot was turned sideways. She walked on her heel. Nothing was done about that in those days.' (Mademoiselle Pagnard speaking) 'She was a very pretty woman, though. Lovely face.'

In the early years of our relationship with Bernardet I knew only that he himself had been brought up not by his parents but by another couple, a circumstance round which had settled in his mind an aura of romance – of a rescue into love. His godmother was his mother's older sister, another daughter of the renowned grandfather who had built his own house after work. She was married to a plasterer, a man therefore several steps up the village social hierarchy, and they lived in an old, one-storey farmhouse with a yard across the way from what is now our house. The ceilings were embellished by the husband with the plaster roses he had learnt to do when he went to work for a spell on the fine new buildings going up in Paris. He also laid new floor tiles: the couple had a grandfather clock that had been made in La Châtre in the middle of the last century and a carved cupboard or two. But no children had appeared to populate this home, and by the time the First World War came, when the plasterer had turned forty-five and his wife was approaching forty, it seemed clear that they never would. One day when Georges was five, this godmother spoke to his mother. 'Why don't we take on little Georges and bring him up? That would be one less mouth for you to feed.'

When this offer reached Paul Bernardet, all he said to his son was: *'Va t'en. C'est une chance pour toi.'* ('Off with you. You're in luck.') This unpaternal remark was retailed with a hint of bitterness sixty years later, even though Paul Bernardet turned out to be right.

Georges moved in with the middle-aged couple, but at first he missed the comfortless house among the fields, which had been his entire world, and the company of his brothers and sisters. Obstinate by nature, he moped, and would not be seduced by his aunt's anxious affection. Eventually his uncle said to him: 'If you stay with us, I'll make you a little wheelbarrow, just your size, and then you can give me a hand.'

A little wheelbarrow his own size! To a child who had never known a toy, or indeed one single possession of his own, the idea was irresistible.

'So I decided to cheer up,' he recounted long afterwards. 'I said to myself: I'll stay here, at any rate till I get the wheelbarrow. Then I'll wheel it all the way home to show them.'

But by the time the wheelbarrow was made, his uncle and aunt's house had become his home. Fifteen years later, transformed into a young man doing his army service in Versailles, his gratitude to the couple who had reared him found expression in the remarkable feat of saving his pay to buy a small house for his aunt in her widowhood. But his sense of obligation also extended to the general desire to perform well. The idea that he had been specially singled out by fortune and must act accordingly seems to have informed his whole life, giving him an underlying confidence that his brothers, struggling into adulthood in a pack, never attained. He worked and saved and gradually built up his own kingdom. The son of the near-landless Paul became known in the Commune as 'The Proprietor'. As the child of a too-numerous family he cautiously limited his own offspring to two. To his own son, he was rather a stern father; less so to his daughter, the first-born. She, as things turned out, was the one who left Chassignolles and made her home with her mechanic husband in the suburbs of Paris.

To our son he was always kind, almost proprietary, like his uncle by marriage long ago, as if his instinct was to try to evoke in this alien child a feeling of loyalty to the patch of territory that meant so much to *him*. 'I'll make you a ladder – then you and your friends will be able to climb into the chicken loft . . . I'll teach you to plant potatoes . . .'

Later, when we built a room on to our house and our son helped us to dig foundations, lay bricks, and mix and apply rendering, Georges Bernardet strongly approved: clearly we were bringing the boy up the right way. Later again a touch of shyness set in – was the boy now too large and foreign to be addressed as *tu*? – and when he began to go off on holidays of his own, Georges Bernardet asked anxiously: 'Doesn't he care for Chassignolles any more then?'

Only after Bernardet himself was gone did I read Daniel Halévy on the French peasantry, but when I did I recognized him:

> The land, the soil itself . . . represents something magic. Even the poorest man hopes that one day he will own a piece of it, and that secret hope illuminates his silent spirit, with its passion that lies concealed beneath a coarse exterior . . . The peasant is proud of his work on the land, and this pride too is a secret treasure . . .

But always to be reckoned with is that haunting fear that this treasure, this land, this proud labour of feeding France, may be becoming devalued in others' eyes. 'The children are leaving the land' – the recurrent cry.

> Their going is the most painful rejection. Many never return, do not even write home: their forgetting makes the rejection still sharper. Others remember, write and sometimes come home on a visit. They are welcomed, fussed over; it is so keenly desired that they should continue to love this corner of the earth that has nurtured them. But they don't care for it any longer – or care only a little . . .

The perennial regret, fresh and keen when Halévy was writing but echoing a lament already heard seventy, fifty and thirty years earlier, and one that has been reiterated with a note of increasing distress between 1920 and our own day. What is always perceived as a new phenomenon is in fact a very long-term one, and more complex than just a matter of numbers. What, exactly, is meant by the 'rural population'? When Halévy was writing *circa* 1920, the people of rural areas still easily outnumbered town dwellers, and out of the entire population of France about forty per cent were still directly employed on the land. Today the population considered as rural, many of whom live in country towns such as La Châtre, accounts for something over one third of the total, but the number who actually *work* the land now is very small. It becomes apparent that the whole subject of rural depopulation is more involved than the immediate perception of it.

Bernardet's son continues honourably to work the family farm, but has not married. If Bernardet had any regrets for the principles on which he had reared the boy he never expressed them, though he mourned the absence of children in the house, understanding what this must eventually mean. Once, there were too many children, but now? The two sons of the daughter in Paris are strangers to the countryside and country ways. When the younger one was a sturdy seven-year-old, sent to his grandparents during the long summer holiday, Bernardet had hopes of making a farmer of him, but the boy has grown up to become a chef in a large urban restaurant. The older boy, always more reserved and studious, has a degree in aeronautics.

('They do not take pleasure in seeing the countryside again so much as in being seen, in showing the town ways they have acquired, their fine clothes and their hands untouched by manual labour.' Halévy again.)

In the early 1980s Bernardet said to me one day: 'If this depopulation of the countryside goes on, fields will be left uncultivated and ungrazed.' The phrase he used, *'des terres en friche'*, evokes images of couch grass and yarrow, then thistles, nettles and soon brambles, invading the clean spaces that have been nurtured for generations where crops or grass should grow. There was horror in his eyes as he spoke. To him, the prospect was a kind of sacrilege, an insult to the whole ethic by which he had lived.

'I went by the field of the slothful, and by the vineyard of the man devoid of understanding: And, lo, it was all grown over with thorns. And nettles had covered the face thereof. And the stone wall thereof was broken down . . . '

Bernardet did not make the connection between the image of desolation that haunted him and the modern increase in farming productivity from which he, like all his generation, had benefited. Indeed the paradox by which land, when more and more efficiently cultivated, may eventually become not more valuable but less, is far from obvious, since it only operates over a long period of time.

In the second half of the nineteenth century land use had already become noticeably more efficient. Then, in the years leading up to the First World War there was a gradual but steady increase in crop yields, as the early machinery began to replace almost everywhere the immemorial scythe and flail. The trend continued between the wars; indeed the spectre of overproduction and falling prices that is so familiar today first showed signs of appearing in the 1930s. It was met with incomprehension by the peasant population, to whom such a concept was against nature. That you could have *too* good a harvest ran counter to all their instincts and traditions, and also counter to the policy of agricultural encouragement that the Government had pursued for the previous seventy years. They refused to believe in the problem and, sure enough, it disappeared with the Second World War and then seemed to be conveniently forgotten. After 1945 productivity continued to increase and to be praised, and the small farmers of the 1950s, '60s and '70s enjoyed real prosperity for the first time in their history: this period is now known, already nostalgically, as 'the Thirty Glorious Years'.

But while, between the wars, farms had still continued to occupy large numbers of people, and the loss of men in the Great War helped to disguise the declining need for labour, the far greater mechanization that came in gradually after the Second World War changed the whole nature of farming. A squad of men out in the fields was, simply, no longer needed. The retreat from the land has, in a large part, been rational: not so much a matter of the boys being seduced away by the bright lights as of them being driven away by the sheer lack of jobs at home.

Today, only two French citizens in each hundred are directly employed on the land, not much more than one million in all, yet they produce double the amount that was produced by six million forty years ago. But it is all too much. This excess of wheat, cereals, milk, meat, richness beyond the imagination of those who worked this land in the last century, has also created a crisis beyond their imagining. The efficient and profitable cultivation of all the available land by a small number of people is one thing; the growing suggestion that this enterprise may not be worthwhile anyway is a different kind of message, and one likely to lead to further mass defection from sheer discouragement.

The prospect of that remaining million of land workers being further drastically reduced raises images of land simply abandoned piecemeal, like some great empire being abandoned by a retreating power and returning to a primeval state. Even when Bernardet's spectre of *des terres en friche* is controlled and made official in the form of 'set-aside' land (dignified in French by the old word for 'fallow' – *jachère*) this in itself is perceived as an insult and a defeat. It strikes at the very heart of rural pride and morality which are, by tradition, quintessentially French national pride and morality.

I feel glad that Bernardet, though he had his forebodings, died before the full effect of the problem was apparent. I am glad he did not live to experience the pain of those who have found that this land they had spent their lives husbanding and cultivating to pass on to the next generation is explicitly regarded as just so much redundant space, a treasure without worth after all.

And I am sorry that he can never have known the extent to which our son, now grown up, has internalized him as one of those fondly remembered, larger-than-life figures from childhood, as permanent and mythic in his way as the fabled grandfather. 'Ah, Monsieur Bernardet would have known,' we say regretfully to each other each time we want to know something.

'My grandfather, now, he could have told you' – how to mend a gate or prune a vine or deal with a hornets' nest; or whom to approach with what offer to buy another segment of land; or who owned each field fifty years ago or why the earth is red near La Croix Pendue . . .

Although the accelerated exodus from the land did not make itself apparent till well after the Second World War, the idea persists that the previous war, with its social and human destruction, marked the real beginning of this trend.

By chance, and the way the generations fell; neither the Bernardet family at one end of the social scale nor the Pissavy-Yvernaults at the other were among those wrecked by the First World War. But in a wider sense not a household in Chassignolles remained untouched by it. The Government's obsession with the need to put a large force on the battlefield without delay to counter superior German numbers, meant that men of all ages were called up in haste without consideration of other needs, even national ones. Again and again tales of that war recounted today by those who were children then dwell on fields left unreaped or unsown, on workhorses summarily requisitioned, grain unmilled, vines unpruned, cut timber left to rot. For four years it was women, children and old men who struggled to keep the farms going.

This was especially hard when an extended family owned bits of land scattered around the Commune of Chassignolles and in neighbouring Communes. Denise Bonnin recalled for me that her family had owned a potato field some five miles distant – the land at Beaumont. At the age of thirteen she was sent to stay there at a cousin's house to dig up the precious potatoes; her father would come and fetch her home on Sunday. She had the whole field harvested by Saturday evening and decided to set off home alone: 'So as to be there all day for Sunday. But I wasn't even quite sure of the way, and nor was the horse. We hesitated at every crossroads and I had to walk, leading him. The only human soul I saw on the way was the baker on his evening round. I was beginning to wish I'd never set out. It got dark and I was afraid. I thought perhaps my home and the village had disappeared, gone by magic . . . I didn't begin to feel a bit better till I came to the lane round the back of the Domaine and recognized it. Then, when at last I got home, the shutters were all drawn and the door locked. My parents had gone to bed. I had to bang and bang. They were amazed when they realized it was me, and not very pleased. But they did get up and help me unload the cart.

'And in the end my poor brother-in-law never did come back to our farm. He was killed, and brought home after the war in a lead coffin as my sister had died too. Our parents took on my little niece – she was brought up in our house like a younger sister to me. When we used to take her to the cemetery, she would scratch at the earth saying she wanted to "see Maman and Papa".' Denise Bonnin said this with horror in her voice.

'Our parents never really recovered from that war. After that, they were old.'

Even when the father, husband, son or son-in-law did return safely to the household, loss still pervaded the air, creating the feeling that nothing would ever be quite as before. Everyone in Chassignolles was mourning, at the least, friends, a godson, a nephew or a cousin. There was also the sense of the absent unborn, those children whom the young men had not lived long enough to father and who loomed so large between the wars in the French imagination. If the 'missing generation' had been there all, seemingly, would have been different. The drift from the land would paradoxically have been less. Perhaps, even, the ancient cults centring on decorated bulls and dances at wayside shrines would have survived. If so many men had not been slaughtered, perhaps country girls would still have believed in tying good luck charms to trees?

From the whole of France, one and a half million died at the front. Something approaching one million had died in the much longer Napoleonic campaigns of a hundred years earlier, but although the dreaded *levées* of that war had passed into folklore, the slaughter of individuals had vanished from living memory. Chassignolles, like the rest of France, was quite unprepared psychologically for the new loss. 'The newspapers kept writing about "victories",' a very old man who was a teenager then remembers. 'But what we heard all the time was "So-and-so's son has gone. And the So-and-sos have heard their boy's reported missing." ' In France, the telegrams from the military authorities went not directly to the families, as in England, but to the Mairie of the Commune where the dead or missing soldier's next of kin was living. It fell to the mayor (Ageorges at that time in Chassignolles) to visit the families in person with the news. 'So people dreaded seeing him coming, poor man.'

There are many entries in the Minute books, particularly for the early days of the war, concerning councillors absent, 'called to the colours'. But though the handwriting of the Minute-taker keeps changing, I don't think that any councillor was in the end killed. They would have been mainly middle-aged men, likely to be deployed in supply lines or at base camps, and often released to return to their socially useful civilian occupations if the Commune insisted hard enough. It was a different matter with the young, who were sent straight to the front. Sixty-six men died from Chassignolles, almost one in ten of the entire male population, but the proportion of deaths among those aged between twenty and thirty was far higher. Out of one group of nine who had gone to the village school the same year and were called up together in 1914 at the age of twenty, only one was still alive at the end of the war: Marcel Yvernault, the son of the inn. In this light, his father Ursin's generous treats of wine and oysters for other young soldiers going off to war take on an extra poignancy, but at least the gesture to propitiate fate seems to have worked. This son lived, to become the father of Suzanne Calvet.

One who did not come home was Anatole Gonnin, the eldest of four boys all born in the 1890s to the family who were then tenant farmers at Villemort. The old miniature castle had descended to country uses: hay was stacked in its medieval chapel and on its Saracen staircase hens hopped. But the Gonnins were a respected family, even if they were not the equal in property of the Graizons, who were established on the one-time Charbonnier property at Le Flets. Villemort was so isolated, except from the new railway line through the wood, that by field paths the Graizons were the Gonnins' nearest neighbours. In the summer of 1914 Anatole, then aged twenty-five, was keeping company with Marie Graizon, an only daughter who would not be seventeen till the November. By November, Marie was pregnant and Anatole was at the front.

In village lore the exact dates have long been clouded in respectful reticence; the sequence of events is recited rhetorically, with much rolling of 'r's' for the story has taken on a symbolic quality and represents all the personal tragedies of that time.

'He came back from the war for just *three* days to marry her – then *three* days more when their son was born – and then that was that. Finished. Gone. Poor girl, she had no married life with him at all.'

In reality, events were a little less apocalyptic if just as bleak, for when Marie went into labour Anatole was already on leave, convalescing with a wounded arm. As the hours went by, he had to report back to barracks in Châteauroux before the child had appeared. It was the Chassignolles midwife who sent a message to him by means of the telephone in the Mairie, to tell him that he was the father of a son. He survived in the trenches for two years more before he was killed. His younger brother had already died there, a third was taken prisoner on the eastern front and returned after the war crippled and 'half out of his mind'. But it is in the rest of young Madame Gonnin's story that the peculiar tragedy lies.

The child Aimé Gonnin was brought up by his mother in her parents' house and the hopes of all three were concentrated on him. From the village school he was sent to continue his education in La Châtre, then to study law in Limoges. He had his bicycle, his dog, his gun, his horse; later, when he was back in La Châtre articled to a local lawyer, he had his own car. He loved his mother and grandparents and was good at drawing. Photographs of him show a solid, short but rather handsome Berrichon with a cowlick of black hair and a noticeable resemblance to the writer Alain-Fournier. By 1939 he was all set to fulfil the family dream and became a successful member of the local bourgeoisie, the equivalent of a Pissavy-Yvernault. About the same time, the old farmhouse was abandoned for a new house the Graizons had built alongside, a home for gentlefolk with four or five well-lit rooms downstairs, each with a decoratively tiled or parquet floor. The aged Jean Beaumont (Apaire) had directed the setting of the roof timbers, and under that roof several good bedrooms with dormers had been planned: plenty of space for a new generation.

The bedrooms were never installed.

Aimé was one of the very few young men of Chassignolles – a handful compared with those of the previous war – not to return from the second one. Before the fall of France, he trod on a mine near the frontier with Belgium. That, once again, was that.

'I remember her arriving at church for Mass the week after he'd been killed. She was like a spectre herself.' Madame Calvet, a generation younger.

Today, more than fifty years later, young Madame Gonnin is old Madame Caillaud, *la doyenne de la commune*. She is a survivor in every sense; in spite of her great age and her failing sight she is a neat, erect figure, dressed in sprigged navy with a small shawl of her own crochet work. Brisk, cheerful, firm in manner, devoted to her flowery garden and to current-affairs programmes on the radio, she lives alone with only a daily visit from the home-help who cooks her dinner – a well-built person on a motor bike described by Madame Caillaud, with a nice social nuance, as 'my little help'. Yet the final, dominating role of her long and variegated life is that of an icon of suffering. She is a village memorial, just as much as the stone one near the church, to both wars together.

'After the second war the Government offered me a decoration. They said it was because I had given both my loved ones to France. I refused it. I didn't give my own. They were taken from me.'

Long after her parents, too, were dead, she remarried. Monsieur Caillaud was a jolly widower and near-neighbour. 'We were supping together most evenings anyway,' he told a male friend. 'All I had to do was push the gate a little further open.'

Then, for about ten years, Marie had, according to her old friend Jeanne Pagnard, 'a proper life':

'They had a little car. Went on visits and trips. Meals out and so on. She was really happy.'

But then he died, as men do. Alone once again, Madame Caillaud lived on, guardian of the house that had been built to contain a future but which had become a museum of memories.

I visited her first on a still, golden afternoon in autumn, cycling past the football field – Stade Aimé Gonnin – that the family gave to the Commune. Leaves detached themselves silently from the horse and Spanish chestnuts one by one. She welcomed me graciously, offered Maxwell House coffee in miniature china vases, wondered energetically in passing if the coffee had been manufactured by that fat, drowned Englishman of whom she had just heard on the radio; wasn't he supposed to have embezzled . . .? But it was clear that her main purpose in inviting me was to show me over her shrine. As we moved through the rooms, the framed photos of her son at every stage and size – as a baby, receiving his first Communion, with friends in a hayfield, with others in a Limoges street, dressed for *la chasse*, at the wheel of his car – were like so many Stations of the Cross, each one requiring its own discourse. There too were his crayon drawings – beloved spaniel, beloved mother – and his qualifying certificate for his final law exams – 'I received that weeks and weeks after he'd been killed . . .'

'We'd only just moved into the house. This was to have been his room.' A bedspread of heavy crocheted lace, Madame Caillaud's own work. Above the bed-head, a large wooden crucifix. She is said to be a devout believer 'in spite of everything'; certainly, in younger days, the Pissavy-Yvernault granddaughter who occupied Mademoiselle Guyot's house, taught the catechism and burnt George Sand's letters, was an object of her particular affection. ('Jeanne Pagnard has always had a fondness for Madame L, but her sister was *my* special friend.') But resigned acceptance of God's Will in the tradition of the dying Louis Yvernault does not seem to form part of Madame Caillaud's piety. I understood that day that this woman is a fighter by nature, not a forgiver.

Also on the walls, numerous tapestry pictures, that same ladylike *gros point* work that Célestine took to in middle life – 'Yes, I did those too. I loved to embroider before my eyes went.' Flowers, a castle like Sarzay, a careful rendering of Millet's 'The Gleaners'. This pretty, silent house is a museum to more than the dead of the wars.

Things are preserved inside Madame Caillaud's head, also, that have disappeared from the visible world. Given her great age, and the fact that she has always lived in a remote part of the Commune, for many years now she has paid only rare and fleeting visits to the centre of the village, and the Chassignolles that exists in her mind is still that of the 1940s and '50s, complete with shops, a barber's and a hairdresser's. She was surprised when I mentioned one day that I wished I could have seen the stone staircase on the outside of the Chaumette-Robin inn.

'But you can. Go and look at it!'

'It's not there any longer,' I and Mademoiselle Pagnard, also present, spoke in unison. Mademoiselle Pagnard, disapproving of such a lapse – lets the side of the elderly down – went on sternly.

'You saw it demolished yourself, when Mesmin Chauvet renovated the place.'

'*Really?*' A rapt, disbelieving look came into Madame Caillaud's near-sightless eyes. Presently she said, with dismissive dignity:

'Nevertheless, I can see it absolutely clearly.'

Of Anatole Gonnin himself, the helpless author of her long-term destiny, Madame Caillaud speaks little, and there is only one picture of him. By comparison with his all-present son, this lost husband seems shadowy, too remote now in time to raise many echoes within her. Or it may be that she never knew him well: as people say, she never lived with him.

This, indeed, is the peculiar poignancy that attaches itself to the names of the young men in the war memorial. *Enfants de Chassignolles*, in French parlance, born out of the very earth of the place, flesh of parents and grandparents raised on its produce, many of them were wiped out before anyone could know them as adults, before they could even know themselves. When people still alive claim 'that first war changed everything . . . the village was never the same after that', I have come to believe that the removal of the young men, their subjection to an alien and terrible dimension of experience, is a large part of what is being indicated. Even those who did come back were not the same; they had been changed. Since they were the chief inheritors and perpetuators of village life, that life could not be the same either. In comparison, the social effects of the second war and France's defeat, however far-reaching, are perceived in Chassignolles as having been much less devastating. The annual ceremony by the memorial each 11 November, though ostensibly a remembrance for both wars, is really concerned with the first one. The roll call is read, and this is known as the *Appel des Morts*, as if the intention were indeed to call up again those children of Chassignolles to their own territory. The impression is reinforced by the deployment of the present-day schoolchildren, lined up with combed hair, to repeat after each name the refrain '*mort pour la Patrie*' – 'died for France'.

I have known several village survivors of the First World War. One liked to mention to us regularly his voyage to the Dardanelles – 'You come from across the sea too, I believe . . . But perhaps not the same sea?' Another, Denise Bonnin's husband, was celebrated for having been for forty days in the charnel-house of the Fort of Douarmont, by Verdun, and having escaped 'without a scratch'. But such oft-reiterated facts form, after decades, their own carapace, a barrier against real memory rather than a continuing key to it.

They are all gone now, these old soldiers, at last joining friends who could, in age, be their great-grandsons. Only in written accounts, today, can one hope to recover some authentic breath of what Anatole Gonnin and his generation experienced.

'At the front, Robert had seen many of his comrades fall, but not till he came back on leave [to his own farm] and saw the snow lying on the meadow did he feel their deaths pressing on his mind.' (*Campagne*, Raymonde Vincent)

Robert thinks of the sown wheat beneath the earth, and of how long it will be till it is grown and harvested. Will he ever enjoy that harvest? And his girlfriend – is she too 'something good that he will never have'? In any case, he himself cannot take things as he did before. He struggles to explain:

' "When I came home, I thought I'd find the house, the fields, the animals and the people as well, all just the same to me as they were before. But it hasn't turned out like that, none of these things have the same weight for me . . ." '

It is as if he has left the place spiritually even before his physical departure. He is sure now that he will not return again, and he is right. When the news of his death inevitably comes, even his father's suffering 'was hardly greater, because he had envisaged the loss of his son so acutely even before it took place.'

The final chapters of the novel are more cheerful. The war is over, the younger daughter marries. The aunt comforts herself with a notion of the circularity of time, which owes less to any Christian doctrine of survival than to an older perception based on experience of the natural cycles – 'Everything comes back, everything begins again. A bad winter never prevented a fine spring.'

In her dreams, Robert's sister goes on expecting him to come back.

'Again and again she thought she saw him. He would arrive on foot, always as the night was falling, so that she never quite managed to see his face.' Sometimes she catches sight of him in the distance, in the avenue of chestnut trees; sometimes he doesn't recognize her; sometimes she is outside and sees him go into the house, but when she runs in the place is empty – or full of people she has never seen before.

This last dream seems to reach beyond the specific losses of war, into the wider territory of time that, in the end, does the same work. It is as if the young girl who later became Raymonde Vincent the novelist had momentarily visited the long future. We all of us, if we live to be old, find the places of our youth are empty, or full of strange faces. For the individual who lasts as long as Madame Caillaud, every single person who surrounded his or her youth has gone, 'ghosts at cockcrow'. I try a tentative question on her.

'Yes, well I have a lot of time these days . . . I quite often catch myself thinking, I haven't seen so-and-so recently. I wonder how he's doing? And then I think, Oh. If I'm the oldest person, he must be dead at present.'

'*Mort à présent*'. Such is Madame Caillaud's phrase. Others too use this formula, a technically correct but slightly archaic French which seems to replace the definite concept of 'now' with the suggestion of a more temporary state. Bernardet in his last years, complaining of ageing, used to say '*Je suis vieux, à présent.*'

Again, that sense of time's circularity, a hint that youth and vigour, the Cavalcade of 1912, the recruits of 1914, the mythic Golden Age, have simply gone for a long winter season, as plants do under the cold earth, and will one day return.

Chapter 16

Three years after the First World War ended, twenty-year-old Denise Apaire married. Her sister and brother-in-law were dead; their parents, left late in life with an orphaned granddaughter to rear, were old and weary. But Denise's wedding cheered everyone up.

She was a pretty girl, and she was also rather lucky. With so many of the younger men gone for ever from Chassignolles and all the other villages, many of her generation remained single. A daughter of a well-established local family, whom I only knew when old age had converted her into a substantial personality, physically and mentally, used to proclaim that she could have married if she'd wanted but husbands weren't worth the bother – 'what with having to do their washing. I'd like one at night, now, to keep me from being scared, but for anything else – pough!' Even Anatole Gonnin's attractive and well-off widow, who had her own reasons to appreciate the power of 'anything else', did not remarry till late in life. But Denise, who had been just too young in the war to mourn a dead suitor, was marrying handsome Georges Bonnin from St Denis de Jouhet, six years older than herself, he who had a fine singing voice and had survived unscathed at Verdun and indeed for an entire four years of war.

I know they made a handsome couple, as I possess a copy of their wedding photo. Like most of those taken in Chassignolles in the 1920s, this one was done by the war widow of a La Châtre photographer, intrepidly carrying on the business. It was rather a new departure then for a family like the Apaires to have a photo taken: the fifty-odd family and guests, carefully rigid on chairs and trestles at the side of the church, seem poised too between rusticity and gentility, and between past and future. In the front row Denise's parents gaze warily out of the past. Little Jean Beaumont, his carpenter's hands uneasy on his knees, wears a stiff, high-buttoned jacket of antique cut, and his thin old wife (who must once have had beautiful eyes) is dressed in the crêpe-trimmed jacket, floor-length skirt and black, ribboned cap of a nineteenth-century bereaved matron. On the other side of Georges, his mother wears the white peasant cap of the region, and another old lady, similarly capped, sports a many-tiered Victorian pelisse and a rolled parasol as an accessory. Meanwhile, up in the back row, young nephews and uncles play it cool in soft felt hats, double-breasted suits and striped ties that could be worn today. One has a cigarette in his mouth; another, who looks about fourteen, holds one nonchalantly between his fingers: the habits acquired in the trenches had percolated through French society. The much-booted and ringletted children look like illustrations from E. Nesbit books of twenty years earlier; while many of the younger women, bare-headed, in dresses run up by Jeanne Pagnard's grandmother and her assistants, seem to belong less to a stereotype of 'The Twenties' than to a timeless near-present. Just one Beauty, in a large-brimmed hat and feather boa, is clearly on her way into a more leisured existence.

Anatole Gonnin's surviving brother married in Chassignolles that year also. So did Victor Pissavy's youngest granddaughter. Sixty years later the three couples posed outside the church after a Mass to celebrate their collective diamond wedding. Beside the rather elegant figures of the Ls from the Domaine and of Lucien Gonnin, who wore a black patch over an eye kicked by a horse, the Bonnins appear diminutive, portly and, as in their original wedding photo, nervous. In daily life, however, they were quite at ease. Between the 1920s and the 1980s their farm prospered and expanded. Eventually they owned or rented bits of land all over the Commune, eighty-odd hectares in all, one of the largest holdings. They laboured from five in the morning till past nine at night, seven days a week, never counting their own toil as part of the equation, but they saw their lives becoming very gradually easier, and the Common Market subsidy system of the 1960s and '70s appeared to them as an endorsement and just reward for all their efforts. By the time profits began insidiously to fall again and the whole utility of peasant farming began to be seriously called in question, Georges was dead and Denise was too old and deaf to bother herself much about such things.

I knew Georges Bonnin for the last ten years of his life. He and Madame L's husband, wed in the same year, died the same winter. When I was brought up to date on these events by a neighbour on our return in the spring I was told, with a nice discrimination of status, that *'le père Bonnin'* had died, while Monsieur L was 'deceased': it is true that the latter august event took place away from Chassignolles. My enduring and rather surprising memory of Georges Bonnin is of him dressed in the regulation black alpaca jacket, striped trousers and clogs, sitting at the kitchen table assiduously reading books. When I was waiting for the milk to be brought in, I would manoeuvre myself behind him to read over his shoulder; it seemed impertinent to question this rather private and authoritative old person outright about his literary preferences. In any case, in age he had become hard of hearing and had reverted in his own speech to the *patois* of long ago. The books were all from the public library in La Châtre, which sends selections to the village Mairies. He seemed to favour popular histories with a military theme and books about explorers, though he was known to try Zola and Dumas. One day I remarked to his daughter, Georgette, how nice it was that he could catch up like this, in old age, on a pleasure he had never had time or opportunity for in youth.

'Well, it's his heart, you know. He likes to feed the chickens and the dogs still, and keep an eye on the calves, but in cold or windy weather he shouldn't go out at all, Doctor says. Stuck in here by the stove, he has to do *something*.'

Yet Georgette herself has inherited much of her father's submerged intelligence, and probably that of her maternal grandfather also, Jean Beaumont, who 'could calculate anything in his head'. It is she and her brother René who run the farm now, another of those brother-and-sister couples like the Pagnards, who, in later life, become undistinguishable from a married pair. Georges and Denise had several children, and the youngest is currently head of a College of Further Education. Once or twice a year he visits the home where he grew up for a Sunday lunch. His sister brings out the best china, kills chickens, arranges tomatoes in decorative shapes, buys good wine.

'He travels the world,' she explains a little sadly. 'It isn't our kind of life.' (Georgette herself has been once to Paris, but only for a day.) 'It was his godfather who set him on his way. He paid for him to stay on at school and go to college. We could never have afforded that.'

Georgette has a son, now over forty. That son, in turn, has a son, young Francis (in the now-fashionable *style anglais*), who comes to the farm for holidays. It is as if some centrifugal force has drawn the most loyal members of this family in on one another in an attempt to preserve a way of life and thought, but in practice their actions make the dynasty more vulnerable to extinction. When Georgette and René are laid to rest, how will Georgette's son manage his substantial property without a woman to share the work and do the accounts? Will Francis adopt the land and ways of his fore-fathers, or will the city of his alien mother, where he spends most of the year, claim him entirely? I am aware, in the cramped, warm kitchen where Apaires have lived and died since before the Revolu-tion, where ninety-two-year-old Denise still prepares the vegetables every day for dinner, and where Georgette lifts the pail of milk warm from the cow to pour it into my can with a generous disre-gard for measures, that I may be witnessing the last stage of a long story. And who, when Georgette is no more, will be there to bear witness to that story? Traditionally, in this as in most societies, men make a cult of minding their own business: it is the women who are the repository of collective memory, who keep the record.

In the eighty-odd years that separate Georgette's birth from Céles-tine's, the village ostensibly changed out of all recognition. It would be tempting to accept the view of all those inclined to say that after the Great War, with the tarmacking of the roads and the rumours of electric light, modernity and rural decline set in – were it not for all the evidence that in the 1920s and '30s village life continued to flourish and even expand, benefiting rather than otherwise from the technical and social advances. There were more shops than ever in Chassignolles: two bakers; five grocers, includ-ing one in Vallet and Jeanne Aussourd's old house with the tower;

several dressmakers, three tailors, and three blacksmiths. No garage as yet, though the war had advanced the petrol engine. The first open-topped country motor buses began to trundle around the Lower Berry; when Chassignolles held another spring *fête* in 1920, eight years after the famous, rain-drenched Cavalcade, a special shuttle service was laid on between there and La Châtre.

Yet much of the work in the fields was still deeply traditional and, in the nostalgic words of a man now old, 'the horse was always with you for company'. Although the reaper-and-binder and the mechanical thresher were now in general use, farming remained a labour-intensive occupation. Indeed, even the most up-to-date threshing machine, powered by a traction engine, required a team of at least fifteen men, sweating from sun-up to sun-down in the noise and the flying chaff. At the other end of the cycle, fields were still regularly sown by a trudging man who scattered seed rhythmically to either side from a pouch at his waist. Indeed I have seen such a Biblical figure myself in the Chassignolles fields, surviving into the 1970s. Between the wars three mills in the Commune were still in regular use, grinding locally produced flour and animal fodder. And domestic life in the farmhouse ran, as ever, on wood chopped by hand for fires or stoves that had to be lit at dawn before any coffee or soup could be heated. All water was still laboriously drawn from wells; piped water did not come to Chassignolles till the 1960s, amazing as that seems today even to the younger generation of rural French. A domestic electricity supply had arrived in La Châtre in 1921; by the end of the decade it had made its way to Chassignolles, hampered by the usual deliberation on the part of the municipal council who wondered at length if 'the sacrifice' – financial – 'would be commensurate with the advantages'. Many of the farms, in any case, scorned 'the line', continuing to use the paraffin lamps that had seemed in their turn such a modern and luxurious amenity at the end of the previous century. Madame Démeure, growing up in the village shop that she was to inherit, remembers that fifty-litre vats of paraffin were kept in an adjacent store house, a focus for constant anxiety about fire, and that, 'especially in winter, people would come in for their five *sous* of the stuff, making all sorts of excuses, just as we were trying to shut up shop. And each time you gave some out you had to wash your hands again in case the smell of it got on to the sugar or the flour.'

When a lighting circuit did eventually creep round most of the farmhouses, people who had grown up with lamps tended to use electricity sparingly, as if it were an unnecessary indulgence. Still today many of the elderly have this view; they are apt to sit, chat, cook and even eat in near-darkness, or by the fire's glow, and only turn on a weak bulb if impelled to by the need to sew, read the paper – or by the arrival of a visitor. People such as the Bernardets and the Bonnins have lived out lives in which the assumptions and expectations of their forebears have remained largely intact, adjusted a little to accommodate modern inventions but not fundamentally changed. The farmhouse kitchens in which they live are still furnished with the oak tables, benches, carved cupboards and cane-seated chairs of their grandparents. No question of a padded armchair, or even a rug. Only the white china-clay sink in a corner, the wood-burning stove lodged in the one-time open hearth and the prominent fly-paper indicate that we are in the twentieth century; only the large fridge and deep-freeze rumbling to themselves in an adjacent lean-to speak of the present day.

Nothing has been taken for granted, and the loss of older comforts – the self-contained and all-providing life of the village in the days before cars – is not readily accepted either. Georgette Bonnin is not one to complain of her lot, but she has been known to remark that the day's work has seemed particularly long and hard when she and her brother have had to turn out in the middle of the preceding night to help with a calving cow in difficulties elsewhere in the Commune.

'It was him over at Les Girauds. There used to be five different people keeping cows there and at Le Flets once, and now there's only him. He had to call us out because he hasn't a neighbour there who'd have known how to help. As I said to René, at least we had the car to get over there ... And what would the poor man have done without the telephone?'

'Well, but Georgette, I think it's partly *because* of cars and telephones and all the rest of modern life that everyone doesn't keep cows now.'

But Georgette was not convinced. She couldn't see how people could be happy to drink nothing but shop-bought milk: it didn't taste right. It was like the water in the tap, with goodness knows what in it, not being as good for gardens as the water in the well. She mourned all those other people, keeping cows, pasturing goats by the roadside, tending scraps of vineyard, filling every house in the Commune, running tiny subsistence businesses in sheds and stables: people who just, mysteriously, weren't there any longer. Equipped from her earliest years with the sophisticated skills needed in a restricted society to get on with everyone without encroaching on their individuality or letting them encroach on hers, she now finds these skills discounted. Their value is lessened in a society fragmented by population decline, extended education, commuting to Châteauroux, television, washing machines, consumerism, package holidays and the questionable belief that individual happiness is a human right and progress is the natural order of things.

The smithy was the traditional gathering place for the men of a village, which is no doubt why a café was so often kept by the wife of the smith. The women got together at the stream where the washing was done. You could be safe there from male interruption, and the fact of literally washing dirty linen in public furthered confidences. It was where the yearnings of the childless were expressed and also the forebodings of others about inopportune pregnancies. Some women in every village specialized in solving such problems and, as an elderly woman has put it to me with nervous succinctness, 'recipes were passed round'. It seems all of a piece that in the myths of the Berry the spirits of women who had destroyed their children, born and unborn, were to be seen at night by the streams frantically trying to wash away the evidence.

By the 1920s the streams had usually been embellished or superseded by a *lavoir*, a purpose-built, roofed shelter with stone or concrete slabs for beating linen, a cistern and drainage runnels. Now the relics of these Lavoirs are solitary places, choked with nettles and brambles, turned into duck ponds or pigsties. They seem in themselves memorials to inconvenience, to unremitting female drudgery, but when they were installed around the end of the last century or the early part of this one they were regarded as a substantial modern improvement. As late as 1922, Louis Pissavy-Yvernault was offering a new one to the village – a generosity that may have been partly influenced by the fact that he already had one on his own land which was supposed to be for the use of his staff and the home farm, but which was used unofficially by half the village.

It is this Lavoir at the Domaine that figures in Adolphine's school drawing book of the early 1900s. A tank drawn square, as if seen from above, shows more clearly than a perspective drawing could a row of stone slabs, each with a scrubbing board and a couple of miniature women at work. By their sides are microscopic bags tied with string. Other women, reverting to horizontal representation, hang on lines between trees rows of long pants, stockings and linen monogrammed 'B-C' – the combined initials of Adolphine's parents. In the foreground, other linen displays more elaborate embroidery based on the same initials, all drawn with mouselike Tailor-of-Gloucester precision.

Madame Démeure remembers the Lavoirs well, but her image of them is less refined. The little muslin bags, she said, held either blue dye to 'bring up' the whites, or the wood ash in which the linen was previously boiled. This was simply collected from the family hearth – 'When we were children, we were always told, "Don't put anything but wood on the fire." No food scraps, because that spoilt the nice clean ash for the washing. For a long time after I began to stock packets of soap powder in the shop, old people would go on calling what was in the packets "wood ash".' The linen was boiled at home, then taken to the Lavoir for copious rinsing. The Dédolin-Démeure family, living in the centre of the village, took to using the newly built Lavoir that straddled a small brook some two hundred yards down the road, but it seems to have been less of a modern improvement than had been hoped.

'It was all right in spring and autumn, but in summer when the brook got low the water in the tank was stagnant. Sometimes you had to rinse the cloths all over again at home in well water to get rid of the smell. And in winter the tank used to freeze over – you had to break the ice on it. The river never froze and it always smelt sweet, so I really preferred taking the clothes there.'

The 'river' was the tributary of the Vauvre whose bridging, on the road to Crozon, had caused the Council lengthy deliberations some fifty years earlier. It was over half a mile from the village. 'Two or three of us used to get our bundles together and take a cart to trundle it down. The donkey we used to have was afraid of water, so we always had to stop a hundred metres short and hump it the rest of the way – you can't force a donkey, it just doesn't work! But bringing the stuff back was the hardest work, because your hands were very cold by then and sore with it.' Madame Démeure laughed gaily, not so much at the memory as at the impossibility of encompassing within one frame of reference that girl with bare hands in the icy river and the old woman in a kitchen full of white machines that she had become.

The Lavoirs were the site of other dramas beyond ice-breaking, chilblains and discussions on the female uses of slippery elm bark. Georgette Bonnin recounted a poignant memory, from her child-hood in the 1930s, of a woman at the Lavoir. Bernardette N (as I will call her) had a kind husband and two small children, 'but used to talk a lot about death. One day, as she stood at her scrub-bing board, she gave a big sigh and said: "I don't like to think of anyone washing me when I'm gone. I'll do it myself beforehand."

' "Tch, tch," said the women on either side of her. "You mustn't think like that, a young woman like you." But she went home and killed herself.'

'. . . Well, I couldn't swear, to be honest, that it was that very day she killed herself, or even the next, but it was soon after: that's why everyone remembered so clearly what she'd said. And I remember it too, because she did it with mole poison. Well, what you gave someone who'd swallowed that poison was goat's milk, to stop it burning up their inside. So when he discovered her and knew what she'd done, Pierre N came running down here for milk. Of course we gave him all we had. But it was no use, she died anyway.'

Monsieur N, another of those survivors of the Great War like Georgette's father, brought up his children and never remarried. ('It hit him very hard, what she did. He'd done his best.') When we first bought our own house in Chassignolles he was a neighbour; he took a benign interest in our first attempts to build a porch, encouraging us with cuttings of wistaria from his own garden, which would not for some reason grow in ours, and with Virginia creeper which grew all too well. He used to address my husband, then about forty, as 'jeune homme', so my husband politely adopted the same mode of address to him. After that, he seemed to visit us mainly for the pleasure and amusement of being called 'young'. His wife lies in the cemetery, where he followed her some fifty years later. There is no mention on the memorial slab of the nature of her death and I expect that the Curé avoided all reference to it.

In the same way, on the not infrequent occasions when the Lavoirs themselves served for death by drowning, local newspapers were at pains to report that it could have been accidental. An unmarried female servant of fifty-one, who died in the new Lavoir in January 1923, shortly after it was opened, comes into this category. So does the man who was found in the same Lavoir only four months later. In his case the paper particularly stressed that he had been engaged in pasturing his cows in that field at the time and that 'any idea of crime or suicide has been ruled out. The death of Monsieur S was accidental.'

Monsieur S. It was not till some time after I first noted this that I realized that Bernardette N's maiden name had been S. Her remark at the same Lavoir a dozen years later appears in a clearer light. A suggestion of a family pattern emerges, a fatal predisposition transcending individual circumstances in a world where all lived at the same rhythm, subject to the same hardships, but in which the occasional person was unaccountably 'not like other people'. Today, as yesterday and a hundred years ago, an apparent suicide does not happen on average every year or even every five years, but it still occurs often enough to form part of the accepted nature of the human condition. 'Traditionally,' as one local friend laconically put it to me, 'they hang themselves, hereabouts.' But the country-healer and fortune-teller who bought the house by the cemetery in the 1970s died with his shotgun in his mouth, on the well-appointed day he himself had long identified – a circularity of destiny which disquieted the village and seemed to defy the usual analyses.

Could Georgette, I wondered, have been unaware of the S family pattern when she told her tale? But of course Georgette was hardly born when Henri S died, and if his death was accounted an accident . . . Fatalities in Lavoirs were not uncommon in that part of France, where few people knew how to swim, though most often they involved small children. But the only body in a Lavoir that seems to have made a profound impression in the Bonnin family annals was not drowned. It was old Denise who mentioned it, quite in passing: such-and-such an event was after the murder in the Lavoir . . .'

'Murder! What murder?'

It turned out to have taken place in the Lavoir at the Domaine: '. . . It was Sunday, see, and the son from La Vergne [a farm hamlet] had died, so everyone had been to his funeral. They were all coming away from the cemetery, in their best clothes, when someone came running and said there was another body, one that had been found. So we all hurried over to the Domaine land and there, on the edge of the Lavoir, with his legs in the water, was a man. One arm was raised and clenched, as if he'd had a stick in it and tried to defend himself. He was in his Sunday suit too, and I thought, when I first looked at him, that he was wearing a great red cravat tied in a bow. But it wasn't a cravat, it was the red blood that had spread out on his shirt front because his throat had been cut. He'd been stabbed as well.' Denise Bonnin shuddered daintily. 'After that, for a long time I didn't like going to that Lavoir.'

'How old were you? I mean, when did it happen?'

She found it difficult to say. It was like her father refusing to drive his cart over his mother's grave: the fact, enshrined in family lore, had become dateless. She thought, on much reflection, that she had still been a child – 'but big. I'd taken my first Communion.'

So, shortly before or during the First World War?

Further lip-munching reflection produced the thought that it was winter time; snow had fallen and that had obscured the murderer's footmarks. 'But the man hadn't been killed at the Lavoir. The Gendarmes said he'd been dragged from over by the woods.'

'Who was he? Did anyone know?'

Denise Bonnin looked surprised at the question.

'Oh yes, he was known. He wasn't from round here, though. He was from the Creuse. He used to work here sometimes. I think he was a builder.'

'And who killed him?'

'Ah, the Gendarmes never found out . . . 'Course, they didn't have all the education then that they do today.'

So, one of that classic out-group, the itinerant labourer from the Creuse. And something in Denise Bonnin's manner suggested to me that, even if the Gendarmes never found out, certain people in the Commune could make an informed guess. She herself resisted further questions and drifted off to another topic, but Georgette said afterwards that she'd always had the impression that it must have been a *crime passionnel*. 'Perhaps the builder was surprised by the husband. After all, the wife wouldn't have told. Would she?'

It occurs to me, also, that far from being concealed this murder was flaunted, as if to make a point. Otherwise, why not leave the body in the wood, rather than going to the trouble to drag it into a public place?

In a society where the theft of a coat from a hedgerow or a pair of shoes from a kitchen could result in a month in prison, a murder should make big news. I looked extensively through the columns of the *Écho de l'Indre*, beginning to wonder if the slaughter of the war had emptied private killings of their power to shock, but it turned up in the end in April 1919: I had been looking for it several years too early, and also too early in the season. The body had immediately been identified as that of a Louis Bachelier, aged fifty-two, from the edge of the River Creuse near Argenton. He was described as a *journalier*, but as having left home the very morning of his death to come to La Châtre 'on business', which suggests that he was in fact something more than a day-labourer. The item ended: 'The forces of the law are looking into the matter: let us hope they will be able to throw light on this mysterious death which has, rightly, upset our peaceable district.'

However, as subsequent weekly editions of the paper confirm, the forces of the law got nowhere. The paper also confirms that April was exceptionally cold, with frosts that damaged the blossom on the fruit trees and sudden falls of snow.

Madame Démeure, a brisk twelve years younger than Madame Bonnin, remembered having heard of the murder as a small girl and being frightened several years later when she took the family cow to pasture near the Lavoir on her own.

'There was one summer evening I saw a man there, on the grass. I thought the famous body had come back, and I ran all the way to the Domaine to get help with my plaits flapping over my ears. I was sure the body was coming behind me! 'Course, it turned out to be just a harvester, who'd lain down for a snooze.'

Madame Démeure dismissed the idea of a crime over a woman.

'The dead man was a horse dealer, so I've always heard. I think it was a row about money.'

A newspaper article later in 1919, referring to this murder and to another unsolved one near Nohant, reflected darkly on the misdoings of gypsies and on the general need to 'control the gypsy problem'. It would seem that views on this unsolved mystery relate to the preoccupations of the speaker as much as to the event. But, as someone who'd spent his life in the area said to me flatly: 'Someone in the Commune, or more than one, knew all about it.'

My own very tentative hypothesis I cannot commit to paper; at least till another full generation has passed to allow the protagonists to drift, like poor Antoine Pirot, away from the proprietary feelings of the living and into the benign indifference of history.

From the eve of the First World War, Charles and Blanche Robin were living in the small house near the Domaine that had been saved from the wreck of the family fortunes. It came as something of a relief to me to hear that Charles remained polite and cheerful on the whole in spite of everything, and indeed was known as 'a bit of a card', a skilled player on the mouth organ and other instruments. Monsieur Chauvet, who later bought the inn that Charles should have inherited, remembers him standing up on the outside staircase with a hunting horn, piping the harvest wagons home.

'What did he actually do in life?'

'Do? Well, he took things as they came, didn't he? He always did. That was just it.'

Perhaps, for a man indissolubly linked to a mad wife, such an apparently feckless attitude was the most intelligent one he could have adopted.

In spite of his reduced status as a *cultivateur* Charles still had genteel aspirations. He laid out the small front garden with box hedges and white rose bushes. 'He had a lot of taste,' said Jeanne Pagnard regretfully. In old age, being considered a deserving case, he was made sacristan like his great-great-grandfather, though it is recalled that he was once drunk enough to fall up the altar steps during Mass. It is remembered also that he used to bring his wife with him when he went to ring the church bells, partly because he was afraid of what she might do left on her own and partly because she enjoyed pulling the ropes herself. Charles has been described to me as a wiry old man, quite tall but thin, with a quizzical eye. Blanche, by that time, was much more substantial than he was, though that apparently did not prevent him once or twice, exasperated beyond bearing, from 'taking a stick to her'. As she accumulated bulk and years, the aura of semi-tragedy that surrounded her dwindled; she came to be perceived as merely comic. Her strength and enthusiasm were, as ever, greater than her judgement, and when excited by the sound of the bells she tugged the ropes so hard that she was carried up off the ground. 'We boys used to gather to watch,' an elderly man told me. 'She would go up on the rope in a flurry of skirt and petticoat, you could see right up her bloomers, which we thought a great joke.' Another man remembered, as a small boy, being held 'among her skirts between her knees' receiving from her a literal crash course in bell-ringing.

Excitement, bells, movement, dancing, heedless sexuality – there seems to be a consistent theme in poor Blanche's eccentricity. Manic depression (so it would probably be diagnosed today) may have run in the family – a genetic pattern like the one suggested by Bernadette N's ending. Jeanne Pagnard recalled hearing that Blanche's father had eventually hanged himself.

She added the irrelevant but thought-provoking detail ('I don't know if it was true but that's what I was told') that after his death his cousins were eager to obtain pieces of the rope he had used. *La corde d'un pendu* had long been regarded as having magic properties, and rural beliefs were not easily given up. It does seem, however, that the theory that Blanche came from prosperous and genteel people should be treated with some reserve.

As in every village in France at the beginning of the 1920s, the war memorial was commissioned and erected in Chassignolles. It stands on a patch of ground, overlooked by the oldest inn, the Chaumette inn, where the road forks as you enter the village. But younger boys – the eager, docile faces in the Bonnin wedding group – were growing up in sufficient numbers to carry on the life others had left for ever. The population never again reached the level at which it had been on the eve of that war, but for a long time the decline was gradual and unobtrusive. The village remained the populous place that it appears in Adolphine's precise drawings, filled not only with people but with handcarts, pony traps, apple presses, small flocks of goats and sheep being herded even in the main street, and the ubiquitous, busy presence of chickens. This crowded life at walking pace, which had not changed radically for hundreds of years, still survived between the wars thanks to the almost complete absence of motor traffic. As young women at the Domaine just after the Great War, Madame L and her sister would prick up their ears at the sound of a car heard far off across the summer countryside – 'Because we knew it could only be coming either to us or to the Duteuils down at Chapin.'

For Madame Démeure, the first car she ever saw was the Duteils': 'You could hear it coming very slowly and noisily up the steep hill from the river, and everybody would rush out of their houses to see it. Later on, there was another car, a great high red thing that we thought was wonderful. It belonged to a gentleman who used to visit La Gazette's mother. That one could only be started by half a dozen boys pushing it out of the Aussirs' stable and down the hill towards Crevant.'

What, I wondered, about the car Jean Chausée had before the Great War? But Madame Démeure was too young to remember that.

'Anyway, after the war Jean Chausée moved on. To La Châtre. You see, he'd found another wife while he was away in the army . . .'

He always had been considered in advance of his time.

In spite of the motor buses, no one as yet foresaw that the private car, that plaything for the adventurous and well-to-do, would eventually become the indispensable tool of rural life, at once its saviour and its destroyer. By one of those familiar ironies of history, this era just before the internal-combustion engine transformed the roads was a time when the convenience and speed of horse-drawn transport was far greater than ever before. The traditional isolation of one hamlet from another, one village from another, that had struck George Sand so forcibly, had gone. The perception of 'neighbourhood', of known and accessible territory, had expanded considerably, almost to the cluster of adjacent Communes that provides today's network. People still walked a good deal – children were expected to walk up to four kilometres to school and back – but longer journeys now became simple and frequent too. Shopkeepers' covered carts delivered goods over wide areas; a general carrier left Chassignolles for Le Magny and La Châtre every morning and returned in the evening. It carried the post, but the carter would also take private packages, messages and persons, and even undertake shopping errands.

You could also entrust him with children who were too young to walk far. The Dédolin grocer's little girl, she who was to become Madame Démeure, was regularly posted back and forth from Chassignolles to her maternal grandparents in Le Magny. She had been wet-nursed in Le Magny, as an infant during the Great War, and spent most of her first five years there. Her father was at the front, and her mother was trying single-handed to keep the business going and look after the elder children.

'I was like a little queen in Le Magny. When I came back to live at home after the war, it took me years to get used to it and feel that it *was* my home. My sister was jealous of me because she hadn't been used to having me there, and my mother had no time to spare for me. I lived for Wednesday evenings, when I could go and spend the night and the next day in Le Magny, because Thursday was a school holiday.'

By and by, the bright child found her place in the family by helping to prepare the packets for the daily deliveries round the outlying farms; her father undertook these by pony and trap, the logical extension of the grocery-peddling business begun sixty years before by Chartier.

'Everything had to be prepared and weighed up separately, sugar, salt and so on, in the exact amounts that had been ordered. Some people would only want to pay for tiny amounts at a time – they didn't use money much in the country then. Washing soda, too – that had to be hacked off a big lump and crushed by hand and if you weren't careful the sharp bits used to pierce the bags. And we often had to grind the coffee as some farms didn't run to a coffee mill . . . But in the school holidays I loved going out with my father. He went all over the place, as far as Crevant and Crozon. People were always glad to see him, and they used to give *me* things as a thank-you to him. I used to get nuts, and the fruits that had been dried in the oven that people used to keep strung up in their attics all the winter. Apple rings and peach rings – lovely! That was before tinned food really came in, of course. Even bottled fruit was thought a bit new by the older generation.'

Today, bottling surplus garden fruit, beans or tomatoes in sealed glass jars, still an almost sacred duty to housewives above a certain age, has in itself become a traditionalist and declining craft. Jars of plums, years old, shining faintly under a layer of dust, accumulate in dark sheds, another treasure whose value is now questioned. One year, Grandmother becomes too old and no more jars are added to the store. Her daughters are too busy, between home and job, or have come to prefer the deep-freeze anyway; her granddaughters do not know how to bottle.

Madame Démeure inherited the shop and spent her life in it while also bringing up, with distracted energy, a tribe of children and foster-children. A complex tension has operated within her, composed partly of a genuine, altruistic desire to create for others the happiness she herself knew as a foster child, and partly perhaps from a lifelong need to be the central figure, the 'little queen'.

'I was really upset when I had to give up the business to claim my pension. I knew the shop would be missed and I missed my customers, they were like my family to me. When you run the shop, everyone confides in you.'

Outgoing by nature, and trained from childhood to look about her and adapt to changing times, Madame Démeure is not one to sit and mourn. The front room that was once the shop is comfortable now with a carpet, well-stuffed armchairs and a tapestry wall-hanging – of a clog-maker, in memory of her husband's trade. Almost alone among those of her generation to whom I have talked, she has a clear perception that though the village was once far more animated than it is today, it was also extremely dirty:

'When I was young, apart from the main street everywhere was muddy. The back lane round by Mademoiselle Pagnard's [part of the site of the one-time burial ground] – that wasn't made up at all till after the second war. And along by the baker's and Madame F's house – the old girls' school that was – there was a great big ditch that sometimes smelt horrible.'

... 'Why? Well, it was partly everyone's slops and no modern conveniences, but it was also the stills. In those days distilling went on for half the year, with people queuing up for their turn. The machines used to stand in the spaces near the church, steaming away, with all the waste stuff trickling off into an open gully that ran across the street then and making a kind of black treacle. Oh, Chassignolles is much prettier and sweeter these days, I promise you – and far more flowers in pots in front of the houses.' Madame Démeure's own flower display, which in her retirement she has plenty of time to cultivate, is one of the finest in the village. You cannot, however, eat flowers.

Like everyone over fifty, she can recite nostalgically the names of the shops and workshops that once lined the street: the smell of coffee and the chocolate wrapped in silver paper in the shop that had superseded Chartier's, the Tabac established in one wing of

the tower-house, the cycles being repaired in another, the three
working smithies with their scent of hot iron and scorched hooves,
the ladies' hairdresser with its discreet sachets of blue-black dye,
the succulently leathery odour of the saddler's workshop. This
litany was enshrined, even at the time, in song. In 1929 the village
staged another of its Cavalcades, and the postman of the period,
Henri Jouhanneau, composed a set of verses and a rousing refrain,
extolling the local amenities to the tune of '*Quand il y aura des coqs
dans un village*'. With the passage of time, this light-hearted piece
of promotion has become a precious record, much appreciated
when the Mairie arranged to have it reprinted and distributed
sixty years later:

> *Hotel de l'ormeau, chez Marcel Yvernault,*
> *Salle pour banquets, noce tout ce qui s'en suit,*
> *La menuiserie, peinture et vitrerie*
> *Dans ces quartiers c'est tout un petit Paris . . .*
>
> *Henri le cordonnier, si vous êtes mal chaussé,*
> *Vous trouverez toujours des chaussures à votre pied . . .*
> *Chez Charpentier des sabots, des galoches*
> *Et sur mesure, il n'y a qu'à commander . . .*
>
> *Si vous avez besoin d'un brancard*
> *Rentrez chez Pagnard, sur la route de Crevant,*
> *Ses ateliers se trouvent de chaque côté*
> *– Un peu plus loin c'est l'épicerie Châtelin . . .*
> *Montez plus haut, à l'hôtel Raveau*
> *Vous goûterez délicieux jambonneaux . . .*

Madame Raveau was currently running the inn which had once
belonged to the Chaumette-Robins and would be bought after the
second war by Mesmin Chauvet, he who demolished the outside
staircase.

> *Où vous pourriez bien vous désaltérer,*
> *Bureau de tabac, cigares et cigarettes,*
> *Du bon vin gris, c'est chez la Mélanie . . .*

Mélanie, estranged wife of Jean Chausée, was now running the
Café-Tabac. The Hôtel de France had passed to the Aussirs.

Presented with this picture of the village as a hive of traditional labour and home-grown produce, it is rather a relief to find that the second half of the refrain introduces a sudden riotous whiff of the Twenties:

> Allons, les choeurs, suivez notre cavalcade
> Et apprêtez-vous à charlestonner,
> Dans dix minutes on va rentrer au bal,
> On va guincher, on va black-bottomer.

So even villagers in central France were not unaffected by fashions from the far side of the world, though I wonder how literally they charlestoned and black-bottomed? And to what? A tinny jazz record by then, perhaps, on a wind-up gramophone? Somehow I cannot quite imagine Bernardet throwing himself into that, dancer though he was. An athletic waltz to an accordion, perhaps, back erect, cap well pulled forward.

When the song was reprinted, the Mairie got someone who remembered 1929 well to add a few notes. These ended with the remark that, although work was long and laborious, 'people took plenty of time off for living; there were a good number of jokers and skivers [farceurs]'.

That too comes as a relief after the stated conviction of many of today's elderly that 'the young don't know what work is'. It also has the ring of truth. Charles Robin, complete with mouth organ, hunting horn and abandoned skill as a chef, fulfils well the description of a joker who took time off to live.

Long before Charles and Blanche had declined into their final role as village oddities, their daughter Zénaïde had left the Berry to embark on a life elsewhere.

The original idea behind her boarding-school studies in Bourges was that she should become a teacher, the classic route into middle-class society for the bright boy or girl. However, once grown up, she went to work in Paris, dans l'administration, the vast, fusty womb of French governmental bureaucracy.

It seems, on the face of it, a choice hardly comparable with Raymonde Vincent's break for liberty in Paris at the same period, but appearances may be deceptive. I do not know that Zénaïde ever embellished her income and her life by modelling for artists, but I would not be surprised; she was a handsome girl and is alleged by those who remember her to have 'moved in bohemian circles'. Paris between the wars, with the cosmopolitan liveliness of its boulevards and the traditional working-class culture still intact in its cobbled side-streets, was one of the better places on earth in which to live. It was a city in which baths were a middle-class luxury but in which a furnished room could be rented for next to nothing, and anyone in regular employment could afford to eat the set meal in one of the innumerable family restaurants. Zénaïde spent many years in a little flat in the ancient Place Dauphine on the Left Bank. With an individual flair that seems to presage the 1960s rather than reflecting her own era, she decorated it with genuine antiques and small pieces of mirror-glass set in patterns. She never married, but I am told she had various gentlemen friends – 'la belle vie, quoi?' The women who stayed in the village, hands reddened and swollen by a lifetime's work, are half censorious, half indulgent.

'Ah, she was a very nice person, Zénaïde, kind, warm, good fun – but a little dotty, not really a good-wife-and-mother type. She was more of an intellectual. And eccentricity ran in the family, as you know.' Jeanne Pagnard speaking. She herself actually visited Zénaïde in Paris, which was a mythical place still to most of the citizens of Chassignolles between the wars; but then trips to Paris ran in *her* family, following the tradition set by her emancipated grandmother.

Another who stayed with her, rather later, after the Second World War, was a boy of ten. He was her distant cousin from the Yvernaults of the inn, who had intermarried with the Chaumettes a full hundred years before, though in the family the precise nature of the connection had been lost. He wrote to me:

'She was a dreamer, affectionate, dynamic – a person out of the ordinary. I was very fond of her; her open-mindedness [son esprit libre] was like a breath of fresh air to me ... She let me go about Paris on my own just as I wanted to, which brought home to me for the first time my own need for independence.' Today that village boy is a university lecturer.

Another child's testimony to her, still more long-range, has reached Chassignolles. One day in the early 1990s a well-dressed lady 'of a certain age' called at the Mairie and revealed that she had been a refugee child in the village during the war. She was passing through the Berry with her husband and wanted to see again the house where she had stayed, which she could only locate by describing its owner: 'Zéna I called her . . . A wonderful person, so kind and such fun . . . I really have a golden memory of those months.'

I think this must have been in 1940 after the fall of France, when Zénaïde, in common with a great many other Parisians, retreated to their country roots for a while. Her parents had died some years earlier: she had kept their house, by now a packed repository of vanished lives.

According to Jeanne Pagnard, who vaguely remembered the little girl, she was the child of Zénaïde's current gentleman friend – 'Not a born Frenchman, no, I don't think so. No, I don't know what happened to him . . .'

Zénaïde met her post-Impressionist painter, whose name was Norman Lloyd, during the Liberation of Paris four years later. By one of those turns of fate that seem to transform the random nature of life, he led her back again to her rural origins, for his own stock in trade was not Parisian streets but landscape. Though he was always referred to in Chassignolles as 'English', his childhood roots lay in the space and light of Australia, which he had left for good as a young man to fight and be wounded in the previous war. After 1944, he came with Zénaïde to Chassignolles for the holidays, and after several years he took to spending whole summers in the place even when she was not there. He it was who built on the makeshift 'English-style' bathroom, added the blue-painted veranda and trellis and embellished the front garden further with a cactus and pampas grass. A new side gate was installed, with a ship's brass bell that jangled and could be heard in the back, and in the end wall above the beehives bits of mirror-glass were set in a pattern.

Charles Robin had not made very old bones. According to the family grave, he died in 1934, not yet seventy. His death does not, however, appear in the Chassignolles register for that year, nor in La Châtre, where relations on his father's side were still living, nor yet in Châteauroux, though he is known to have been there in the care of the nuns around that time. He is remembered singing a potato-pickers' song at a Christmas party. So exactly where he was at the end is a small mystery. It was an era when, in the country, most people still died at home – but where indeed was home, with his only child far away in another life? The mould was broken. The Chaumettes, once so numerous in the village, were all gone. If Blanche survived him, she would hardly have been capable, by all accounts, of caring for him in his last illness, but I think she may well have been dead herself by then.

I do not know because her name does not appear in the Chassignolles Death Register either, for any year in the 1920s or '30s. Nor does she figure on the gravestone. For some time I believed that, as she got madder and her husband declined in vigour, some of her relatives must have appeared from elsewhere and mercifully reclaimed her. Perhaps they did – but she cannot have gone far, for in death she was returned to Chassignolles to lie with the family to whom she had caused so much inadvertent harm. Both Monsieur Chauvet and Monsieur Aussir were adamant that she was 'down there too'.

'Are you sure? Her name's not there.'

''Course I'm sure. They're both there. I helped carry her to the cemetery on my shoulders. That was how it was still done, then.'

'I should say so. It was me who made Blanche's coffin. A big coffin for a big fat woman.' Monsieur Aussir. He added casually: 'The cemetery's full of my handiwork, you know.'

The shiny black plaque, which now lies broken in the dust, was engraved all at one time, replacing various earlier inscriptions whose indecipherable traces still faintly mark the stone.

It can only have been put up after Zénaïde's own death in 1954 because Zénaïde is on it. The initiator was almost certainly Norman Lloyd, he who inherited the small house and all the hoarded family chattels that it contained. So the stone commemorates not so much the actual bodies who lie there – Silvain-Germain, Zénaïde's great-grandfather, is mentioned though the cemetery did not exist when he died – but rather those whose memory was revered and had been handed down.

It would seem that, over the years, Zénaïde had spoken to her companion of her grandmother Célestine. She must have spoken too of Célestine's by then mythical father, first innkeeper, first Secretary of the Mairie, but she did not much mention, it seems, her own mother. Whether poor Blanche's name was ever, briefly, on the grave I do not know. But after Zénaïde's death from cancer of the breast (a repeat of Anne Laurent's seventy years before) the outsider who was the one person left to preserve her memory simply omitted Blanche from the record. This fact is in itself an eloquent comment.

But what of Célestine's last years?

Because the packet of letters from her distant youth had surfaced in the small house, I assumed for a long time that she had returned to live there in her widowhood with her feckless, ageing children. She is certainly remembered appearing in Chassignolles in the years after the Great War, wearing the white cap tied with ribbons beneath the chin that by then most women had abandoned – mistakenly, one might think, for it was a becoming article of dress. But Jeanne Pagnard was adamant that she did not live in the village. 'Oh no, not with Blanche!'

Sure enough, the Chassignolles census for the period does not list her. I found her in 1921 in La Châtre, still in the Rue des Chevilles, where Pierre had died in November 1914. The alley had declined further during the years of the war. The roofer and the clog-maker who had been there earlier had moved on, several houses were derelict or used for storage. Célestine was one of only three inhabitants, all old women, each living on her own. One, of seventy-three, is described as a 'servant' and another of seventy-eight as a *journalière* – a casual worker. There was no safety-net then for such marginal members of society. It is something of a relief to find that Célestine, also seventy-eight, is described as 'without occupation', but on what did she live? On some relief fund for the widows of indigent licensed victuallers? Or on the charity of her husband's relatives?

There is, however, a happier note on which to end Célestine's story. According to both Mademoiselle Pagnard and the Bonnins, she had 'a friend' in La Châtre who lived very near by. The word Jeanne Pagnard used for this person was *bon ami*, the traditional term for companion-lover: she at once corrected herself, but the general message was clear – 'Of course they were both old people by then, and he was the retired Curé from Crevant! But he was her special friend and they spent their days together.'

So perhaps it was choice rather than absolute necessity that made Célestine remain in that ramshackle street behind La Châtre's church. Her life had been spent largely in thrall to the demands of others. The passing years had denied her the happy family of descendants she might reasonably have expected and had taken from her almost every advantage she had known in better days; but, like the granddaughter who followed after her, she finally made her own unconventional arrangements. It is satisfying to know that she who had been reared for something better than a life of peasant labour, and who was so sought after in girlhood, was not after all bereft in old age of the company and affection of a suitable man.

By 1931, when Célestine was approaching ninety, her companion had died – it is thought, during the particularly severe winter of 1929. She had become too old to sustain independence any longer and had moved to Châteauroux, to the charity home run by the Little Sisters of the Poor. Charles was quite without any resources and had Blanche on his hands. There were no other near relatives who could look after her and nowhere else she could go. Her granddaughter had her life and her job in Paris, and even the provincial French respect for family duty did not demand that Zénaïde abandon everything to care physically for her grandmother. It is, however, remembered that Zénaïde, 'who'd always been fond of her old Granny', paid for Célestine to have some extras that the Sisters did not provide, including a cup of sugared milk every evening.

Célestine died at last in February 1933. The motor hearse that brought her from Châteauroux back to Chassignolles travelled at a matter-of-fact speed over roads that she had once known as muddy tracks for donkeys and packmen. The few personal possessions she still had with her were similarly returned, and were stuffed into the already-full oak presses without anyone examining them.

Célestine was laid away in the cemetery that was new when her mother was buried there. Her son followed her only a year later. They joined many Chaumette cousins, Jeanne Pagnard's grandmother, the pedlar great-grandfather who opened the first shop in the village, many Apaires, Bernardets, Pirots, Yvernaults and others, named and unnamed, whose lives and labours and aspirations had gone to form the village Célestine had known, and where she herself had played such a central role over many decades.

Chapter 17

Sixty years have now passed since Célestine's death, another life-time of physical change and social evolution. Born to the first stirrings of a new era, she died also on a cusp. Looking back now at the rural France of the 1930s, it seems to us and to the nostalgic survivors of that period that the intricate, well-peopled structures of traditional country life were then still intact, the archetypal world that we have lost. And yet the number of cars on the roads was increasing year by year, the first tractors were appearing on the bigger farms, the wireless and the daily paper had installed themselves even in remote farm kitchens. Planes appearing in the skies above the fields no longer occasioned excitement and wonder; within a few years, another war and a psychologically traumatic Occupation would move France on once again. Combine har-vesters, Family Allowances, medical insurance for all, secondary education, television, declining Church attendance, efficient contra-ception, bathrooms in every home – all these phenomena of the later twentieth century were already waiting in the wings when Célestine took her last ride.

And yet the Chassignolles we first knew in the 1970s still retained – retains even today – much from a far older world. Pictures without date, drawn from the last twenty years, assemble themselves in my head. Because they express survival and con-tinuity, it takes me a while to realize that some of these images in themselves have insensibly acquired the patina of vanished things, absent persons.

I walk up the road from our house to the village, bound for the baker's. A thin old woman falls into step beside me, our neighbour. Her husband – he who had once crossed the sea to the Dardanelles and wondered politely which sea we had crossed – died a year or two back. His widow is lonely in her big, dim farmhouse with only her vegetable garden to scold. Too old now to keep goats, she wages an obsessional war against the mice in the shed who eat her potatoes: there is usually a petrified corpse strung up in the cobwebby window like a villain on a gibbet. Its beady eyes are open, it holds a fragment of cheese in its pitiable mouth. Marie D calls it, with satisfaction, a 'scarecrow'.

'You're going for the bread? I'll keep you company.' I resign myself to ten minutes of her random reflections on life and mice.

At the next corner we are joined by another pensioner, a man with a trim white moustache and a stick, whom at this time I know only by sight. He is in fact Monsieur Jouhanneau, retired postman. Cheery greetings are exchanged, for it is a beautiful spring day with a hint of summer warmth to come and may flowers once again whitening the bare hedgerows.

We embark on a ritualistic conversation about the season being advanced but treacherous, and about the risk of night frosts to the early fruit blossom. Marie D opines that people are at risk too – far too early to think of leaving off woollen underwear: ' "*Pentecôte, découvre côte*" – that's what we always said, wasn't it, Henri?' ('Don't uncover yourself till Whitsun.')

The old man assents politely, but I see that inside this vulnerable old figure there is hidden away the strong man, impatient of women's fussing, that he once was.

Having secured another listener, Marie D suggests they let me go on ahead:

'Your legs are younger than ours. We can't walk at your pace. We're old just now [*vieux à présent*].'

The old man says: 'It's lucky you and I have already been young once, Marie, for it won't come back again.'

He speaks with a faint incredulity in his tone, as if he, like others accustomed all their lives to the regular renewal of the seasons, finds it hard to believe that his own youth and vigour will not, like the may and the swallows, return.

Henri Jouhanneau, the composer of the Chassignolles Song, tramped the Commune on foot for years with his wallet of letters. Later, when the lanes were better surfaced, he took to a bicycle. Now another postman, another strong young man making the most of a routine job, roars round the same lanes on a PTT motor bike. When in a good mood, he matches the drama of this with a histrionic manner of delivering the mail – 'Voilà, Madame! Encore une lettre de votre amant.' He hands a circular for pig food or an electricity bill to a housewife, who may be flattered but is certainly disconcerted to be told it is a letter from her lover. Monsieur Gallant (an approximation to his genuinely dashing name) takes no account of who else may be within earshot. Mademoiselle Pagnard says: 'Really, he shouldn't say such things. After all, they might be true . . .'

By and by Monsieur Gallant's own domestic situation becomes complex, and he abandons Chassignolles post office for the life of a supply postman over the whole Department, an itinerant existence that may suit his temperament better. But with the passing years he moves up several grades into a grander, advisory role, and re-establishes himself with a second wife and a young family. He builds himself a cottage from a pattern-book, in the middle of a field with a fine view, and settles down to grow leeks and asparagus like anyone else. Turned forty, and still never short of a joke, he is well on his way to becoming a prized old-timer, like Jouhanneau before him.

We ourselves, like migratory creatures following our own natural cycles, come back to Chassignolles at predictable intervals. Doing this, we become peculiarly conscious of the changing seasons, though their reassuring pattern tends to lull us into the false belief that no real change is in process. The cowslips that speckle the ditches if we arrive at the right moment in early April have disappeared like les neiges d'antan by May, when the buttercups are taking over the under-occupied pastures and the Remembrance poppies suddenly spot the growing corn fields. By high summer another transformation has taken place: neat rows of vegetables have been conjured from the soil, and our garden is temporarily surrounded on two sides by a dense curtain of greenery. Behind fruit trees, studded with early red apples as in a tapestry, rise oaks, and behind them two poplars. They mark from far off the marshy, willow-hung site of a duck pond, once fed by a stream and a spring where the occupants of our house used to fill their jugs. Pond, stream and spring have now dried up; they are casualties of the falling water-table from which the new water-towers and pipes have sucked their fill.

In the closed attic that we left swept bare, where the summer heat is trapped, a miniature drapery of cobwebs has grown, powdered with the dust of the outer air: leaf and blossom dust, pollen, the spoil of the occasional woodworm. Fresh droppings are scattered on the boards, and when we open a shallow drawer a terrified dormouse, with the black-and-white striped face of a mime artist, leaps out and runs for her life. Left behind, her children make squirming, sucking motions from the centre of a perfect nest constructed of moss and chewed dishcloth. We carefully move nest and occupants to the chicken loft, to Bernardet's incredulity and civil scorn. Later, when the charming dormice have become a plague – nibbling fruit from a bowl in broad daylight, preening their whiskers on beams within our sight, gorging themselves on blackberries whose seeds then reappear in blobs on the kitchen tiles – we harden our hearts and buy poisoned wheat. The dormice sensibly refuse to touch it. Years later again, we hear there is talk of declaring these exquisite little pests, now apparently rare, a protected species.

The sheer volume and variety of seasonal life remains a source of wonder as it noisily ebbs and flows. Where does it all go in the long, cold, silent winters; by what intricate regeneration does it return? Crickets, cicadas, butterflies, dragonflies like miniature helicopters – some years the eerie lights of glow-worms appear after dark around the ditches and the ivy, but other years there are none. Several times a hedgehog has occupied the garden, snuffling round like a full-sized pig. Always the lizards reappear, benign spirits possessing the house's southern face, rustling among the vine. The year we built a wall of hollow pot bricks, they colonized that as a safe labyrinth: we dreaded that in rendering the wall-ends we might entomb some of them, and our luck along with them.

Some summers there are brown field mice and even sleek rats, some there are none. Sometimes flying ants or mosquitoes or moths

255

lay siege at dusk, moles build subterranean systems under the grass, and one memorable year hornets nest in the chimney. Lighting a fire on an evening of sudden, lashing rain, we provoke an angry hum; for days afterwards we are wary, people tell us stories of death by stinging; fragments of giant honeycomb with no honey, dry and sinister, plop on to the hearth.

One year, and not again, a nightingale sings passionately all night. Other times a screech owl nests in a nearby field; its rasping voice sounds at a distance like a giant breathing. Another year, when poultry are living in an adjacent orchard, a yellow moon hangs so bright and low in the sky that the witless chickens think it is the dawning sun and crow and cluck all night. They are irritably hushed every fifteen seconds or so by the hissing geese, whose intelligence must be marginally greater.

In the days of the chickens, they escape into our garden and lay us eggs under the hedge of lilac and hornbeam. We find this some compensation for the lettuces they peck, but Bernardet does not. He disapproves of the chickens, not just because they attack the vegetables he has planted but by association with their owner. When people have sat on the same bench together at school, a rivalry or an enmity begun then settles into a fixed attitude long after its origin has been forgotten. I have often become aware, in the village, of a steel cobweb of old resentments or reticences, just as tough as old alliances, which someone from another world can only treat with the greatest circumspection.

So-and-so 'speaks ill of others'.

Such-and-such is 'as lazy as a dormouse'.

'He favoured the girl too much.'

'That woman never ought to have married him.'

In a society where a forebearing tolerance of others' weaknesses, vanities or eccentricities has important survival value, such judgements are not passed lightly, but once they are they become part of a moral construct, epitaphs on a whole lifetime.

'What the father built, the son wasted.'

'The daughter-in-law was the ruin of that family.'

In autumn, the vibrant wild life of the high season is retreating into death or hibernation. A vivid stillness possesses the landscape, a breath drawn in before the November storms. Transfigured by the first night frosts, the red and yellow leaves hang as brilliant as those of the New World against a high, mild sky. It is as warm as an English summer. The wood behind the Domaine is particularly golden, for it consists almost entirely of Spanish chestnuts. Bicycling through it, I come upon Madame Bernardet; her own sit-up-and-beg bike is parked in the ditch, there is a cloth bag on her arm. She is in conversation with a middle-aged man, similarly equipped, whom I vaguely recognize. They greet me cheerily but with a slightly self-conscious air: could they possibly – at their age? But no, of course, I realize they are gathering chestnuts, and that the appearance of conspiracy is because the trees actually belong to the Domaine . . . But no one from there is going to bother to gather them . . . Pity to let them go to waste . . . The habits of their own youth and of all the generations lying behind them are impossible to resist. One does not, if one is wise, refuse nature's bounty. So chestnuts and walnuts are picked, even if they are not strictly needed, just as huge quantities of vegetables and fruit are harvested even when there is a glut and firmly bestowed on acquaintances too old or too urban to have a glut of their own. 'Harvest' and 'picking time' – *la récolte* – are words with a moral glow surrounding them. The fact that the most important harvest of all, that of the wheat, is so highly mechanized these days, has not dimmed this aura: rather, it is as if people feel obscurely cheated by the speed and sureness of combine-harvesting and therefore transfer their necessary emotion to other crops. Enjoyable crises develop over the exhausting need to pick, prepare and freeze the haricot beans before they swell too far, or the obligation to get the damsons in before the wasps descend.

In the old tradition of the villager doing well, as distinct from merely scraping a living. Bernardet maintains his own vineyard, in the favoured place on a well-drained southern slope towards Le Magny. There, very early one Sunday at the beginning of each October, the Bernardet clan gather *pour les vendanges*, the numerous descendants of the hard-pressed Paul justifying their existence. Many of the younger ones are builders, electricians, mechanics and even teachers: they enjoy the day's labour in Uncle Georges's vineyard, punctuated as it is by a hearty picnic breakfast and lunch, but they enjoy it consciously as a ritual belonging to a way of life they themselves are leaving behind. When Bernardet is gone, the vineyard will go too, and with it the little wooden barrels of purplish wine with its own distinctive taste. Looking after a vineyard, keeping it weeded and sprayed and trellised, is labour-intensive; economically it can hardly be worth it today, with *vin ordinaire* in every supermarket at a few francs the litre, though Bernardet himself swears his own wine is healthier than 'all this treated stuff'.

The old subsistence economy, with its procession of duties that become rituals, forms a calendar that is distinct from the official one but cohabits with it, so that an old seasonal marker may reappear under a new guise. One year, on the eve of 11 November, when the church bells are tolling cheerfully for men dead sixty years and more, I go down to the Bonnins. Old Monsieur Bonnin is there, more talkative than usual, indeed positively jolly, making lunges at the stomach of a frequently pregnant neighbour. Another moustached old man breezes in – 'I hear tell there's some new cider going!' The remains of the apple crop have just been pressed and bottled. We all have a glass of this volatile liquid, still fermenting in its own sweetness. An atmosphere of discreet celebration reigns. Although both men are old soldiers, and will stand at agèd attention by the war memorial the following day, well wrapped up in scarves, I sense that something older than Armistice Day is being marked here. By and by it comes to me that 11 November is also the Feast of St Martin. Since St Martin's Day was always a quarter day when bills were settled and employments entered into or terminated, it is also therefore far older than St Martin himself. It is the autumn solstice, one of the four natural turning-points of the ancient world, a time for purificatory bonfires that were once sacrificial in intent. Here in the warm kitchen with the glasses of apple juice and the jokes about the pregnant neighbour, something very old is being subliminally recalled.

We are not always there ourselves in autumn. The grapes over our door are eaten by blackbirds, much to Bernardet's justified disgust. '*Les merles les auront . . . C'est dommage.*' One year, knowing that I am due to come, he cuts them for me and strings them up in the house complete with their leaves, where they greet me with a Bacchic air, musky, just beginning to bruise. With laborious care I transport a few bunches back to London: bounty must not be rejected. But even Bernardet can see that when we come without a car we cannot carry apples home across the sea. Most years our apples fall with soft, unregarded thuds on to the composted earth of the vegetable patch, which they enrich further in their turn.

But then the bounty of acorns falls unregarded in this century from the oak trees all round, and even Bernardet does not try to harvest these. Once eagerly snuffled up by the pigs that wandered free in the villages, they now just drop with a tiny crack on to the tarmac roads. One buries itself in the hedge between us and the neighbouring chicken run, and takes root. It is four foot high before Bernardet and I discuss it, and we decide to leave it there. It flourishes year by year, it is taller than our growing son, then taller than any of us. Bernardet says several times, 'That tree will live longer than me.'

'It'll live longer than me too, I hope. Longer than anyone now alive. Much longer.'

But Bernardet still wears an elegiac expression.

'I've had a good life. But just now I'm old [*Je suis vieux à présent*].'

I tell him he surely has years of health and strength ahead of him yet, partly because that is what I want to believe myself and partly because I assume that this is what he wants me to say. He looks gratified but shakes his head – 'No, no, my place is in the cemetery now.'

'Oh, I expect he just says that to keep the bad spirits away [*pour conjurer le mauvais sort*].' Mademoiselle Pagnard, in placid amusement. She, in any case, is seven years older, and looks death in the eye unafraid.

Bernardet's concern for the oak is unusual in a farmer. One winter morning in the early days, the first time I ever stay at the house on my own, I wake with a jump in my cocoon of blankets. There has been a great thud that leaves the earth vibrating. The air feels threatening. I dress hastily and go out, to find that big trees that must have taken several hundred years to grow have been felled in the copse at the end. Why? I ask the woodcutters, hoping that some special purpose lies behind this slaughter. They are vague. 'Oh – for repairs.'

A couple of the inevitable old men in striped trousers have come down to look too. They gaze at the fresh stumps with the brutal appreciation of huntsmen admiring a quarry. One is Monsieur Chezaubernard, old soldier, owner of Barbary ducks. The other, an elderly clog-maker known as 'La Gazette' from his aptitude in passing round village news, has generously shaken his plum tree for us the summer past, scattering ripe fruit at the feet of our delighted child.

They opine that that's what trees are for – cutting down as needed. Always have been.

Another night at this same time I am asleep near the embers of the fire and wake with a start. An oak log shifts in its ashes, sending up a small spurt of flame, and it seems to me in that moment that a short, stocky old man in a cloak has crossed the floor, glancing at me as he goes with a shrewd amusement.

A trick of the firelight.

'An old man covered with a mantle', as in the Book of Job.

Our house was called 'the Pope's House' . . .

Another time, the ghosts I momentarily see are not men but the vanished pigs who once consumed the acorns. One evening at Les Girauds, as dark is coming down, I suddenly glimpse these antique pigs, hairy and long-snouted as in *Les Très Riches Heures du Duc de Berry*. Great boars, sows and little ones are together in a herd, rooting under the trees of a small copse. I make for home by an uneasy wind and a rising moon, seriously wondering if, for a moment, I have seen through a rift in time. Suppose it should happen again? Rags of black clouds transform themselves ahead into George Sand's cavalcades of unearthly huntsmen. The road seems solid enough beneath my feet. But suppose it should disintegrate into a muddy track, and the lights of the village ahead reduce themselves, as I approach, to weak pinpoints of candle flame . . .

A few days later I learn that a new enterprise has recently been established at Les Girauds. It rears wild boars, free-range, to sell their meat as a delicacy for Christmas and the New Year.

'La Gazette' has been gone for many years now. So have Monsieur Chezaubernard and Monsieur Bonnin. Indeed, all three of the husbands in the 1981 diamond wedding photo, Messrs L, Bonnin and Gonnin, were dead by the middle of the decade, leaving their wives as testimony to the superior female powers of survival. The year comes when, on 11 November, there are no men of the first war standing to attention any more: the Old Soldiers are the youngsters of the second war, who are themselves now heavy and grey-haired. A few years later comes the Armistice Day when the mayor announces: 'For many years, as you all know, it has been Maxime Démeure, in his capacity as a leading member of the *Anciens Combattants* and ex-prisoner of war, who has read out the names of the dead. Since he is now no longer with us, let us remember him, also, in our two minutes' silence.'

I think it was not until then that I realized that the old men in striped trousers, once so numerous, had, like the striped dormice, disappeared quietly from the scene one by one. They had become the past, even as the last old men in smocks did in the 1920s or others in breeches and cloaks did in the 1850s.

Old Norman Lloyd the painter had gone too, sadly separated at the last by debility from the people he had so nearly made his own. With memory loss, his command of French, always self-taught and eccentric, had gone. Now that they could no longer communicate with him, he became even to the kindest villagers something of an object of fear and aversion. A primitive distaste for the old and worn out, whether a tool, a beast of burden or a human being, asserted itself in their voices. Some maintained, according to their own preoccupations, that he didn't eat enough, or didn't keep himself warm, or that it was unnatural to live alone – or again that he'd had some financial blow which had 'turned his brain' – but all were insistent that he must somehow be spirited off to whatever distant relatives he possessed elsewhere. Ultimately, in France, the family is everything. With a sense of treachery in our hearts, abetted by his disappearance and then reappearance in a state of shock in a Paris hospital, we set this removal in train. For years, the Bonnins in particular would faithfully ask us for news of him, evidently conceiving of the United Kingdom as a fairly small, cohesive place.

Monsieur Chezaubernard, long a widower and used to looking after his own health, lived snug as a dormouse in his own house with a roaring wood stove. Then, one November, he wasn't there. 'He'll be back in the spring,' people said. 'He's just in the Old People's Hospital for the winter, because it's difficult for his daughter to get over from Le Magny in bad weather to keep an eye on him.'

In the spring the weather was still bad. Easter came early, cuckoos shouted unseasonably across the cold green fields. On the weekly bus going into La Châtre, well wrapped-up old women assured one another that it was 'no day for washing shirts outside'. They knew – they remembered. On Good Friday came a sudden fall of thick, wet snow, just as it had fallen another early April, the time of the murder in the Lavoir. At the Bonnins that evening,

Georgette said: 'Have you heard? Le Père Chezaubernard is near the end . . .' She said '*au plus mal*', the time-honoured French phrase for announcing an imminent death, the phrase sent in the telegram to Paris when George Sand lay dying in the Berry a hundred years earlier.

Later that night, the hospital sent him 'home to die'. In reality, he was gone already, but the rural hospitals know that people like their dead to lie in state at home and, since it is theoretically forbidden to transport a corpse anywhere but the morgue, a polite fiction is maintained. All the long weekend, while snow endured outside and the stove made the inside disquietingly warm, Monsieur Chezaubernard lay at ease on his own bed. He was covered with a lace-edged sheet, sprinkled with white carnations as for a country wedding breakfast, and above it his face appeared like the face of a doll, a matchbox propping up his chin. His moustache, the bushy one of a *poilu* of the '14–'18, was the most real and familiar thing about him.

His daughter, till then shy and taciturn with us, never forgot that we came to pay our respects to him. Many years later, if I went on foot through Le Magny's one street, she would pop out of her house like a small, benign witch. 'It's you! Where's your car – your husband? . . . Walking on foot back to Chassignolles? All the way from La Châtre? . . . *Ma pauvre dame!* You must have some coffee to keep you going . . .'

We were not to pay our respects to Bernardet at the last. We were not there. I regret that.

Jeanne Pagnard reported that he 'looked handsome in death [*Il faisait un beau mort*]'.

In 1988, the same spring in which he had written to me 'Your primroses are a marvel to see', he planted forget-me-nots and marigolds near our front door. Though he maintained that he had handed everything over to his son now, and worked less and less, he seemed to us as busy as ever. As always, each time we returned our garden was neat, weeded, clipped or dug according to the season. Only the grass caused a perennial difficulty, because lawn-mowing did not enter into Bernardet's concept of good maintenance. Grass was hay to him, and therefore should be scythed, but only at long intervals. And in any case, he explained, scything tired him inexplicably these days.

'My place is in the cemetery now.' Jovially.

'No, no, Monsieur Bernardet, not yet. Fine chance!'

Over the scythe, he experienced a revelatory moment. It quite often occurred, when I was talking to him, that I would hesitate about the gender of an unfamiliar word such as 'scythe' (*une faux*) and ask him if it was masculine or feminine? He always politely supplied the correct gender, but with slight puzzlement. Finally he conveyed to me that he did not understand why I did not know, since it must be the same in my own language?

When I explained that gender is attached to the word, not the object – that is varies from one language to another, and does not anyway exist in the same way in English, he looked thoughtful. Later he said to me, 'You've made me realize words aren't what I'd always taken them for.'

I think he enjoyed his last summer. The weather was very good, which in farmer's terms meant hot sun punctuated by providential showers of rain. He even swapped his cap, habitually worn indoors as well as out, for a straw hat, and his much-mended black alpaca for the blue dungarees of his son's generation. We talked often, about our children, about his own childhood.

That autumn, a roofer was supposed to come and mend a leak round the chimney of the kitchen stove. There had been some difficulty about the roofer not knowing what was wanted so I telephoned Bernardet to ask him to sort it out. (The telephone had been installed at Les Béjauds about five years earlier.) He listened attentively, assured me, 'I will do my very best, Madame', playing trusted old retainer. It was, intermittently, one of his favourite roles, though at other times he could be unyielding and it did not do to presume on him.

'Will you be coming after Christmas?' he then asked.

'Not this year, Monsieur Bernardet, no, because my husband will be in India for two weeks then.' (He always liked to hear of our travels. It made him feel glad that he did not, himself, have to make such traumatic journeys to such savage places.) 'We'll be back in Chassignolles in March.'

I sensed obscurely that he was disappointed. This was exceptional; he had a countryman's patience, the knowledge that things happen when they happen and cannot be forced. But the reason for his anxiety to see us was not clear to me at the time, so we did not change our plans as we should have done.

At the New Year I received, again exceptionally, a little note from him on squared exercise book paper.

'Wanting to wish you and all your family a good and happy year. In Chassignolles, for the moment, everything's going on nicely and the weather is very fine. Please accept my best wishes, and I look forward to seeing you soon.'

'It was his goodbye to you, Mum,' said our son when, only a few days later, we received a written *faire part*, the traditional French notification of a death:

'*Madame Bernardet et ses enfants vous font part du décès de M. Georges Bernardet survenu le mardi 3 janvier décedé à la suite d'une très courte maladie.*'

'He knew he was ill and he wouldn't do nothing about it. Wouldn't even see the doctor.' Madame Bernardet in March, tearful, still shocked.

'Georges Bernardet was always tough with other people and tough with himself too.' Mademoiselle Pagnard, to me. 'And Madame Bernardet's the same. Look how hard she's always worked herself. She wasn't the person to persuade him to stop in bed. Look at me – I had my operation and it's been worth it. But Georges didn't see things like that. He wouldn't go to hospital and that was that.'

I learnt later that during the autumn Bernardet had lost weight and often complained of a pain in his side.

'He was tired.' To Madame Bernardet, as to many of her generation, all illness is fatigue. 'He didn't really do much any more. Just the gardens.' Theirs, ours and another one near ours belonging in theory to his Parisian daughter.

But on the morning of New Year's Day he was up before dawn, helping his son with a calving cow in difficulties. The calf was safely born. He breakfasted as usual, then rode his mobylette over to our side of the Commune. He spent the morning tidying, snipping, hoeing: a last look round. The winter sun, bright in a blue sky, melted the hoar-frost, but to each of the several neighbours who saw him at work that morning and passed the time of day, he complained of feeling unaccountably cold.

'Ah, you want to take care, then,' they said comfortably. 'You never know . . .'

As always, when the church clock struck midday, he cleaned his hoe and spade, got on his machine and rode back to Les Béjauds.

But for once in his life he refused his dinner. 'Not hungry. Don't feel too good.'

Nonplussed, Madame Bernardet suggested he might take the unprecedented step of lying down for the afternoon.

In the evening, she roused him.

'You ought to get up and try to eat something now. Keep up your strength.'

He got to his feet. As he reached the kitchen an explosion, expressing itself as a massive haemorrhage all over the floor tiles, felled him to the ground. He did not get up again. Although an ambulance was called and he was carried off to the hospital he had so far avoided, he did not know it. He never regained consciousness.

In the village, where the unexpected death carried small shock-waves of fear and self-reproach, younger people said: 'Of course, if only he'd seen the doctor earlier . . .'

'They can do a lot now. Look at Mademoiselle Pagnard.'

'Dreadful that he wouldn't look after himself, when you think . . .'

But I thought that it was Bernardet's own conscious decision. Once again, from within the context of a life apparently circumscribed, he had acted with foresight, independence, and his own sense of priorities. It wasn't just the idea of going to hospital. He hadn't hesitated, a few years earlier, to have a cataract operation, which had been successful. He was quite informed enough to know that an operation and treatment for his growing malaise might prolong his life. But he had evidently determined in his own mind that the life of a frail old man, doing well all things considered, was not for him. His inherited lack of sentimentality over the worn-out horse, the old cow gone dry, the useless mouth to feed, was consistent. Since he felt as he did, one cannot say that the choice was anything but clear-sighted and right.

Il est mort – à présent.

He has his own place in the cemetery now, a new grave, one of the line of glossy granite bedsteads that have filled up the western side in the last twenty years and are due to invade the field next door. He has simply his family name on the stone, along with Madame Bernardet's awaiting her tenancy: on tombstones as in letters the French are more formal than the English. He has a fine array of memorial plaques from relatives, friends and neighbours, testifying to his standing in the community. He has mop-headed chrysanthemums each 1 November – All Saints, a major day for family reunions, when even unbelievers docilely visit their dead and make offerings that cut through fifteen hundred years of Christianity to an older set of beliefs. For the rest of the year he has plastic flowers, which I cannot feel he appreciates. Indeed the whole cemetery seems physically so alien to the values and habits by which his life was lived that I have difficulty in believing he lies there. With his cap, as ever, on his head? I suppose not. With a rosary, then, between his finger bones? Even less suitable: he did not set any store by such things.

Il faisait un beau mort . . .

For me, he is far more present in the night sky over the house opposite ours, the house where he grew up, when the Plough stands low and clear above the roof-tree. And he is present in all those other roofs he helped to raise including our kitchen one, and in all the gates, ladders, outhouses, racks, handles and wheelbarrows he has left behind.

Once, finding the remains of an old stool and what seemed to be part of the shaft of a wooden plough among a load of mixed firewood, I pointed them out to him.

'Ah, people have laboured over those,' he said nostalgically (*des gens ont peiné là-dessus*). 'What can you do, they're only bits? But I agree, I don't feel right either, putting on the fire something someone has taken trouble over.'

Bernardet's going brought home to me that a culture of conservation we had taken as part of the basic fabric of Chassignolles was in inexorable decline. Fewer and fewer people were replacing broken fence palings with carefully whittled new ones, patching worn clothes, mending bicycles with string, laying windfalls out in attics, carefully fixing padlocks to small stables and byres for which they had no real use. Fewer people now thought grass was for hay, or that the roadside verges were the natural habitat for chickens, or that there's nothing like a few sheep in an orchard to keep it tidy.

The layout of the fields and gardens has remained unchanged, since the area escaped the *remembrement* of the 1960s that destroyed so many old hedges on the plains of the northern Berry; instead, the change has been more subtle and recent. The communal grazing field, where Marie D once used to take her goats and where our son and others played football in the evenings under the elms, has sprouted a crescent of council houses and a mown expanse of purely decorative green. Not till about 1990 did the strimmer make its appearance, but when it did an unnerving sleekness began to invade the ditches alongside the farm gates. Pots of flowers have proliferated. The numerous wayside crosses, neglected since the Great War, are now decorously encircled with marigolds and pansies. On the rough expanse where the *alambic* has always stood in autumn, and where Monsieur Chezaubernard used to keep his ducks in a free-range idyll, the young village schoolmaster has organised a nature trail, complete with little labels.

'When we were young we didn't need to be taught about Nature. We saw it every day, walking to and from school in all weathers.' Thus, anyone in the Commune over forty.

The old conservation habits born of poverty and endeavour are being replaced, even here in the most traditionalist part of France, by Conservation. The castle of Sarzay, which has been falling down for most of the last two centuries, was acquired a few years ago by an impassioned restorer, who realized that he could afford to buy it if he sold his modest house in the suburbs of Paris. Employed by the national electricity company, he drives frenetically round to read the local meters and spends the rest of his time deep in mortar, moat-excavation and wrangles with the bureaucracy of the Heritage industry.

The mill at Angibault has been rescued also. For years a deserted, haunted place, hard to find even as in George Sand's day unless you knew exactly which green lane to take, it has now been bought by its local Commune as a place for *fêtes* and school exhibitions. The rooms have been cleaned of mouldy flour, grain and rubbish and painted white. The wheel has been renovated and turns merrily – at least on Sundays – in the newly dredged stream. When we visit it, a fellow-visitor who worked there as a young man, before the war, can hardly contain his delight. 'It used to be such a hole. And the man who ran it, he was a hard master, I can tell you. But look at it now. Wonderful!'

Another time, I take Madame Bernardet there. In spite of a work ethic as rigorous as her husband's, she enjoys expeditions and her life has not provided her with enough of them. She was twelve before she even managed a brief train ride into La Châtre – to be presented with her school leaving certificate – although she had seen the trains pass every day as she worked in her father's fields. She confides a wish, never likely now to be fulfilled, to 'see the great vineyards in the south'. Meanwhile we make do with George Sand landmarks. After Sarzay and the mill, she wonders if we could see 'La Mare au Diable' – the Devil's Pool. I am afraid that this famous marshy lake, which I have heard is more or less dried up, will disappoint her, but I have a detailed map and we embark on a search. At the junction of two woodland paths we encounter a child; Madame Bernardet, diffident in some societies, feels confident here and is transformed before my eyes into a character from a folk-tale herself.

'*Petit garçon, petit garçon* – can you tell us the way to the Mare au Diable?'

Fortunately he can. He, to complete the picture, is looking for his father in the big wood. Have we seen a man on an orange tractor?

On the way home in the car, Madame Bernardet says: 'There now, I can say I've actually seen it! I've always wanted to.'

She has spent her entire life about ten miles away from it, but such cultural expeditions did not, till very recently, enter into the Chassignolles scheme of things.

Culture-consciousness has invaded the local fairs too. Twenty years ago, many of the traditional Assemblies where goods and livestock were once traded and where Célestine and her contemporaries danced the evening away to bagpipes and flutes, had descended to canned pop music and drum majorettes. Perhaps the old men in striped trousers liked looking at the majorettes' legs, but this sort of thing is now frowned on as 'not folklorique'. Instead, medieval jugglers do a turn ('Lords and Ladies, I last passed by here in 1293 – no, no, I tell a lie: it was 1295') and children have rides on a prototype roundabout that consists of a horizontal wooden wheel turned by real trotting ponies tethered to it. The bagpipes are back; hefty young Berrichons in blue smocks or long skirts and lace caps self-consciously perform traditional measures, while stalls on all sides proclaim old-style Berrichon produce to crowds sated with an even more traditional Sunday lunch. As if the past were all one country, it is also manifested by a row of turn-of-the-century pony traps and gigs, their hoods in tatters, combined with an array of interwar reapers-and-binders and early tractors disinterred from local barns. At one *fête*, a threshing machine is persuaded to function again, disgorging grain into sacks still marked with the name of the miller who went to war in 1914. A team of men all past fifty retrieve without difficulty movements and gestures that have laid dormant within them for thirty years.

People love these old and not-so-old machines. Gratified to find themselves suddenly tourists in their own past, they stand in front of them and reminisce. The Bonnins particularly appreciate them, unabashed by any idea that their own current lifestyle might almost be considered, by people elsewhere in France, as a repository of bygone customs and skills. It is they who still milk nonchalantly squatting on their haunches, without so much as a stool, they who will spend an hour or more coaxing in from the field a cow who is being difficult. It is they who, come sun, cold or rain, take themselves off to the Bois de Villemort on May Day to gather wild lilies of the valley, in unself-conscious commemoration of the days when the annual selling of the lilies in the local market town was an important source of female pin-money.

I feel divided in my mind about the dancers in smocks at the *fêtes* and the loving reconstruction of Sarzay. On the one hand, there is the simple perception that if places, objects and customs are not preserved, then they are lost, and that therefore preservation efforts must on balance be a good thing. But there is the more sophisticated knowledge that to preserve things deliberately, for the sake of doing so, is to lose them in another way, and to risk keeping the shell of a world at the expense of its meaning.

A degree of double-thinking inhabits this page. Indeed, it has inhabited the whole book. We cannot help knowing, even if others do not, that our very presence in Chassignolles is not an unmixed blessing. However low a profile we keep, however much we cherish and support Communal endeavours, we are in ourselves harbingers of profound and continuing social changes. When we first arrived, the phenomenon of the holiday or weekend home was barely known in the Berry. 'Off again so soon?' old Marie D used to say in disappointment. 'But what about all those carrots in your garden you haven't finished yet?' Twenty years and several autoroutes later, the part-time householders (invariably known, whatever their origins, as 'Parisians') are an accepted fact of life in central France, and, as for us, people in Chassignolles are used to us. But I become more and more aware that when there were twenty-seven different shopkeepers and artisans in the centre of the village, there were no spare houses for outsiders to buy up, and that this was, for the village, a healthier situation.

A descendant of the Pissavy-Yvernaults, encountering me in the Mairie one morning with old Minute books piled around me, says shrewdly:

'You've taken over one of our houses. Are you taking over our past too?'

Stricken with guilt, I protest.

'But you didn't want it! *You* could have done this research. But you haven't.'

He relents.

'Quite true. I haven't . . . Maybe we need you. Maybe you are giving our past back to us.'

I rest my case. For me, to give back in this way, with interest, something of what Chassignolles has given to us, is a matter of pride and satisfaction. But so many people are not there to receive my hopeful gift. It has been estimated that, over the length and breadth of rural France, taking one area with another, one in sixteen of all habitations is standing empty, not even in occasional use – this, in a country where pressure on dwelling space in the larger towns remains unremitting. The figure cruelly contradicts the entrenched rural belief that property is what counts and that one can do no better thing than leave a snug house and a patch of ground to pass on to those who come after.

Moreover, this progressive desertion is the more sinister in that it is not immediately obvious. On a lonely road you come upon a cluster of buildings, nicely positioned so that the living quarters and barn face the south and a rolling view, while the store house is on the cooler north side under shady trees. There is a covered well, perhaps a donkey-stable or cow-byre, a pigsty and a dog kennel. The gate into the yard has been carefully secured with twine, so at first sight the place seems well looked after. The tiled roof is in good shape, smoke might be about to come from the chimney. There is firewood enough for several winters neatly stacked by the side of the house under old plastic fertilizer sacks. The shutters are shut, the inhabitants seem to be out in the fields . . . But then you see that the grass is growing lush in the yard, undisturbed even by the separate tracks elderly feet should have made to the well, the byre, the store. It grows green and long too round collapsing bean and tomato stakes in the undisturbed vegetable patch. The vine along the front of the house straggles unpruned. The hay visible in the dormer of the barn is blackened: it has been there years. A padlock on the great door is beginning to rust.

Someone took the trouble to put that padlock there, that string on the gate. There was a day when someone carefully secured the shutters before going out of the house, perhaps to hospital or to stay with a daughter 'for a bit', leaving the pots, pans, table and chairs in the place, switching off the electricity, meticulously locking the door over whose glass panel a lace curtain still hangs petrified within. Someone that day believed the place to have value and importance, a continuing existence ahead of it. But, ever since then, the silence has remained unbroken. By and by, if it continues, the mice and the rats, the spiders and the birds, the wind, the rain, ivy, brambles and time itself will begin to do their work of dismantling.

Yet to see the long past as constant and only the future as broken and dark is, in itself, a misperception. The fact is, great cycles of growth and decay have occurred before, and settlements have been destroyed and rebuilt hereabouts before, several times over. This time, too, is only a stage.

The period in which nearly all land in the Berry has been perceived as valuable, worth draining, clearing, enclosing, cultivating, has been a relatively brief one: it has lasted less than two hundred years. When Célestine was born, about one third of the land in the whole area was unused at any one time, either lying fallow or simply unclaimed. The prospect of returning again to something like this figure – allowing heath and marshland to creep back and forests to reclaim outlying fields – implies such a profound revolution in thinking that it is too much to ask of any individual farmer today, yet it may be what the future holds.

Today the Domaine in Chassignolles, though carefully maintained, is shut up much of the year. Madame L is too old to stay there alone, and only comes for a few weeks at a time when she can be accompanied by a posse of her numerous descendants. In the wood nearby the Virgin still holds her Infant aloft, serenely indifferent to time and solitude, keeping her secret. Occasionally, not quite certain what depths I may be stirring, I bring her a bunch of wild flowers.

At the Domaine's home farm, the young and go-ahead tenant has installed an all-metal building with an automatic grain dispenser in which to rear ducklings *en masse*. Here, in an eternal well-lit indoors, the ducks are safe from wind, cold, heat, foxes, dogs, cats, birds of prey and passing cars, but I think that the Barbary ducks on the waste land used to lead a richer life all the same. .

Marie D has been gone for years. Her house, empty for some time because her children could not agree among themselves what to do about it, has now been acquired by a younger branch of the Domaine family as a holiday home. 'Parisians' occupy Villemort on a similar basis: for the first time in a long while the chapel and the Saracen staircase are treated with respect. So, too, is the tower-house in the centre of the village: once an abbot's lodging, then the Sieur Vallet's and his lady's, later a grocery, a Tabac and a bicycle-repair shop, it is now being restored very slowly with authentic materials by a maker of musical instruments. He was drawn to the area from far away by the bell-ringing tradition in St Chartier and by the musical recitals that take place every summer in Nohant in memory of George Sand's liaison with Chopin. I wonder what Jeanne Aussourd's wraith thinks of that.

The big mill at Le Flets where the Charbonniers were once millers has lost its wheel, and its millpond has silted into a green bog. A little higher up the hill a tributary of that stream has been dammed to make a series of lakes, complete with ducks, perch and carp, whose owners picnic and fish on Sundays. Le Flets and Les Girauds are much depopulated, but at Les Béjauds several new houses have risen from the earth, neighbours with young children for Madame Bernardet. She is cautiously gratified by this, while continuing to assert that nothing is as it was, and Les Béjauds' own particular annual festival has been revived.

Madame Bernardet herself, aided by her son but driven by her own need to maintain things 'as they were in the Mister's time', continues to plant vegetables and flowers in our garden for us. She carries water in pails from the well across the road, having no faith in hosepipe water for making things grow. If she needs to clear garden rubbish, she digs in a pitchfork and twirls up a great load which she then carries away on her back as she always has done, a bent figure from an old lithograph. In view of her advancing age, none of this can last for much longer, and we regard each garden season that passes as an unlooked-for benefit.

Over the way, at the back of a derelict property, the one-roomed cot where Le Mère Philomène and her old-age pension ended her days is appropriated one winter by an antic figure who is to be seen striding round the roads talking to someone invisible or huddled up with a book under the shelter near the Mairie. He has also been observed painstakingly throwing bits of china into the river. It is said that he used to be employed *dans l'administration* in La Châtre and to be 'so clever that his wits have turned'. There is a good deal of anxiety about him, but it is generally agreed that he is 'a citizen like anyone else' and harmless, and he remains in his chosen lodging. In the charitable tradition of long ago, when ragged wanderers were common in the countryside, offerings of food are occasionally left at his door.

Nearby, Monsieur Chezaubernard's snug house has been taken on by Monsieur Aparicio. He came originally from Spain, an itinerant labourer trying his luck in the usual way in the richer lands to the north. But that was forty years ago; Monsieur Aparicio has long held French nationality and now, in his retirement, is settling down with the approval of Chassignolles to become an old fellow who is good at fixing things. He has enlarged his vegetable plot over the empty site next door, where once there stood the house of the carter who carried packets and children to and from the neighbouring villages – the house we saw become a skeleton and return again to the earth. Monsieur Aparicio has another stake in the earth of the Berry. A stepdaughter of his, killed in a road accident, lies in the cemetery.

The village's remaining café-hotel has been bought by the Commune some time after Madame Calvet's retirement and done up with the latest in lighting. A tenant has been installed, but people shake their heads and wonder if the place can be made to pay these days by anyone not possessing Madame Calvet's enormous energy and devotion to duty – 'The young, you know . . . Tcch.'

The small house that occupies a patch of land originally the property of François Chaumette (born 1795), the house to which Charles and Blanche moved just before the First World War and where Zénaïde lived out her idyll with her painter, has already completed a whole cycle of change. Embellished by Charles Robin with box hedges and by Norman Lloyd with trellis and a veranda, it has now had these pruned away again. It was sold (I am told for a figure that just about covered the stamp duty) to a retired farmer, and is once again an unremarkable slate-roofed French dwelling, as basic as a child's drawing.

The large, monographed napkins that formed part of Charles and Blanche's ill-fated marriage gifts are in our house on the other side of the village, carefully preserved from mice and moths. They are used on special occasions.

The cat embroidered by Célestine a hundred years ago is in a house in London. The wool is worn, but the picture is still distinct. The silk, more fragile, has gone from its eyes – had done so before the stool ever came into our possession. Shall I restore those eyes to their original brightness? To do so might be to destroy the object's integrity. And yet to add my own labour to a past one is another way of perpetuating that past, the things that people '*ont peiné là-dessus*'.

The letters to Célestine are in a filing cabinet. Each one, in its time, represented substantial trouble and pain. By all the odds, they should have been consigned to oblivion long ago, as lost as forgotten rain. Yet, like ladders and wheelbarrows, benches and ploughshares, they have turned out more durable than the lives and endeavours they express.

So too do houses and barns, gate posts, hedgerows, field slopes and the lie of paths, persist and persist, even when people that created them are earth themselves.

Afterword

Among the joys and frustrations of writing a book such as this is that, once published, it attracts further items of information. On its initial appearance in hardback I bestowed a copy on someone whose help and interest had been of great value to me and who (exceptionally for an inhabitant of Chassignolles) would be able to read it in English – Jacques Pissavy-Yvernault, descendant of the family who figures often in its pages. As he worked his way through it, he began feeding back to me further childhood memories of the area and its people.

'I wish you'd told me this before!'

'Yes, I'm a fool. But you didn't ask me that before!'

'But how do I know just what to ask you unless you tell me?'

Among the things he passed on to me too late to be incorporated into the body of the text was a mid-nineteenth-century manuscript memoir (*see page* 102). Apart from its intrinsic charm, its value for me is that it confirms and illustrates conclusions previously reached by other means, which is why I translate passages from it below. It was written as a young man by Paul Pouradier-Dutheil, he who was a friend and relation by marriage of Louis Pissavy-Yvernault and who went on to have a distinguished if chequered military career: he and Clemenceau disagreed about the conduct of the Great War. The Dutheils were a local family (there is a Moulin du Theil a few miles from Chassignolles); Paul's father and grandfather were both lawyers in La Châtre and there the family lived, but they possessed a hunting lodge together with a farm and lands bordering on the Commune of Chassignolles – the Domaine of Chapin, where they spent the long summer vacations when the Court in La Châtre was not in session. One of Paul Dutheil's earliest memories, however, was of the time when the family journeyed there in a very different season. He was born at the end of 1854, and this event seems to belong to 1859:

'One winter's day of snow and biting cold Fanny and I were rolled up in layers of quilt and blanket. [Fanny was his little sister. She later married the banker son of the Pissavys', a brother of Victor, who was almost a generation older than herself, and lived with a certain ostentation in a large house on the edge of La Châtre.] Looking like two parcels, with only our small heads with wondering eyes poking out on top, we were installed in a donkey cart that belonged to Le Père Soudit from whom the family bought wine ... At that date you could not get all the way to Chapin in a four-wheeled cart. [Indeed, the long-delayed widening and improvement of that road out of Chassignolles in the direction of Crozon were not to be completed for another twenty years.] In winter, especially, you could travel only on foot or with a very sturdily built two-wheeled conveyance. I have retained a vivid memory of that journey, which was decided upon suddenly and undertaken there and then: not so much a move, you might think, as a flight. At the time, I did not wonder much what was going on; I was too busy chattering and joking with Fanny and our mother and with our father, who walked beside the cart talking to Soudit. It was an exciting journey, for on the way down to the Ris Blanc [the small river below Chassignolles, where, seventy years later, the young Madame Démeure and her friends took clothes to wash] one or other of the two men had to hang onto the back of the cart, for the slope was so steep that otherwise cart, occupants and donkey could all have ended up in the river. Even I was a little scared at this point, and was hardly reassured when, as we forded the stream at the bottom, I saw the water come more than half-way up the cart wheels and almost to the boards on which we were sitting. Finally we made it without mishap, but it was almost nightfall when our procession entered the farmyard at Chapin where everyone was standing around waiting for us: Langlois' wife and Sylvain in front, behind them young Louis, Le Père Langlois, François and the rest.

'A roaring fire had been made in the big farmhouse fireplace, a hearth built to burn whole tree trunks with a high, wide chimney leading straight up to the stars that could accommodate the entire family gathered round for a *veillée*. It seemed to me like something out of a fairy tale . . . In my surprise and delight I went rather too close to the flames, spreading out my small, cold, stiff hands to them in the way that seemed to me right. All of a sudden I was seized with that awful pain called an *onglée* which results from too quick a change from icy cold to heat, and my day ended in tears. Luckily my father had a remedy for everything; he took me on his knees (perhaps the best bit of the remedy) and wrapped my hands in a warm handkerchief till the pain wore off.'

For the rest of that cold season Paul, Fanny and their mother stayed at Chapin and hardly went out. They were entertained by Charles, Louis' child, who 'had the Berrichon shepherd boy's special talent for making little carts, miniature water mills to put over rivulets, toy fences, gates and so on'. The father went back to work in La Châtre: 'On the three days a week on which he appeared in Court, he came back to Chapin afterwards to dine, sleep and spend the following day there working at home. He has often told me that this period was one of the happiest times of his life – "I would arrive, having come all that way on foot; I was young, I had spent the day representing someone in Court and so earning a bit of money to feed my family and there you would all be gathered to welcome me on the threshold."

'I have learnt since that our removal to Chapin was quite literally a flight. That year a terrible epidemic of croup broke out in La Châtre. ['Croup' is properly the description of a symptom, an inability to draw breath because of swelling in the throat: here, it would appear to indicate an outbreak of diphtheria.] Over the course of several months, this disease carried off more than eighty young children: their graves fill one whole side of the cemetery. When I was older, my father took me several times to visit that patch of ground where I myself would almost certainly have been laid to rest along with Fanny if Chapin had not been there to save us. I seemed to feel coming from him there in the cemetery a kind of pleasure mixed with horror as he contemplated the tragedy that had been averted . . . A single fact may convey a graphic idea of the ravages caused by that disease. Long after, in the year when many of those boy children who were my contemporaries would have reached the age of twenty, there were only a handful there for conscription into the army so the usual recruitment could not take place . . .

'My first cousin, another Paul, died then in Châteaumeillant [a town some ten miles from La Châtre]. He was six or seven years old. I can remember us playing together on the wide pavement in front of our house. The last time I saw him he was wearing a little straw hat with a blue ribbon and we ran races together.

'One day, after we had come back again to La Châtre, my aunt came to our house. She was in mourning. She picked me up and sat me on her lap, looking at me for a long time in an odd way. Then she asked me "Do you remember your cousin Paul, *mon chéri*? You won't be playing any more with him: he's left Châteaumeillant . . ." And, in tears, she hugged me so hard she almost smothered me.'

(It will be noted that this catalogue of childhood mentality relates to the densely populated country towns. No such cluster of deaths appears in the Chassignolles registers for the fatal year. This confirms the general picture, already conveyed by the birth and death records, that a child born in the village had, contrary to the twentieth-century mythology on the subject, a very good chance of surviving to grow up. Indeed I have been told, and have no reason to disbelieve it, that the lowest mortality rates of all occurred among children reared on isolated farms, whose contacts with anyone beyond their own extended families were minimal. It was these youngsters, however, who tended to succumb to illness in early adulthood, when they were called up into the army or went into service in a town and encountered alien microbes for the first time.)

In subsequent years the annual migrations to Chapin were less dramatic but considerably jollier. 'When we went through Chassignolles the journey became a fête, almost a triumphal procession. As we reached the edge of the village our father would greet his old friend the Curé, Normand [this was indeed the name of the incumbent described in the censuses for 1856 and '66 as the 'mass-server' – perhaps a piece of bureaucratic secularism]. The old man would come to hear our news over the hedge of his garden, which bordered on the lane, with his housekeeper, to be sure, following on his heels. He was the first, and then it would be someone else and then the schoolmaster Monsieur Charbonnier and then Dédolin the clog-maker.'

(Charbonnier, then a young man in the early days of his career, is a familiar figure. Dédolin the clog-maker was the great-grandfather of Madame Démeure, she who kept the grocery shop till the 1980s. His son and one of his grandsons were to follow the same calling: the dynasty is still remembered in the village. So the tapestry picture of a clog-maker's workshop, painstakingly stitched as an anniversary present by a daughter-in-law, which hangs today in Madame Démeure's main room, commemorates not only her late husband, Maxime's, trade but her own family tradition also. Today, a one-time clog workshop in Chassignolles is occupied by a foster son of hers, a young man whose lost family origins lie in eastern Europe but who has taken on the mantle of village carpenter.)

The later pages of Paul Pouradier-Dutheil's memoir, which was written largely in 1879, when he was a homesick young military officer on a foreign posting, seem to be addressed to the girl who was later to become his wife. Describing the egalitarian nature of life in La Châtre, where the young workmen with whom he had played as a boy at the same school were still greeting him on his visits home as an old and intimate friend, he wrote:

'You will probably be amazed, *amie*, at this way of life, which is that of a small town which has, up to now, lived much cut off from the world on account of its lack of communications: there is no railway line for a full ten leagues all round. Indeed, I think that when there's hardly a stage-coach or a coachman left in the world the La Châtre tackle will still be running ... A town that has its stage-coach can retain its old, simple manners and that genuine brotherliness of which I spoke just now. Sadly, these pleasant things are disappearing with the passing years. I admit that at moments, and in certain circumstances, I have something of a horror of Progress. Of course I am impressed and made happy by scientific developments. I love taking my ease in a fine carriage in an express train that slices through distance [three lines vigorously scratched out here – perhaps as being of too intimate a nature for public consumption?] ... But, on the other hand, without being able to explain why, I dread the disappearance of my old stager from Châteauroux to La Châtre, my *Grand' Voiture*. I can't imagine arriving home another way than perched on its top next to —— or ——

[two named coachmen]. How will I manage when I can no longer ask them, as we trundle along, to fill me in on recent deaths, marriages, births and scandals – when I won't have a charioteer to regale me with all the gossip, interspersed with encouragements to the horses, cracks of the whip and special manoeuvres each time we go down a hill? I shall have a lump in my throat the day that I arrive at La Châtre by railway train without having seen, as one does from the coach, the whole of the beautiful Black Valley spread out below with its villages, its church towers, the river and the blue distance. I pity with all my heart the generations of Berrichons who will never experience the vision of the sunrise as they reach the heights of Corlay.'

The railway was at last making its way to La Châtre as Dutheil wrote; the station opened three years later. To George Sand, born fifty years earlier than Dutheil and a friend of his grandfather, the stage-coach itself and the road it ran on represented modernity and progress compared with the unmapped heathlands of her own childhood. Now in turn the railway line, winding along the valley of the Indre from one village to another, has become part of that lost country of the past. Dutheil himself was, in the fullness of time, to help introduce the first telephone to Chassignolles and one of the first cars.

Bibliography

While it would be impossible for me to list every book that has, over the years, formed part of my reading on the subject of central France and her recent history, the following is a list of works which I know to have contributed directly to the writing of *Célestine*.

Published works

Alain-Fournier, Henri, *Le Grand Meaulnes*, Paris, 1913

Ardoun-Dumazet, *Voyage en France* (No. 26 in series), Paris, 1901

Audebert, B. and Tournaire, J., *1900, La Châtre et la Vallée Noire*, Editions Souny, Limoges, 1985

Balzac, Honoré de, *L'Illustre Gaudissart* (1833), *Le Curé du Village* (1839), *La Rabouilleuse* (1841), *Les Paysans* (1844)

Baroli, Marc, *La Vie Quotidienne en Berry au Temps de George Sand*, Hachette, 1982

Berducat, Jeanine, *La craie pour l'ecrire* (1989), *Léonie, femme de la terre* (1992), *François, le maçon* (1993), *Octave, le déraciné* (1994). All published by Editions La Bouinotte, Châteauroux

Bernard, Daniel, *La Fin des Loups dans le Bas Berry: histoire et traditions populaires*, privately printed in Châteauroux, 1977

—— *Itinérants ambulants dans l'Indre au XIX siècle*, Extract No. 11 from 'Le Bulletin du Group d'Histoire et d'Archéologie de Buzancais', 1979

—— *Hier en Berry: les Habits du Peuple des Campagnes*, privately printed in Valençay with the assistance of La Guérouée de Gatines, 1985

—— *Coureurs et Gens D'Étranger en Berry*, privately printed, 1984

—— *Le Berry de George Sand*, Editions Gyss, Châteauroux, 1989

—— *Paysans du Berry dans la France ancienne: le vie des campagnes berri-chonnes*, Editions Horvath, Roanne, 1982

Braudel, Fernand, *L'Identité de la France*, Flammarion, Vol I, 1986; Vol II, 1988; Vol III (not completed) 1990

Bury, J. P. T., *France 1814–1940*, Methuen, 1949

Burnand, Robert, *La Vie Quotidienne en France 1870–1900*, Hachette, 1943

Chastenet, Jacques, *La France de Fallières*, Fayard, 1949

Cobb, Richard, *A Sense of Place*, Duckworth, 1975

—— *Promenades*, Oxford University Press, 1980

Devailly Guy (ed.), *L'Histoire du Berry*, Editions Privat, 1980

Duguet, Claude-Charles, *L'Histoire d'une Petite Ville qui n'a pas d'Histoire: La Châtre avant la Révolution, XVII Siècle*, privately printed in La Châtre in 1896, reprinted by Res Universis, Paris, 1991

Dyer, Colin, *Population and Society in Twentieth-Century France*, Hodder & Stoughton, 1978

Faith, Nicholas, *The World Railways Made*, Bodley Head, 1990

Febvre, Lucien, *La Terre et L'Evolution Humaine* (4 vols) Paris, 1924

Flaubert, Gustave, *Madame Bovary*, 1857

Gaultier, Jean, *Histoire de la Châtre et du Berry*, Éditions le Vagabond, 1982

Guillaumin, Émile, *Paysans par Eux-Mêmes* and *La Vie d'un Simple*, Paris, 1904

Halévy, Daniel, *Visites aux Paysans du Centre (1907–1934)*, first volume 1907, complete edition Grasset, 1935

Héron de Villefosse, René, *Histoire des Grandes Routes de France*, Librarie Perrin, 1975

Hervier, Denis, *Cafés et Cabarets en Berry de 1851 à 1914*, privately printed in Châteauroux, 1980

Hoch, Lesley Page, *Paths to the City: Regional Migration in Nineteenth-Century France*, Sage, California, in co-operation with the Social Science History Association, undated

Jouhandeau, Marcel, *Mémorial* (6 vols), Paris, 1948

Le Roy, Eugène, *Jacquou le Croquant*, Paris, 1899

Mendras, Henri and Cole, Alistair, *Social Change in Modern France: Towards a Cultural Anthropology of the Fifth Republic*, Cambridge University Press, 1991

Nadaud, Martin, *Mémoires de Léonard, ancien garçon maçon*, Paris, 1895

Navarre, Emmanuel, *La Châtre et son Arrondissement*, privately printed, 1896

Pagnol, Marcel, *L'Eau des Collines*, Paris, 1949

Pairaux, Maurice, *L'Indre au Siècle Dernier – Le Conseil Général, La Vie départmentale*, privately published in Valençay, *circa* 1900

Sand, George, *Le Meunier d'Angibault* (1845), *La Mare au Diable* (1846), *François le Champi* (1847), *La Petite Fadette* (1848), *André* (1851), *Histoire de ma Vie* (1879)

Smith, Adam, *The Wealth of Nations*, 1776

Vidalenc, *La Société Française de 1815 à 1848*, Paris, 1773

Vincent, Raymonde, *Campagne*, Paris, 1937

Weber, Eugen, *Peasants into Frenchmen: the Modernization of Rural France, 1870–1914*, Chatto & Windus, 1977

—— *France, Fin de Siècle*, Harvard, 1986

—— *My France, Politics, Culture and Myth*, Harvard, 1991

Young, Arthur, *Travels in France During the Years 1787, 1788 and 1789*. Republished by Cambridge University Press, 1950

Zeldin, Théodore, *Histoire des Passions Françaises* (5 vols), Éditions du Seuil, 1980–81

—— *Les Français*, Fayard, 1984

Zola, Émile, *Au Bonheur des Dames* (1883), *La Terre* (1887)

In addition, I have made general use of the two excellent periodic reviews that are published in the Berry, *La Bouinotte* (Châteauroux and Le Blanc) and *Berry Magazine* (Bourges).

I have also made extensive use of various newspapers of the nineteenth and early twentieth century (referred to in the text), which are today kept either in the Bibliothèque Municipale in La Châtre (my thanks to the staff) or in the Departmental Archives of the Indre, in Châteauroux

Unpublished sources

Baucheron, Hypolite, *Recherches Sur la ville de la Châtre et sur quelques localités environnantes*, manuscript held in the Departmental Archives of the Indre.

Le citoyen d'Alphonse (Préfet de l'Indre), *Portrait du Berrichon de l'Indre en 1803*, printed extracts from a Report made by the Préfet, held in the Departmental Archives

In this Archive I have also made extensive use of nineteenth-century Census records, certain judicial records of Court cases, certain military records, land registry records (those of the Service des Cadastres) and maps. My gratitude to all those members of staff who patiently found and carried heavy volumes for me and allowed me to keep several of them on my desk at once.

I am also indebted to the staffs of the Historical Service of the French

Ministry of Defence, and of the Research Service of the Archives of France, who kindly provided me with records relating to the obscure lives of Auguste Chaumette and Antoine Pirot.

My warm thanks also to the Secretary of the Mairie in Chassignolles, who, as custodian of the Civil Registers and the Municipal Registers, was generous with her time and her interest.

I have also, through the kindness of Jacques Pissavy-Yvernault, been privileged to consult manuscript Notes on the Pissavy-Yvernault family, compiled in the 1950s by Henry Fougère, also a manuscript entitled *Souvenirs Laissés par Madame Louis Yvernault sur la Mort de sa Fille* from the same obliging source. Also, thanks to the present Mayor, the manuscript family tree of the Pirots.

A further manuscript, *Souvenirs d'Enfance*, written by Paul Pouradier-Dutheil *circa* 1880, only came my way once this book was going to press, but happily I have been able to include it in the present edition (*see* Afterword). My thanks to his descendants, especially to his grandson, Étienne Triat.

My thanks also to those readers of the hardback edition who have indicated various minor misprints and errors, or apparent errors, especially in the transcription of French words. Many of these have been rectified in the present edition. Others, however, have been allowed to stand because they are not my errors or oddities but those of the original register-keepers, letter-writers, etc. for which correction is inappropriate.

Index